WRITING

MODERN ENGLISH

Robert M. Gorrell
University of Nevada

Charlton Laird
University of Nevada

PRENTICE-HALL, INC., ENGLEWOOD CLIFFS, NEW JERSEY

Library of Congress Cataloging in Publication Data

GORRELL, ROBERT M
  Writing modern English.

  1. English language—Rhetoric. I. Laird, Charlton
Grant   joint author. II. Title.
PE1408.G67   808'.042   72–12865
ISBN 0–13–065243–1

Printed in the United States of America

10   9   8   7   6   5   4   3   2   1

Prentice-Hall International, Inc., *London*
Prentice-Hall of Australia, Pty. Ltd., *Sydney*
Prentice-Hall of Canada, Ltd., *Toronto*
Prentice-Hall of India Private Limited, *New Delhi*
Prentice-Hall of Japan, Inc., *Tokyo*

Acknowledgments

The authors are grateful for the following permissions to reprint copyrighted material.

Extract on p. 80 from Denis Brian, *Tallulah, Darling*, New York, Pyramid, 1972.

Extract on pp. 26,30 from Margaret Bryant, *Current American Usage*. Copyright © 1962 by Funk and Wagnalls Publishing Company, Inc. With permission of the publisher.

Extract on p. 170 reprinted from *A Clockwork Orange* by Anthony Burgess. By permission of W. W. Norton, Inc. © 1962 by Anthony Burgess. Copyright © 1963 by W. W. Norton & Company, Inc.

Comic strip on p. 49 from The Chicago Tribune, May 9, 1972. Reprinted by permission.

Cartoon on p. 7 from *The Saturday Review*, 55 (March 25, 1972), p. 19. Reprinted by permission of Robert M. Hageman.

Extract on p. 8 copyright © 1969 by Lillian Hellman. Reprinted by permission of Harold Matson Company, Inc.

Extract on p. 149 from John Hersey, *Hiroshima*, New York, Knopf, 1946. Reprinted by permission.

Extract on p. 207 from Robert Jungk, *Tomorrow Is Already Here*, New York, Simon and Shuster, 1954. Reprinted by permission of Simon and Shuster and Alfred Scherz.

Comic strip on p. 53 © 1972 Walt Kelly. Courtesy Publishers-Hall Syndicate.

Extract on p. 25 from "An 18-Year-Old Looks Back on Life." © 1972 by Joyce Maynard. First printed in *The New York Times Magazine*, Apr. 23, 1972. To appear in the book *Looking Back*, by Joyce Maynard, to be published by Doubleday.

Extract on pp. 9,11 from James Michener, *Kent State; What Happened and Why*, New York, Random House, 1971. Reprinted by permission.

Extract on p. 181 from Bill Moyers, *Listening to America*, New York: Harper & Row, 19 . Reprinted with permission.

Extract on p. 59–61 from Robe   rs, *A Linguistic History of English*, Boston, Houg   ifflin, 1968. Reprinted by permission.

Extract on p. 102 from Lord Ra   *The Hero*, London, Watts, 1949. Reprinted wit   ission.

Extract on p. 29 from the book *B   ichard J. Daley of Chicago* by Mike Royko. Copy   1971 by Mike Royko. Published by E. P. Dutt   Co., Inc., and used with their permission.

Illustration on p. 5 from C. L. Su   er, *World War II*, New York, American Heritage   ss, 1970. U.S. Coast Guard photograph reprinted b   ermission.

Extract on p. 134 from Carroll L. Wilson, "The Fragile Climate of Spaceship Earth," *Intellectual Digest*, 2 (March, 1972), 78. Reprinted with permission.

PREFACE

The habit of expression leads to the search for something to express.
HENRY ADAMS

Writing Modern English attempts to cultivate "the habit of expression" and to stimulate "the search for something to express." That is, it is intended to help students learn methods of using language and to suggest ways of finding and controlling things to say. Although the exercises are usually designed for simple correction, they are not mainly tests or drills in correcting errors but are rather guides for practice in writing techniques. So that it can serve as a complete text for the composition course, the book includes a concise handbook and a reference system for use in revising papers, but even the portions of the book concerned with revision are directed toward showing the student what he can now do to improve his writing, not much with reminding him of past slips that would better have been avoided.

The book is based on the following principles:

1. To write well an author must have something to say and abundant detail to say it with.
2. Good writing develops more from practicing what to do than from being told what not to do.
3. Studying the way a language works helps a writer to use the language well.
4. Use of language cannot be reduced to a set of rules defining "right" and "wrong"; writing must be judged on whether or not it does what it purports to do.

These principles are applied in the discussion of four aspects of composition.

Rhetoric, Grammar, Diction, Mechanics

Samuel Butler, in *Hudibras*, makes fun of rhetoric—

> *For all a Rhetorician's Rules*
> *Teach nothing but to name his Tools.*

As a study of techniques for clear expression, however, not as a series of "rules," rhetoric promotes the study of writing, and, we trust, the practice of writing. Thus the early chapters of the book look toward providing the student with a sound, though brief, grounding in a rhetorical approach to writing.

The first chapter propounds the essential notion of good writing, that it is a continuing process that comprises three overlapping stages—prewriting, writing, and rewriting. Most good writing passes through at least these three stages, although, since none but the final draft usually appears in print, students may not appreciate that if the written page is to be any good, even seasoned professional writers face a long and arduous job.

Accordingly, in Chapter 1 we have viewed writing as a serious and also rewarding activity, practical as a tool for communication and satisfying as a means of self-expression. We suggest also that a topic is something more than a title that can be inscribed at the top of a page. In Chapter 2 we have tried to show how the purpose and direction of a topic can be made clear through topical devices, especially the topic sentence.

Most frequently, weak writing is weak not because of what it has, but of what it does not have. It remains weak because it lacks development. Accordingly, we have intended Chapters 3 and 4 to show how writing can be built up with fact. Particularly in Chapter 3 we have relied upon the resources of the writer himself, using the approach of commitment and response—a device that we have found widely useful. It will reappear frequently throughout the book. Chapter 4 stresses sources outside the writer, especially reference works.

The next three chapters, 5–7, concern the handling of material. In Chapter 5 we treat analysis and classification, both as means of restricting a topic, and as major tools for developing composition. In Chapter 6 these techniques are made more specific and adapted to the outline, but here we have tried to encourage an awareness of an outline as a working convenience, not as an extra burden that the student feels he has to prepare in order to keep the instructor happy, just because teachers tend to be outline-prone. Chapter 7 treats topical material, and we have given particular attention to beginnings and endings. In Chapter 8 we consider paragraph patterns with emphasis on the structure and writing of the standard expository paragraph, hoping the student will see that good paragraphs are, in effect, brief compositions, and that they can be developed and controlled in accordance with the same principles and practices that make for good writing generally. Chapters 9–11 concern three ways the mind works, ways that have special uses in writing: definition, inductive reasoning through evidence, and logic through deductive thought.

With Chapter 12 we start another major portion of the book, that of treating the sentence. Here we have relied on an approach that we have found works for students, we believe because it relies on an essentially sound analysis of Modern English sentence structure. We emphasize the core of predication, noticing what the Danish scholar Otto Jespersen called *nexus*, the working together of the subject, verb, and complement. Especially in Chapter 12 we urged the informed choosing of subjects, a study that has been neglected in much study of composition, being confused with the identifying of subjects. Chapter 13 concerns another neglected subject, precise predication. These two chapters provide a basis for Chapter 14, which shows the student how to use passive and expletive structures, and how to avoid misusing them. Chapters 15 and 16 encourage the use of coordination and subordination in writing, so that, for the student, the handling of the basic SVC pattern and development through coordination and subordination provide a simple but comprehensive way of writing English sentences. Chapter 17 describes the means of gaining coherence within the sentence, and Chapter 18 encourages excellence in sentence writing through a study of emphasis.

Chapters 19 and 20 consider language and writing. Clearly one of the great needs of students, especially those who are likely to have some trouble with English, is a larger and more precisely usable vocabulary. Unfortunately, growing a vocabulary is a long process, and accordingly we have approached it on a broad basis. We have recognized the utility of prefixes and suffixes, and we have tried to make use of etymology and language history. Students are likely to be intrigued by the concept of Indo-European, but only with help can they make much use of it to improve their own writing vocabularies. Presumably everybody has the vocabulary he deserves, but by studying words he can deserve more. Chapter 20 discusses word choice and use of the dictionary. Chapter 21 brings together the discussions of sentence structure and word choice into a consideration of broader topics like point of view, style, and tone.

We have tried to suggest throughout the book that writing can have many forms and uses. In the next three chapters, 22–24, we select three of these as having special utility for college students. Chapter 22 is directed toward the examination and the impromptu paper, but develops these types of writing as extensions of the familiar question-answer sort of discussion. (The student may elect to work through this chapter early in the course; it could improve his grades, and in courses other than English.) Chapter 23 gives hints for the very large problem of how to write about literature. Chapter 24 treats objective writing, one of the most practical kinds of writing for business and professional people as well as scholars and scientists. Here we have given special attention to note taking and the avoiding of plagiarism. We have used the second edition of the Modern Language Association *Style Sheet*, since it is standard for many subjects.

The mechanics of writing, although often arbitrary, are nonetheless significant for expression. An example is provided by an incident involving the rival boom mining camps, Aurora and Bodie. According to the editor of the Aurora newspaper, when a family was moving from Aurora to the rival camp, a child perched upon the load of the departing family's household goods was heard to pray, "Goodbye, God. We're going to Bodie." The Bodie editor, however, accused his rival of various sorts of perfidy, including the misrepresentation of an innocent child's delight. According to the Bodie editor, the girl had said, "Good! By God, we're going to Bodie." Spelling and punctuation can change meaning, and accordingly we have devoted Chapters 25 and 26 to the mechanics of the writing system, including punctuation, spelling, and manuscript form.

We would call attention to the treatment of spelling problems, pages 231–237. Fortunately, many bright persons learn to spell almost unconsciously, but some—and some of the best students—have great difficulty. The problem may be compounded by unsound learning methods; the student, with or without instruction, develops the habit of looking up words and forgetting them, looking them up again and forgetting them once more. The result is that instead of learning to spell he comes to believe that he cannot learn. In this he is likely to be wrong. We have become convinced that practically all young persons who are ever likely to get to college can learn to spell if they will use a good method persistently. We have found that the method of diagnosis and cure described in Chapter 25 will work for almost a hundred per cent of the so-called "bad spellers" if they apply it seriously.

In Chapter 27 we have provided a statement about usage and a glossary of troublesome words and phrases, along with definitions of grammatical terms. In discussions we have preferred the terminology of the conventional grammatical statement on the theory that it is likely to be the most useful for most students. We have also included some terms from more recent grammars, particularly those using generative transformational theory. We have not provided a separate chapter on grammar, since research has shown that no amount of grammatical knowledge will alone help composition very much, but we have tried to show—notably in Chapter 12—how a knowledge of Modern English grammar can promote good sentence structure, and we have suggested here in Chapter 27 that an awareness of grammar can help the learning and ordering of terms in accordance with standard usage.

We are grateful—

The comments of many teachers all over the country who offered suggestions about the manuscript were helpful to us, especially the suggestions of the following professors of composition who, at the instance of the publisher, read the book in manuscript: Judith Wolfert Chodos, Los Angeles Trade-Technical College; Truman W. Grandey, Mt. Hood Community College; Walter Mosley, Northwestern State University; and B. L. Smith, Kent State University.

We owe many debts to the staff of Prentice-Hall, including Mr. William H. Oliver for his continuing and zealous belief in the utility of this book, Ms. Robb Reavill for her skill and acumen in bringing into being a volume that is typographically exasperating, and Ms. Susan J. Anderson for her thoughtfulness in attending to all the thousand and one ills that the flesh of authors seem to be heir to, especially while giving birth to a book. Many of the sentences in the volume, both good and bad, are the work of our students, and though these authors remain anonymous, even to us, we are grateful to them. Our wives, Johnnie Belle Gorrell and Helene Laird, have not only suffered talk about the book without flinching but have tried the exercises without complaint; we are grateful.

ROBERT M. GORRELL
CHARLTON LAIRD

The Revision System:
A Note to Students

Some students will not believe this, but their professors probably would: "Most teachers of composition would like to write a long letter every week to each student, discussing the student's writing and how he could improve it." Of course teachers do not write such letters, at least not in anything like that quantity and length. They could not. Most of them have a hundred students or so, and along with classes, committee meetings, preparations, conferences, staff meetings, and the like, they could not write a hundred letters a week, each of which would take at least a half hour.

Many of them even find themselves reduced to penning cursory comments like "Good. Your best so far." or "Carelessness. Please correct spelling errors." Such notes can be discouraging for the student, particularly if he has made an honest effort to produce a paper he feels is worthy of serious attention. And the teacher probably does not feel happy about them, either. Teachers, in spite of some rumors to the contrary, are likely to be human beings, even rather considerate human beings who like to believe they are doing a hard job well.

Accordingly, we have tried in this book to devise a system whereby the instructor can, in effect, write the student an individual letter without investing the time that such a letter would ordinarily consume. It works in this way. Let us assume that the instructor has noticed that the writer has written a weak topic sentence. If this is only an occasional slip, and one that can readily be remedied, he is likely just to revise the sentence, as being the easiest and clearest way to show the writer how to strengthen his topical matter. If, however, he observes that the student rather regularly writes weak topic sentences, that they ramble, are not very precise, and sometimes lack transitional material from earlier in the paper, he may write **2b** in the margin.

Each of the two parts of this symbol, the number and the letter, has its own significance. The number **2** means that the student is being referred to something in Chapter 2 of the book, and to the second numbered portion of that chapter, designated as **b.** If the student will now turn to the front inside cover of the book he will find a block labeled **2**, with **2b** under it, and the information that this passage occurs on pages 9–10. If he then turns to page 9, he will find the following heading, ruled above and below:

2b Phrasing Topic Statements   **TS**
*Revise to strengthen topical matter; a carefully phrased theme
or topic sentence will help.*

This means that the instructor is saying, as a minimum, "In my judgment, your topic sentence is nowhere near so good as it could be. I suggest you try to write a better one."

If the student is cognizant of topic sentences and has tried hard to write good ones, he may mutter something to the effect, "Obviously. Should have seen it myself." He probably needs no more instruction, and he has only to revise. But if he does not know how to improve his topic sentence, then the instructor has, in effect, told him, "If you are still puzzled, work through the remainder of this section to see if it may help you." The instructor probably will have particularly in mind that the student might notice the four sorts of things a good topic sentence can do (page 10) and he could use them to see what is weak in his own topic sentence. He now has, for all practical purposes, a letter to him from the instructor describing topic sentences and what he should do about them.

The instructor may choose another way to get the same effect; he may write **TS** in the margin. This is what is called a copyreading mark, standing for *topic sentence*. For this symbol the student should turn to the back inside cover, where he will find **TS** in a sequence of symbols listed in alphabetical order. Here, also, he will find reference to pages 9–10. Hence, the instructor is implying what he would have meant if he had written **2b.**

Or consider another case. Let us assume that the student has written, "He took a course in Biology." The instructor might write **Sp** beside this, particularly if he assumes that the student knows better, but was a little careless. The student's reaction may be, "Sure. Should have known *biology* is a common noun there and isn't capped." If so, he has little more to do than make the correction. But if the student is weak in spelling, the instructor probably has in mind the passage in italics on page 238, under **26b** and **Sp** *"Correct the misspelling and consider whether a principle of English spelling or the violation of a specific rule is involved."* In that case, the student will do well to read and ponder the subsequent paragraph, and notice that he is given cross references to more extensive treatment. If the instructor doubts that the student understands how to capitalize, he may write instead, **26c,** **Cap,** or **lc.** Any of these will direct the student to the problem of capitalizing.

One set of symbols is likely to appear somewhat differently. Let us assume that the student has written ". . . like I thought he would." The instructor might circle the *like* or otherwise flick it to attract attention, and write either **27** or **Gloss** in the margin. If the student will turn to Chapter 27 he will find that it contains a glossary of usage and grammatical terms. Since *like* has been flicked, he should turn to *like* in this alphabetical glossary, where he will find suggestions as to usage. If he is in doubt about the whole problem of usage, he will find a discussion at the beginning of the chapter.

In short, the correction system is intended to help the student make minor corrections quickly, but, more importantly, it is intended to give him constructive advice about strengthening his writing.

CONTENTS

Objectives: (1) To begin to see composition as prewriting,
writing, and rewriting. (2) To restrict a topic by analysis.
(3) To begin using a journal to record "ideas" for writing.

You do not have to face a firing squad in order to write a paper for an English class. Nor need you be condemned to a living hell in Siberia. But knowing how the presence of death entered into one man's writing may show something of how anyone turns experience into writing. Here is the story:

Fyodor Dostoevsky was a bright young engineering student in Czarist Russia, with sympathy for the peasants who were being beaten down and impoverished. Young Fyodor read a letter aloud to a liberal meeting—not his own letter. He just read it. But it attacked the government, and for this act he was arrested, tried, and condemned to death.

The execution squad had their rifles aimed when an aide dashed in, bringing a partial reprieve from the Czar. Fyodor was sent to a prison in the frozen tundra of Siberia, from which few men returned alive and well. Many died; some went insane; others were invalids until their early deaths. Fyodor was lucky; he was paroled to the army, and after a few years more, allowed to return to European Russia, a free man.

Some time later he published a book, the title of which can be translated *Notes from a Dead House*—in Russia, a "dead house" was a building in which bodies were kept while awaiting burial. The *Notes* pictured the Siberian prison as a "dead house," in which the men officially living could be readily confused with those officially "dead."

Notice what had happened to create this book. Fyodor had faced execution and then endured a sort of living death in Siberia. During all these experiences he was observing his surroundings, storing his mind with impressions. When he was paroled to the army, he had time to write and had access to writing materials. He made notes for himself, wrote letters to his friends. When he got back to the Russia he considered home, he collected these scraps he had written, revised them, and put them into a book.

That is, he had gone through the whole normal sequence of writing when it is done in an orderly way. First, he had gathered material, which was consciously or unconsciously preparation for writing. We shall call it prewriting, the sort of experience one must go through in order to write, to have something to say.

Next, he had written. While in the army he had written down bits he could remember and had reported his experience in letters. This is the second part of the writing experience, physically putting words down on paper so that they become what one wants to say. But at the same time, Fyodor was prewriting; reliving his experiences as he recorded them, he also recalled what he had almost forgotten, and thinking about his past he was able to see it in another and clearer light.

Back home, he collected what he had already written and did some more writing, but he found also that he could now improve what he had written earlier. He "rewrote." In short, he had now completed the cycle needed for most good writing—prewriting, followed by writing, followed by rewriting. In fact, much bad writing can be traced to the writer's neglect of one step or more of this sequence. Most frequently, the prewriting or the rewriting or both is neglected.

Thus prewriting, writing, and rewriting are separate procedures, each leading to the next, but they also blend into one another. To see how this sequence and blending work, let us look at Dostoevsky's later writing—he was by now no longer young Fyodor, but a mature writer. When he collected his *Notes from a Dead House* he did not know he was prewriting for a novel. But he was. Rethinking his experiences and his accounts of them, he saw the whole more clearly and produced a work we shall call *Letters from the Underworld*. The prewriting for it had been done in the course of producing his *Notes*; now he had to write, and of course rewrite.

But that was not the end. As he penned the novel *Letters* and grew in his experience as an established author, he was, in effect, prewriting for what would become some of the finest stories in the world, *Crime and Punishment, The Brothers Karamazov*, and the like. Each time he was prewriting by using ideas from his Siberian days and wrestling with material during the writing process that had produced earlier books. This prewriting led to new writing, which led to more rewriting, perhaps to several written versions before the book was ready for the printer.

That is, in part, Dostoevsky became the novelist he was because his whole life developed into a pattern of prewriting, writing, and rewriting. Suffering in prison was prewriting for *Notes; Notes* was prewriting for *Letters,* and *Letters* was prewriting for *Crime and Punishment*. And of course each was a writing job, a job that was not complete until the manuscript had been rewritten, in some instances many times.

That is the way professional writers work, and beginners can well learn from them, very much as young basketball players study professionals and learn from them, either directly or through a coach. In writing, the first part of the prewriting-writing-rewriting sequence starts with choosing a topic.

Prewriting: Restricting a Topic

Every college student has had experiences enough to suggest dozens of themes—he has known people, participated in sports, gone to school, read books, had childhood adventures, played music, engaged in protest marches, participated in clubs, or worked at a job. Furthermore, he has interests that suggest subjects he can investigate—from stamps to jet engines. And often subjects are assigned, after college as well as in college. An oil executive says to his exploratory geologist, "We have taken an option on some properties on the Alaskan north shore; fly up there and get us a report." An instructor assigns a theme to be based on an essay the class has read. But even when a subject is assigned, for a business report or a student theme, the writer must adapt it to his own purposes.

1a Restricting a Topic Top

Your topic is too broad; to restrict it, consider using analysis.

In particular, he must limit it. A three-page paper on "Sports in America" or "The Life of Edgar Allan Poe" can be no more than a general survey or an inadequate outline. Analysis provides one good method for limiting a subject. By analysis a writer can break a subject into its parts and find a manageable topic. A diagram of the process might look like the following:

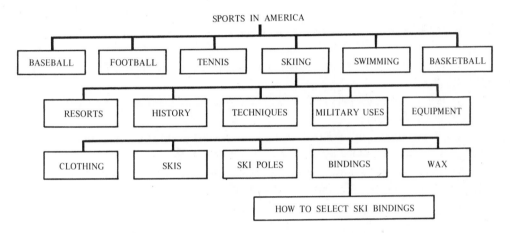

The student interested in sports in America might subdivide his topic into individual sports and from them select skiing. He then might subdivide skiing —into, perhaps, history, techniques, military uses, equipment. He has worked in a sporting goods store and knows something about skiing equipment. He continues to analyze and ends with a topic: "How to Select Ski Bindings."

Restricting a topic need not be, of course, as formal as a diagram, but practice with such a regimented procedure may help the writer to discipline his thinking.

A Journal as Prewriting and Writing

One of the best ways to do both prewriting and writing is to keep a journal, jotting down notes on everyday occurrences. Here is one journal entry:

> Going back home after lab today I saw a kid zipping down the street on a bike with his hands in the air, showing off. I learned to do that when I was a kid, though once I got dumped when I had to brake suddenly on a wet pavement. It reminded me of a guy I knew in boot camp. We had just

been inducted. The officer handed him a note, and said, "Take that bike and deliver this to Commissary, Barracks B." Barracks B was only about a mile away, but the guy didn't come back for nearly an hour. He was dripping sweat, pushing the bike. "What's the trouble?" the officer asked, "have a blowout or something?"—"No, Sir," the guy said. "I just don't know how to ride a bicycle."

This kind of writing provides both practice and usable material. The writer recounts an event; he also comments on what he has gone through or seen or heard or read as ideas come to him. The notes also serve as prewriting, because later a writer can go back to them and use them as the basis for more careful writing.

If the student has trouble finding material to record in a journal, he might try asking himself simple questions about the people and things around him, about himself, about what he has done. Questions like the following may be useful:

1. *What happened?* A lecture is a happening; so is a meeting on the campus.

2. *What was it like?* What could be seen, heard, or sensed in some other way?

3. *Who were these people?* Where did they come from and why were they acting as they did?

4. *Was it important? What does it mean?* Most events may not matter much, but some mean more if they are examined carefully.

5. *What was your own reaction?* What did you think or feel? Can you guess what others were thinking or feeling?

Rewriting

As we have seen, professional writing almost always results as a sequence of three activities that are to a degree independent, but that also merge with one another. In college courses the rewriting usually takes place in part through the directions of an instructor. He is likely both to correct faulty practices and at the same time to recommend means of improvement.

He may rely in part on conferences with the student, either individually or through a writing laboratory. He may write notes of advice on the student's paper. Or he may make use of a system of key symbols that will direct the student to printed statements that are applicable to the paper in hand—as a matter of convenience or necessity, most instructors utilize some combination of these three. The present text provides two key systems that the instructor may use to recommend rewriting (see "A Revision System: A Note to Students," p. vii).

1A You have been advised to ask yourself questions about what you have experienced. Study the picture below and try to answer the questions that follow it.

1 What is the occupation of the men?

2 Where are they?

3 What may they have been doing?

4 Why do they look the way they do?

5 Are there any ways in which they are markedly different? Or do they seem to have something in common?

Try to draw further conclusions about the men and the scene from clues in the picture. Then write a short paper recording your observations, putting together the most interesting things you can say about the men and the situation.

1B Fill in the following charts, like the one on page 3, with topics that might be subdivisions in an analysis to restrict a general subject to a limited topic. The first chart provides the topics that the writer chose; fill in possible alternatives that would have been discarded. The second chart needs to be entirely filled in.

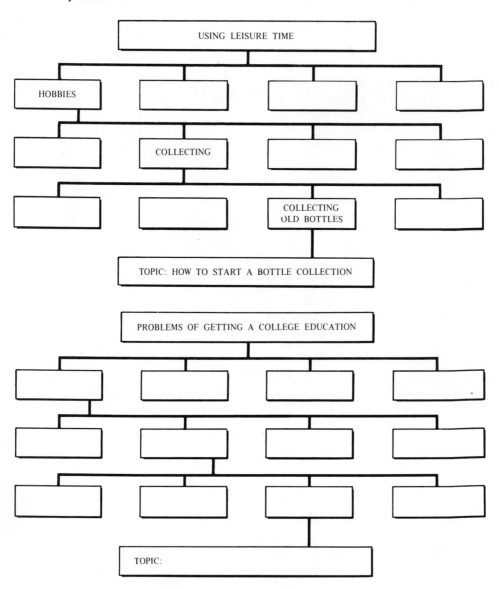

Objectives: *(1) To focus writing on a central idea, an individual interpretation. (2) To write topical statements so that they provide transitions and help the writer organize his material.*

Any body of information, any set of facts, can be interpreted in various ways. A piece of writing gets its individuality as the writer interprets his material, as he focuses on a central idea that gives a particular meaning to his facts. Consider, for example, the information in the following cartoon:

In a general way we can readily see what the cartoon is about. A girl and her apparently illegitimate baby are being turned out into the storm by her father. In one of the old melodramas he would have been saying something like, "Never darken my door again," or "From this time forth I have no daughter."

But apparently the cartoonist is focusing attention on something more, because another woman, probably the man's wife, is saying something, seemingly in protest. What she is saying provides the unifying idea for the cartoon. What would the picture mean if she is saying, "But Harold, don't you remember what we did before we were married?" How would the focus, the interpretation, of the details be different if she is saying, "But Harold, the poor little thing is not to blame, and it's our only grandchild"? As originally printed in the *Saturday Review* the material was given a still different interpretation, intended to be funny. The federal income tax exemption had just been raised, and the caption of the cartoon read, "But, Harold, it's a six-hundred-seventy-five-dollar tax exemption."

2a   Unity About a Theme or Thesis Idea   U

Revise the passage, focusing it clearly on a central idea.

Like the cartoonist, the writer should have a central idea and unify his writing around it. In a journal, a familiar letter, or any spontaneous writing, the writer may not have decided on the significance he wants to give his material, and may jot things down as they occur to him. But even in a reminiscence, as the writer works with what he has done, he directs his writing toward a controlling idea. The following is an incident from childhood told by the dramatist Lillian Hellman in her autobiography, *An Unfinished Woman*.

> I had been sleeping on a bench that night in Montgomery, Alabama, so I don't know when I first saw the three figures—a young, very thin Negro girl, and two white men. The men were drunk, my father said later, and maybe that accounted for the awkward, shaggy movements, their sudden twists and turns. The girl would move to a bench, sit, rise as the men came toward her, move to a wall, rest, slide along it as the men came near, try for another bench, circle it, and move fast when they moved fast. She was trying to stay within the station lights and, as the train came in, she ran down the platform toward it. But she miscalculated and ran outside the lights. I saw one of the men light matches and move in the darkness. When he caught the girl he put the lighted matches to her arm before he kissed her. The girl dropped her valise and there was the noise of glass breaking. I have no clear memory of the next few minutes until I heard my father say, "Let the girl alone." Then he hit the man and the other man hit my father, but he didn't seem hurt because he picked the girl up and shoved her up the steps of the train, came running back for me, shoved me up the steps of the train, got in himself and suddenly began to yell, "My God, where is your mother?" My mother was on the ground repacking the girl's valise. The two men were running toward her but she smiled and waved at my father and put up her hand in a gesture to quiet him. She had trouble with the lock of the valise but she seemed unhurried about fixing it. My father was halfway down the train steps when she rose, faced the two men and said, "Now you just step aside, boys, and take yourselves on home." I don't know whether it was the snobbery of the word "boys" or the accents of her native Alabama, but they made no motion as she came aboard the train.

The girl was invited to share our basket supper and she and my mother spent the next few hours speaking about the nature of men. I went into the corridor to find my bored father.

Like most other children, I had learned you usually got further by pretending innocence. "What did those men want to do with the girl?"

The incident is clearly told, and the reader can interpret its significance in various ways. It is like the cartoon without its caption. But Hellman had a specific controlling idea in mind for the entire passage in which she uses the incident, and she supplies a caption. As the narrative proceeds, young Lillian recounts the incident to her nurse, a wise old black woman; when the woman says nothing, Lillian comments "Papa was brave, wasn't he?" The older woman agrees but adds, "Things not going to get themselves fixed by one white man being nice to one nigger girl." The old woman's comment supplies the caption, gives the incident the interpretation the writer wants for her autobiography.

| 2b | Phrasing Topic Statements | TS |

Revise to strengthen topical matter; a carefully phrased theme or topic sentence will help.

Usually the central idea will be clear to the reader, and even to the writer, only after the idea has been carefully phrased, most frequently in a sentence, or for a long composition in a paragraph. The following is part of James Michener's attempt to find out what happened when some National Guardsmen fired on students at Kent State University and killed or maimed several of them:

A visit to Jack Albright's new home at 3304 Marsh Road does not clarify the matter. He appears at the door, a very tall man who looks exactly like a young Dick Foran. He smiles affably, is most courteous, leads the way into a tastefully furnished living room of which he and his petite blond wife are obviously proud. "I've told this story a hundred times," he begins, "and no one believes it. I'm tired of telling it." When asked for one more repetition, he says with keen interest, leaning forward as he speaks, "You understand, I'm on the Guard's side completely and everything I say is intended to bolster up their case. The college kids were behaving insanely. They'd have overrun them at the pagoda and taken their guns away, that's for sure. The Guard were a hundred-percent right."

"Did you hear the command given to fire?"

Jack Albright sits back. His enthusiasm vanishes, "Well, there was a lot of noise, a lot of screaming. I was about 150 feet away, and what could I hear?"

"Did you hear an officer say, 'Turn around and fire three rounds"?'

"Well, I heard . . . well, yes. I heard it."

Kent State: What Happened and Why

The first sentence is obviously a topic statement, summarizing the theme of this passage—which is in effect a paragraph, although because of conversation it is broken up in printing.

The following is one author's statement of the four things a topic sentence is most likely to do:

1. It expresses the main idea of the paragraph, focusing attention on it. That is, it introduces and may summarize the content of the paragraph.

2. It usually provides a transition, referring to what has preceded and leading the reader into the new part of the total discussion.

3. It may indicate how the paragraph is to be organized, pointing ahead to subdivisions, for example.

4. It is often the most general statement of the paragraph, but it is still as specific as possible in clarifying the paragraph's main idea.

Examination reveals that Michener's topic sentence accords in part with these requirements. (1) His sentence both introduces the subject, mentioning "a visit," and summarizes the discussion, notably in the phrase "does not clarify the matter." (2) It provides a transition, referring to "the matter," that is, to the question of how decent young men in the Guard came to shoot down young people, at least some of whom were innocent of any wrongdoing, and whether the Guard was ordered to shoot. (3) The sentence gives some suggestion of organization, that the paragraph will be made up of evidence at least partly contradictory. Thus we expect evidence for and against the Guard, and that is what we get. (4) The topic sentence is clearly the most general. On the other hand, it is quite specific about where and with whom the interview took place. The term "matter" is general and could have been made more specific, but the whole question is complex. Michener had already analyzed it in detail, and he apparently thought that a reference to this earlier specific material was exact enough.

Name_____

2A

OBJECTIVE: To analyze a topic sentence and define what it does.

INSTRUCTIONS: Examine topic sentences in the following selection in connection with the paragraphs to which they relate, and note how much is done
in each topic sentence.

EXAMPLE: For an example of the method, reexamine page 10 above.

EVIDENCE: The selection here is the passage in Michener's book that
follows the account quoted on page 9. It can be thought of as a single paragraph broken into three parts or as a brief composition made up of three
paragraphs.

It is important to visualize the condition of the Guard as they begin
their retreat. They have been on duty for nearly a week, sleeping at odd
times and in odd places. They have eaten irregularly and been sub-
jected to taunts and ridicule. They are bewildered by the behavior of
college students and outraged by the vocabulary of the coeds. It is
hot. They have been stoned. They have chased a lot of oddly dressed
kids back and forth and have accomplished nothing except the in-
dignity of having their own tear gas thrown back at them.

And they experienced irritating physical limitations. Private Paul
Zimmerman told a reporter from the Akron *Beacon Journal*, "It was
hard to see through that plastic. To look behind you, you'd have to
turn your head all the way around. I was hot and sweaty."

Sergeant Dale Antram, and any other Guardsman wearing glasses,
had to take them off in order to get the gas mask on: "We would be
marching up the hill but we would be thinking behind us. We were
always watching over our shoulders, and guys were saying, 'Back
there!' 'Watch it!' 'Here comes a rock!' "

CONCLUSIONS: For each sentence that you consider topical in the passage, write a statement or two specifying which of the four things listed on
page 10 the topic sentence does.

2B Although the following paragraphs have central themes, their opening sentences do not reveal them. For each paragraph, construct a unifying statement of the main idea to replace the italicized opening sentence, and write your sentence in the space.

1 *Pollution is a very important problem in this day and age.* For the first, pollution of the sea occurs both near the beaches and far out into the ocean. Clams, oysters, and even shrimp have been killed in great numbers near the shore, and far out to sea many fish have been contaminated with mercury. Thor Hyerdahl's *Ra* sailed through miles of oil gobs. For the second, lead and other dangerous chemicals are building up in the earth and are finding their way into the food one eats and the water one drinks. For the last, air in the cities has been turned to smog laden with exhaust fumes and the ash and filth from factory chimneys.

2 *The party was very interesting.* Fierce Captain Kidds and their ladies moved about in gay costumes. Wooden cutlasses decorated the walls, and the Jolly Roger hung from a chandelier in the middle of the room. Cardboard ship's wheels formed a screen in front of the chairs along the walls. The punch bowl on the table was masked in paper to resemble a treasure chest, and its contents seemed as attractive to some of the guests as pieces of eight to buccanneers on the Spanish Main.

3 *The subway is one notable aspect of America.* Apparently no one ever walks toward the turnstiles. Commuters at the rush hour seem torn by a frantic, unreasoning compulsion to be ahead of someone else. They seem not even aware of practical motives like getting a seat or making a connection or keeping an appointment. One feels that if a steep cliff lay just beyond the turnstile, nothing could stop the panic mass from plunging over. The people are charmed by the mad rush and roar of the train itself, bursting out of nowhere, stopping with a protesting clatter, and then roaring off into the darkness.

4 *Every baseball player has to bat.* The batter must develop an automatic sense of time to convert the signals from his eyes into the moments he must wait before starting his swing. His sense of timing must blend with a sense of direction so that the bat moves mechanically into the spot toward which the ball is moving. And muscles of arm and leg and back must be co-ordinated in a rhythmic pattern that accumulates their full force in the contact of the bat on the ball.

2C   In the following paragraphs from Robert H. Thouless's book *Straight Thinking in War Time*, the initial topic sentences have been omitted and replaced with a note in brackets of the general subjects of the omitted sentences. Read each paragraph; then in the space after it construct a topic sentence that seems to you to introduce what you have read. Your instructor can supply the original topic sentences for comparison.

1   [arguments of our enemies] .... It is certainly not difficult to find fallacious thinking in the German propaganda broadcasts in English or in Hitler's speeches, or even in some of the neutral comments on ourselves. Such a task is made easier by the fact that we are particularly inclined to see the fallacies in the case against ourselves. We may be quite right in our detection of them but such a mental exercise will be of little practical value. Our criticisms will have no effect on our enemies unless they read them (which we may be certain they will not) and the effect of the criticisms on ourselves is likely to be only to confirm us in our prejudices and rather to darken our judgment than to enlighten it.

2   [emotional words] .... The practice of using such words to deflect judgment from its straight course is particularly rife in time of war. Examples are to be found in every newspaper and in every propaganda speech. During the fighting in Malaya, for example, a British newspaper commented that "it was necessary to exterminate the vermin at their source." The word "vermin" here means (factually) the Japanese, and the factual meaning of the passage is that it was necessary to kill the Japanese in Japan. This rendering of the passage, however, is by no means equivalent to the other. It omits the emotional implication of hatred and contempt conveyed by the word "vermin." It has the same factual meaning but a different emotional meaning.

3   [emotional meanings and speech] .... So by change in manner of speaking we may indicate a simple fact, a sneer, or warm approval. These inflexions may also sometimes be implied in print. For example, at the same time that our papers were reporting that British troops in Malaya were being withdrawn in accordance with plan, they were also reporting that the German armies in Russia were withdrawing "in accordance with plan." The factual meaning of the report was the same in both cases: that the armies were withdrawing. The difference in emotional meaning was conveyed by putting in inverted commas the phrase *in accordance with plan* when it referred to the enemy. This corresponds to the sneer which might be conveyed by an inflexion of the voice in speech and suggests doubt of the statement that the enemy's plan was to withdraw. Factually the situation was probably the same in Malaya and in Russia; the army leaders would have preferred to be going forwards rather than back, but presumably every army leader, whether British or German, also makes a plan as to what he will do if he is forced to retire.

2D Following are five topic sentences; read them carefully.

1 First I want to make it perfectly clear that I consider this topic most important; I would hardly have chosen it to write about if I had not, would I?

2 Not only did American cryptographers contribute to winning the war by breaking the Japanese naval cipher, but in doing so they founded a whole new school of cipher-making and cipher-breaking.

3 Before we can evaluate the program to bring Lake Erie back to life, there are some other things that are aspects of the problem.

4 Illicit drugs get into the United States mainly through three channels: direct from the Orient, from the Orient by way of southern France, and from various sources by way of Latin America.

5 The next move is anybody's guess.

At least one of these is a poor prospect for a topic or theme sentence. In the following space identify it and explain why you think it is likely to provide inadequate topical matter.

At least one of the statements might make a good topic sentence for a paragraph or a theme sentence for an article. Pick the one that seems to you the best candidate and explain why. A topic or theme sentence can be appropriate only if it fits the paragraph or essay it introduces, but for this study you may assume that the content will be adequate to the topic or theme sentence.

Something can be said for each of the three remaining sentences. Identify them by number and indicate what seems to be good about each and what seems to be inadequate.

2E Read carefully the following numbered bodies of evidence:

(1) In Washington, D.C., a pet skunk, cured of cold with whiskey egg-nogs, thereafter refused milk unless it was laced with bourbon. (2) In New York, Geiger, African beer-drinking parakeet, celebrated by destroying $150 worth of bottled goods. (3) Near Lamont, France, a hired man gave horses wine instead of water; they wrecked the barn. (4) Near Kalamazoo, Mich., a heifer constantly follows a farmer who poured a pint of whiskey down her to warm her after she had broken through thin ice. (5) In Illinois, motorists were warned of cows drunk from eating fallen windfall apples. (6) In Natchez, Miss., it is illegal to give an elephant a stein of beer. (7) At Windsor, Ont., some 20,000 bees invaded a distillery, produced whisky-flavored honey. (8) At Oberhausen, Germany, Fiffy, an escaped monkey, gave up after sampling a bottle of schnapps. (9) In South Africa, a defendant apprehended with 100 bottles of stolen cognac explained he mixed cognac with chicken feed; his 1,000 hens laid nine more eggs per day. (10) A Connecticut housewife, disturbed by her chickens clucking off key, remembered having thrown out a brandy-soaked cake. (11) In Tennessee, officers sometimes discover stills by following tracks of reeling hogs, which lead to mash piles. (12) In France, a man pulling a supposed hose out of a cask, found it to be a snake, too blissful to strike at him. (13) In Southern England, pedestrians feared a dazed and staggering Airedale had been run over, but noticing confetti on the dog's coat, smelled its breath and concluded it had attended a nearby wedding party. (14) In Paris, extensive research at the Sorbonne led to a report which includes the following: "Whisky-drinking cats made no protest when a mouse tickled their whiskers."

1 In the space below, write the numbers of the passages that, if rewritten, could be built into a composition. Put them in the order you would expect to use. You may see possibilities for more than one composition; in that case, write more than one sequence of numbers.

2 Write five topic or theme sentences that might be suitable for one of the compositions you have planned. Underline the best one.

3 On a separate sheet of paper, write your best topic sentence and follow it with the composition you have planned. You may further improve the topic sentence if you see a way to do it.

Objectives: (1) To distinguish between fact and judgment.
(2) To develop an idea with adequate specific details,
employing varying methods.

A topic or theme sentence, as we have seen, is a commitment. The writer tells himself what he expects to do. When he writes this statement down on paper he has, in effect, promised his reader what he will do. Much of writing involves the attempt to keep a series of such promises. Notice the following:

> In spite of rigid bumpers, faulty brakes, and fragile wheel bearings, the most unpredictable part of an automotive assembly is likely to be the person who controls the accelerator.

The first part of the sentence seems to be transition; apparently the writer has discussed mechanical failures as a source of automobile accidents. The second part of the sentence is commitment; in effect, the writer is now promising his reader to discuss drivers as a cause of accidents, especially irresponsible drivers.

Now suppose the next sentence reads, "More than half the deaths on major highways last year can be traced to the irresponsible acts of drivers presumably competent." The writer has responded to his own topical statement, but he has also made further commitments. He has, in effect, said to the reader: "I will treat the subject in part statistically, and I will distinguish between reckless drivers and some others—for example, incompetent drivers."

Now suppose that the second sentence were made to read as follows: "More than half the deaths on major highways last year can be traced to the acts of irresponsible drivers, especially to drunken drivers." How would the commitment change? Or suppose the sentence were made to read this way: "Statistics make clear that of all segments of the population, those that cause the highest percentage of fatalities on the highway are the young males under twenty-five." What would now be the commitment?

That is, much orderly writing is a series of commitments, which lead to responses. These responses, in turn, lead to more commitments, often to more specific or detailed commitments. A good writer should be careful to commit himself only to what he expects to do, as we have seen in the preceding chapter. Then he needs to respond to the commitment, the promise, he has made. This response we shall call development.

3a Distinguishing Fact and Judgment   Fact

The writing lacks factual development; try limiting it to
one judgment and developing that with fact.

The same event may prompt different comments. We may report what happened: "John got A in chemistry." Or we may use what happened for a more general statement: "John is the brightest boy in his chemistry class." The first may be called a factual statement, a report of a happening or state of affairs. Facts result from measurement or observation or calculation. Facts can be tested or verified. The second is a judgment—an opinion, a pronounce-ment, a decision, a conclusion. Judgments characterize or classify; they express approval or disapproval; they conclude.

Compare the following:

FACT: Willie Jones stole an apple.
JUDGMENT: Willie Jones is a bad boy.

FACT: I heard a story of an elephant who charged a boy who had fed him chewing tobacco two years before.
JUDGMENT: An elephant never forgets.

FACT: Some human traits tend to reappear throughout history.
JUDGMENT: You can't change human nature.

Many statements are not so easily distinguished as these, containing elements of both fact and judgment. The person who says, for example, "The city government has become completely corrupt" sounds as if he were stating a fact and may have some facts in mind, but his comment is largely judgment.

Both facts and judgments are useful. Judgments may be the topic state-ments or conclusions of an essay; opinions are the proper results of careful thinking. But irresponsible judgments are all about us, and writers are fre-quently tempted to rely on them and avoid the hard thinking, observation, or research necessary to collect facts. The writer who has "no more to say" after a line or two usually has brought himself to a dead end by stating only a series of judgments and failing to collect facts. The student who wrote the following was understandably unable to continue; he had made enough judg-ments for half a dozen themes, but he had not provided facts to develop any of them.

> Much of the current criticism of comic books is nonsense. It is written by people who have no sympathy for them. The critics use only the bad comics and never talk about the good ones. They forget the other kinds of comic books. They forget also the bad literature they read as children. Plenty of people read comic books and do not become juvenile delinquents. Many comics provide good relaxation. The critics should worry more about slum clearance and less about comic books.

Types of Development

Pieces of writing, paragraphs or longer compositions, can be developed in many ways. Of course, no experienced writer says to himself, "First, I'll develop a paragraph with details. Then I'll develop one with an example, and then just for variety. I'll use analogy." The method of development usually rises naturally from the information the writer has and the needs of his audience. In fact, most writers use several methods, mixed together or in sequence. But types of development are various, and running through them may be helpful. Here are some of the most common:

1. *Giving particulars, details, examples, illustrations.* Most frequently, paragraphs are developed with specific details; notice the following, the opening sentence of a paragraph by John Dos Passos:

> The backyard was the only place you could really feel safe to play in. There were broken-down fences, dented garbage cans, old pots and pans too nearly sieves to mend, a vacant chickencoop that still had feathers and droppings on the floor, hogweed in summer, mud in winter; but the glory of the McCreary's backyard was Tony Harriman's rabbit hutch, where he kept Belgian hares.

Although relatively still brief, not all details are so brief as "dented garbage cans." A recent description of smuggling heroin into a Latin American country says that "some means of shipping drugs are bizarre," and gives as an example that many tons have been imported stuffed into the corpses supposedly shipped home for burial.

2. *Incident, extended illustration.* An incident or example may be so extensive that it provides development for a whole paragraph or a brief composition. For example, the illustration in the preceding paragraph could be treated as an incident, in which the writer recounts how a corpse was acquired in France, filled with heroin, and shipped and how the contents were accidentally discovered.

3. *Cause and effect.* A writer might start with the causes of a student riot and go on to the results, to the effects. Or he might start by describing effects, as Michener does in the quotation in Chapter 2, and then try to trace these effects back to their causes.

4. *Analogy.* Analogy is the device by which we try to explain something not understood by relating it to something well known. For example, a student revolt might be compared to a plant. It has roots in abuses that need to be corrected; it grows, blossoms into flowers, and even may produce seeds. Such a treatment would include development by analogy, although at the same time the writer may use details, examples, incidents, and the like.

5. *Comparison and contrast.* Almost anything can be compared to something else and contrasted with something else. Competitive skiing can be compared to track in that it relies mainly on individual performances in a variety of events; it can be contrasted with basketball and baseball in that it does not rely on handling a ball.

6. *Restatement and enlargement.* A writer may restate his topic or theme sentence. Notice the following:

> The woman's lib movement is mainly social. A woman may find herself discriminated against in her legal rights, in her salary, in her professional and business opportunities, in the way her community treats her.

The second sentence provides a restatement of the first with added details. This sentence, in turn, could be enlarged with more details, examples, incidents, and the like.

Prefer specific material for development.

The terms *general* and *specific* are relative. An idea or statement cannot be classified as absolutely general or specific, but it can be said to be more or less specific than another. *Dwelling* is more specific than *structure; ranch-type house* is more specific than *dwelling*; and *a green-shuttered ranch-type house with redwood trim* is more specific still. The specific expression singles out an individual item, specifies it.

Writing, of course, requires both general and specific statements. Some kind of general observation is usually the ultimate purpose of writing, the conclusion of a composition. A generalization often states the main idea of a paragraph. Usually, however, the general statement lacks conviction and clarity until it is explained or exemplified or illustrated specifically.

3A The following paragraph describing the convening of a college chapel service is printed as Professor Theodore Morrison did not write it. The italicized passages are less concrete equivalents of what Professor Morrison wrote, and the words of the original will be found below the paragraph, not in their original order. Try to reconstruct the paragraph by writing into the blanks at the right the number of the appropriate and more specific passage; that is, the answer to be written in blank 1 is *5*.

Andrew (1) *looked* back through the (2) *somewhat generally subdued light* of the (3) *solidly built religious structure* as he and Connie guided Muriel to (4) *their seats*. Attendance had (5) *increased to a degree*. (6) *A number of members of the* faculty had turned out to swell the (7) *relatively small number* of (8) *older people* who sat (9) *very straight* in the (10) *more or less unpopular seats toward the front*. Rather more (11) *people of college age* than usual, (12) *with both of the sexes represented*, (13) *were going to church in accordance with the official requirement*, but going in the morning instead of waiting for the (14) *afternoon service in the middle of the week which was quite popular*. They (15) *made their way in* and sat (16) *more and more close together* as the rows (17) *went farther toward the back of the church*. (18) *Repressed voices and some evidence of movement*; (19) *good-natured faces not clearly seen in the lack of light*. Neckties (20) *tied quite a way down the fronts of shirts* that were open at the neck; (21) *just enough to get past* a rule of dress. Someone should have thought to (22) *make provision for* (23) *the control of the kind of clothes the girls wore so that they would look all right in church*. Andrew could make out a girl in a coat over shorts, (24) *laughing a little and endeavoring to conceal her lower extremities from view.*

1 _____
2 _____
3 _____
4 _____
5 _____
6 _____
7 _____
8 _____
9 _____
10 _____
11 _____
12 _____
13 _____
14 _____
15 _____
16 _____
17 _____
18 _____
19 _____
20 _____
21 _____
22 _____
23 _____
24 _____

1. giggling and covering up her legs
2. stone chapel building
3. bare conformity to
4. meeting one third of their weekly chapel requirement
5. gave a quick glance
6. the presidential front pew
7. faithful elder dignities
8. pushed in
9. knotted half way down shirts
10. vague pale grins
11. ordinarily crowded Wednesday vespers
12. appropriate chapel costumes for coeds
13. picked up a little, not much
14. a few additional
15. legislate
16. mutterings and jostlings
17. in denser clusters
18. undergraduates
19. sparsely populated advance pews
20. scattering
21. receded in the twilight perspective
22. morning dusk
23. on upright spines
24. male and female

3B Distinguish the following statements by writing *F* in the blank after each one that is primarily fact and *J* after each that is primarily judgment. Some may be more easily distinguishable than others, and some of your decisions may be debatable; be prepared to discuss elements of fact and judgment in questionable statements.

1 The atomic weight of tungsten is 183.92. _____
2 Love makes the world go round. _____
3 George has run the 100-yard dash in ten seconds. _____
4 The peak of Mount Everest is more than 29,000 feet above sea level. _____
5 A stitch in time saves nine. _____
6 The word *fond* meant "foolish" in the sixteenth century. _____
7 Democracy leads to the worship of the mediocre. _____
8 A mother is the holiest thing alive. _____
9 Most of the newspapers in America are Republican in their political attitudes. _____
10 Allegory is extended metaphor. _____

3C Consider which of each of the following groups of expressions is the most specific; then write its letter in the blank.

1 (a) disease, (b) disease of fowls, (c) illness, (d) pip, (e) unhealthiness. _____

2 (a) Joseph Conrad, (b) novelist, (c) human being, (d) writer, (e) English novelist. _____

3 (a) She was strangely dressed; (b) She wore a bright orange evening gown, a feather boa, and a wide-brimmed hat decorated with a flame-colored ostrich plume; (c) She was dressed in extravagant old-fashioned clothes in clashing colors and inappropriate styles; (d) She had an unusual assortment of unsuitable clothes; (e) She wore an evening gown that was curiously colored and styled, a strange, outdated neckpiece, and a hat that certainly belonged to another era. _____

4 (a) The table was loaded with a fine array of tempting viands; (b) Many foods of various kinds were spread before us on the tempting table; (c) The table held large quantities of well-selected foods designed to provoke the appetite of the most critical; (d) On the table was a large ham surrounded by bowls of pickles, olives, stuffed celery, and potato chips; (e) The roast held the center of the table, but it was surrounded with a variety of appetizers and snacks suitable for the occasion. _____

5 (a) The movie has some exciting, realistic effects that make it interesting; (b) A series of colossal and sensational shots make the movie breathtakingly exciting; (c) Mainly contributing to the interest of the movie is a panoramic presentation of a significant battle of the late Middle Ages; (d) The most interesting scene of the movie shows the Battle of Agincourt of 1415, with French cavalry falling before hissing English arrows; (e) The movie was extremely interesting because of the brilliant and realistic effects of one of the scenes that shows a life-like and exciting presentation of a battle that had important significance on the course of history. _____

6 (a) ground-to-air missile, suitable against aircraft traveling at low altitudes and supersonic speeds; (b) modern weapon; (c) one of the most highly effective instruments in the modern arsenal; (d) as a discovery, terrific! (e) the Air Force's new knockout drop. _____

3D In the spaces make notes of three specific instances or examples that might be used to illustrate each of the following general statements.

EXAMPLE: The rights of students may be ignored by the administration.

Answer: (1) students may have little control over the curricula they take; (2) if students try to appeal they may have nobody to appeal to; (3) the dean of students may order dormitory rooms searched without a warrant.

1 I often associate colors with particular things.

2 Some television programs are very much worth seeing.

3 Even in an age so dominated by social and economic forces as the present, certain men have emerged as world figures.

4 Some comic-strip characters are actually funny.

5 I still remember many of our favorite childhood games.

6 Slang can be expressive and clever.

7 Fashions in dancing change rapidly.

8 Popular songs often remind me of events of the past.

3E In the spaces write notes for an incident or story that might illustrate each of the following statements:

1 A demonstration for peace can become pretty warlike.

2 The first days in college can have their moments of embarrassment.

3 High school pranks and practical jokes often have a serious side.

4 Legend is often quite different from the facts behind it.

3F The following statement suggests an analogy: A hen can be a profitable machine. Obviously, a hen is not like a machine in all ways—it is not made of metal or plastic, for instance—but it is like a machine in that it turns a less valuable product into a more valuable product. The analogy could be developed by telling what feed, living quarters, and care of the hen cost and what eggs are worth. Select one of the following statements suggesting analogies and in the space write details that would make the analogy clear and revealing. (1) A fraternity is like a department store. (2) A political party reminds me of an automobile, ancient but reparable. (3) Pets are like people. (4) Cleaning a room is like a military operation. (5) A tuxedo is like a strait jacket. (6) Long hair can be a rubber stamp. (7) Trying to get equal job opportunities for blacks is like trying to make a permanent dent in a pillow. Or you may have a more engaging analogy. Then, on a separate sheet of paper, write up what you have in mind.

Objectives: (1) To apply details from personal experience to develop an idea. (2) To use library facilities as a source for material to develop writing.

A writer may start with an idea—which almost inevitably will develop as he works with it—but most of his writing develops ideas. Generally speaking, the writer can get materials for development from two sources: he can re-examine his own background, dredging up things he can remember, or he can use materials that other people have already recorded.

4a   Adequate Development   Dev

Provide more adequate development by increasing detail.

Much weak writing is inadequate because it lacks detail. The writer may get more detail in many ways, but usually the readiest source is himself. He has only to examine his own background or his awareness more carefully. The following is a paragraph from an account by Joyce Maynard of her high school experience, written when she was a freshman in college:

> Marijuana and the class of '71 moved through high school together. When we came in, as freshmen, drugs were still strange and new; marijuana was smoked only by a few marginal figures while those in the mainstream guzzled beer. It was called pot then—the words grass and dope came later; hash and acid and pills were almost unheard of. By my sophomore year, lots of the seniors and even a few younger kids were trying it. By the time I was a junior—in 1969—grass was no longer reserved for the hippies; basketball players and cheerleaders and boys with crew-cuts and boys in black-leather jackets all smoked. And with senior year—maybe because of the nostalgia craze—there was an odd liquor revival. In my last month of school, a major bust led to the suspension of half a dozen boys. They were high on beer.
>
> *The New York Times*

The writing is familiar, natural, but it includes detail and what could have been a dull account has come to life.

4b   Development through Outside Sources   Sources

Provide additional detail by consulting reference works or similar sources, including those in a library.

For much material, reference works and other collections in public and personal libraries provide the readiest means of development, in fact, the only practical ones. Much writing relies almost entirely on details collected by others, and even highly personal accounts may require supporting and checking through printed materials.

To use the work of somebody else, however, the writer must learn to take notes carefully, Jumbled notes may lead a student to inaccuracy or even to unintentional plagiarism, stealing another person's work and treating it as one's own. Fortunately, a little care and the appropriate techniques will solve this problem.

Let us assume that a student is writing a paper on usage and consults the following selection from Margaret M. Bryant's *Current American Usage.*

> INVITE, n. *Summary*: Invite *is normally a verb, but it is frequently used humorously as a noun in speech. In formal written English, however,* invitation *is usual.*
>
> *Data*: One study (Gitter) recorded as an example Bob Hope's remark on the "Colgate Comedy Hour" (Apr., 1956); "There's no need for a book of Who's Who! You're somebody if you got an *invite* to the Grace Kelly wedding. . . ." The study cited above found this use of *invite* in 18% of the written occurrences and in 38% of the spoken ones.

Now let us assume that the student takes the following note:

> INVITE. Invite is normal as a verb but it is frequently used humorously as a noun. Bob Hope used *invite* in connection with a Kelly wedding. *Invite* is used in 18% of the written occurrences and in 38% of the spoken ones.

This note is a mess. Any alert student can find many things wrong with it. The note-taker did not understand the passage before he started taking notes on it. When he did, he copied scraps without distinguishing what he was quoting as Bryant's opinion, what he was summarizing (inaccurately) from a remark by Bob Hope, and what Bryant attributes to another piece of research. Compare this note with the following one:

> Margaret M. Bryant, *Current American Usage* (New York: Funk & Wagnalls, 1962), under *invite*, concludes, "*Invite* is normally a verb, but it is frequently used humorously as a noun in speech. In formal written English, however, *invitation* is usual." Bryant gives several quotations including one from Bob Hope, "You're somebody if you got an *invite* to the Grace Kelly wedding." Bryant refers to a study she calls "Gitter," in which *invite* was used "in 18% of the written occurrences and in 38% of the spoken ones."

This note is much better. The note-taker apparently tried first to understand the entry; actually, a little more work would have turned up "Gitter," too, which is explained in Appendix E, but reference books may be hard to understand at first, and a student should not pretend, especially not to himself, that he knows more than he does. If the student needed to quote material, he quoted it accurately and put it within quotation marks. When he summarized he used his own words, and he distinguished sharply between what Bryant concludes and what she quotes from someone else.

4A Following are statements that might serve as the main ideas of paragraphs. Using a book on American history, an encyclopedia, or a summary like that in the back of the *New International Dictionary*, second edition, find three facts that might be used to develop each of these ideas and state these facts in the spaces.

EXAMPLE: A few days after the inauguration of Roosevelt in 1933, Congress, in special session, began passing emergency legislation.

Answer: (1) On March 13 the rapidly prepared Emergency Banking Act ended the Bank Holiday. (2) A bill authorizing the Civilian Conservation Corps was a first attack on unemployment. (3) In May the Farm Relief and Inflation Act was the first of the bills attempting to solve some of America's agricultural problems.

1 At the close of the French and Indian Wars, a series of British bills levying taxes on the American Colonies did much to develop the unrest that led to the Revolution.

2 The first administration of Jefferson could boast of a number of accomplishments that strengthened the national government and the Republican party.

3 The character of American life in the twentieth century owes much to the scientific advances of the late nineteenth century, particularly to inventions that were to affect the lives of most people.

4 The "muckrakers" of the early 1900's built much of their influence through a series of notable books and articles exposing corruption of every sort.

5 During the first half of the nineteenth century, transportation changed significantly in America.

6 Problems of financing the War Between the States developed ways of raising money that were to influence the country for many years.

7 A series of events in 1917 caused enough resentment in the United States to make the public sympathetic toward a declaration of war against Germany.

4B Following is a paragraph from Mike Royko's *Boss: Richard J. Daley of Chicago* (New York: Dutton, 1971), p. 108. Assume that you are writing an article on police corruption in cities. In the space below take a note from this paragraph, summarizing at least some of it and quoting some of it exactly. Be sure you distinguish quoted matter by using quotation marks appropriately. For treating quoted material see **25i**.

That's the way the Police Department was in 1955, when Daley became mayor, and it was the same, and maybe worse, in 1960. He knew about it because it would have been impossible not to. He grew up in politics and the police force was part of the Machine. But nobody was complaining, at least nobody of importance. When *Life* magazine wrote in 1957 that Chicago's police were the most corrupt in the nation, Daley raged about the "unwarranted slur" and defended his police as being among the finest in the nation. They were among the finest only in the cut of their civilian attire and in their choice of cars and diamond pinky rings. Even if Daley had wanted to reform them, and there was no indication that the idea crossed his mind, it would have been an unpleasant job. Some policemen worked as precinct captains. Others were assigned to watch polling places on election days, to assure that there would be no interference with the acts of fraud. They were a source of income and influence for his ward bosses. To tamper with the Police Department would have been politically unwise. And in January 1960, he had enough problems without looking for others.

4C Following is the entry for (IN) BACK OF, BEHIND in Bryant's book, cited earlier. Take an appropriate note from it of the sort you might use if you were writing a paper on several disputed usages. Identify sources. Be sure to distinguish fact from opinion and use quotation marks properly; see **25i**. The names of persons in parentheses are graduate students and others who collected examples of usage; if you need the names of these research workers they are, in order, John N. Winburne, Dominick Bongiorno, Joseph J. Roach, E. P. Gross, Cecilia A. Hochner, Lillian Karlin, Russell Thomas, and Jean Malmstrom.

(IN) BACK OF, BEHIND

Summary: Once frowned upon as colloquial, (in) back of (*as a substitute for* behind) *now occurs in both spoken and written English; in formal writing,* behind *is used.*

Data: One investigator (Winburne) cites this example of the usage: "The artillery was usually a few miles *back of* the front line infantry . . ." (Ernie Pyle, *Brave Men*, 1944, p. 97). *In back of* has likewise struggled up to standard usage and now one hears it employed on all sides, by performers on radio and television, by graduate and undergraduate students, by teachers, professors, and college presidents (Bongiorno) as in ". . . he was aware of a presence *in back of* him" (*McCall's*, Nov., 1959, 88). However, a study conducted in 1961 (Roach) found twenty-two examples of *behind* in writing, only one of *in back of*, suggesting that most writers, if not speakers, prefer *behind* in formal situations. Four other studies (Gross, Hotchner, Karlin, R. Thomas) also found more examples of *behind*. Nevertheless, *in back of* is standard usage now, patterned on *in front of.*

According to a study of the Linguistic Atlas records (Malmstrom), in the context of "The broom is *behind* the door," *behind, back of,* and *in back of* are used by informants of all types in all areas: New England, Middle Atlantic, South Atlantic, North Central, and Upper Midwest States. *Behind* strongly predominates but the other forms are frequent also, especially in Northern areas. *Back of* is used much more often than *in back of*, especially in Type III (cultivated) speech, but evidence points to divided usage, nationally distributed.

*Objectives: (1) To analyze a subject to provide a plan
for organizing and developing writing. (2) To classify
material consistently, using a single basis. (3) To distinguish the relationships revealed by coordination
and subordination.*

Analysis and classification are everyday ways of thinking, useful when we
deal with broad topics and with masses of detail. By analysis, we divide something into its parts for fuller understanding—history into periods, faculties
into departments. By classification, we group items under heads—articles in
a grocery store in different sections, members of a faculty into different departments. The two are companion processes; in writing they work together
to provide order and organization. By analysis a writer narrows his subject
(see Chapter 1) and then finds the main parts of his topic, the main subdivisions of his composition; by classification he assigns scattered details to
approximate subdivisions.

For example, a student recently arrived in a college or university might
decide to capitalize on the thinking he did during the summer and write
something about the problems of selecting a school. He might recall what he
had considered in making his decision. He might remember that he had
compared tuition costs, living expenses, and the availability of part-time work.
He had considered where schools were located, their distance from his home,
and the nature of the country around them. He had tried to find out about
the qualifications of the faculty and the kinds of courses offered. He had
tried to find out about extracurricular activities and social life at the school.
He could examine these recollections and realize that he had, by a process of
analysis, broken his subject into four general parts: (1) financial, (2) geographical, (3) academic, and (4) social. Thinking further about these topics,
the student would realize that each part could be further analyzed, and that
any one of them would supply enough material for a fairly long paper. He
might, for instance, pick the third, academic considerations, and break it
into parts. He would find his ideas falling into categories like qualifications of
the faculty, library and laboratory facilities, admission policies, and curricula. Each of these could be further analyzed to produce a more limited
topic, or they could serve as main divisions for a paper on academic criteria
for selecting a college. The paper could be organized by the analysis. And
details could be classified under the main headings the analysis had produced.

Types of Analysis

Almost any subject can be analyzed, and most topics can be analyzed in
more than one way. Following are some of the commonest approaches:

1. *Division in time.* Past events, whether thought of as history or just as related incidents, can usually be well analyzed by time. Things happen at the same time or one after another; relating them in time provides ready and often useful analysis.

2. *Space or area.* Time and space are fundamental facts of the world we know, and basic ways of looking at things. From one point of view a community is a pattern of spaces—the inner city, residential districts, suburbs, shopping centers, manufacturing and wholesaling areas, and the like. Space may be linear, with towns strung along a river or a highway.

3. *Purpose, use, adequacy.* Most things have use or purpose, and they satisfy the purpose more or less adequately. Community colleges and junior colleges differ in part because they have somewhat different purposes. Similarly, some colleges may do a great deal for students, whereas some may not.

4. *Parts of a system, institution, mechanism, or area.* A major league baseball team is part of a system called a league, and the third baseman is part of a system called a team. An admission system is part of an institution, and a disc brake part of a mechanism.

5. *Parts of a discussion.* Every idea, every argument, every effort to decide what to do can be broken down into parts. The analysis above, in which the student considers how to choose a college, is an example.

6. *Parts of a process.* Processes, practices, techniques, ways of doing things, can be analyzed. Anybody who has learned to start a car knows that the major action can be broken down into lesser actions, into steps in the action. Even actions that are called "automatic," such as the working of the automatic gear shift, are part of a series.

7. *Aspects of character.* People are common subjects of writing, and people have many traits. They may be more than the sum of their apparent traits, but noticing the traits can help.

Any extensive analysis is likely to require a breakdown on more than one basis. The description of a college or university would be likely to require some analysis in terms of time, considering the various periods of growth. Analysis in terms of space and the nature of an institution would also be necessary. But only one basis of analysis should be used at a time; birth control devices can be broken down into mechanical, chemical, and temporal devices, into those that are effective and those that are not; but the bases should not be mixed. One cannot divide such devices into mechanical, chemical, and ineffective—some of both the mechanical and chemical may be ineffective.

5a Analysis and Writing   An

*Use analysis as a means of limiting a topic or consider
it as a means of development.*

By breaking a subject into its parts, that is, by analysis, any subject can be reduced to workable size. Beginning writers tend to attempt subjects too large, so large that adequate development becomes impossible. Analysis can save them. If necessary they can break a subject into parts, and then break these parts into their components, and can continue breaking it down until a topic is the right size. They need observe only one caution: analyze on only one basis at a time. A writer may analyze the first time on the basis of purpose and a second time on the basis of usefulness, but he should not mix the results.

Likewise, analysis can provide a means of development. Our hypothetical student discovered that on the whole colleges and universities have three sorts of admission policies. If the writer is preparing a paper long enough, this tripartite division would provide a good basis for development and organization.

5b **Classification**	**Class**

Reexamine classification; be sure it is consistent and made on only one basis at a time.

Classification works with analysis. Analysis provides the topic, the heading, the group, or the subject. Classification supplies the details to be included in the group, the information that provides the development of a topic. In the example above, once the writer had decided by analysis that he wants to discuss the problems of a black ghetto student confronted with admission to an institution of higher learning, he has a basis for knowing what to include and what to exclude. Among others, he could exclude the problems of white students, the difficulty of getting part-time work, the relative value of various diplomas.

Almost everything can be classified in more than one way, because almost everything has more than one characteristic. But items should be classified under only one heading at a time. People may be classified as adults and minors if the classification is made on the basis of legal age; as Democrats, Republicans, independents, and members of minor parties if the basis of classification is voter preference; but they should be put into only one classification at a time.

Coordination and Subordination

Coordination and *subordination* are terms used to describe the relationships revealed by analysis and classification. They can be applied to real-life events or situations or to writing. In a business partnership, for example, two people may share control, with equal responsibility and authority; in an analysis of the structure of the business they would be considered coordinate. In this analysis, everybody working for them would be considered subordinate to them in some way. These labels, however, would apply only to the relationships among these people as they functioned in the business; the terms would apply only to one way of analyzing and classifying employers and employees. They would not necessarily describe the inherent abilities or characteristics of the various individuals. The two partners, for instance, might both be members of a military reserve unit, one a captain and one a private. In analyzing the organization of the unit, they would not be considered coordinate; the private would be subordinate to the captain. Or a secretary, clearly subordinate in a description of the business, might be more beautiful, more intelligent, and better informed than her boss—his equal or superior except in the business structure. He might propose marriage, producing a quite different set of relationships outside the business.

Similarly, in the analysis about questions to be considered in selecting a college, the six main divisions of the subject—financial, spatial, geographical, and so on—are coordinate, but are all subordinate to the main topic.

In writing, coordination and subordination express the particular kinds of relationships the writer wants to stress, the results of his individual analysis and classification of his material. Consider the following paragraph from a discussion of the future of the English language.

> We have seen that a language may be considered from the point of view of its words, its sounds, its inflectional endings, and its patterns of word order. We know also that for the last several centuries the vocabulary of English has been very large, that some words have been borrowed from languages in almost every part of the world. Certain languages, principally Latin, French, and the Scandinavian tongues, have contributed heavily to our present lexicon. Moreover, the dictionaries of the English language at various periods of its history seem to reflect a consistent present lexicon. Moreover, the dictionaries of the English language as it was used approximately 1000 years ago, contain about 37,000 words. A fairly complete dictionary of Middle English—that is, of the language of 500 years ago—would have between 50,000 and 70,000 entries. It is likely that a dictionary of Early Modern English, the period of Shakespeare and his contemporaries, would contain at least 140,000 words, and it is a well-known fact that unabridged dictionaries of present-day English have approximately half a million entries.
>
> ALBERT H. MARCKWARDT, *American English*

Marckwardt has chosen to analyze the general subject language into four subdivisions, indicated in the opening sentence. These are the divisions he finds useful for his particular purposes, discussing the future of the language. He might have analyzed in different ways—for example, history, influence, ease of learning—but the divisions he has chosen work. They are coordinate, subordinate to the main topic, language. The remainder of the paragraph develops the first subdivision, words, starting with one topic subordinate to words, the size of the English vocabulary. Then the size of the vocabulary is developed by a series of details coordinate with one another, but subordinate to the subtopic, size of the vocabulary.

5A Using a common quality or characteristic as a basis, classify the items in each of the following groups. Head each class with a title that indicates the basis on which you have classified.

EXAMPLE: cod, swordfish, pickerel, rainbow trout, mackerel, black bass

Fresh-water fish	*Salt-water fish*
pickerel	cod
rainbow trout	swordfish
small-mouth bass	mackerel

1 sonata, tragedy, sonnet, epic, comedy, lyric, fugue, concerto, farce

2 (Classify in their relation to war.) ambition of rulers, imperialist designs, disruption of industry, destruction of cultural facilities, fear of invasion, over-production of armaments, loss of life, lack of international understanding, development of false economy, dissipation of natural resources.

5B Make two separate classifications for the items in each of the following groups, classifying each time on a different basis.

1 leather helmet, shoes, cotton ankle socks, leather mittens, wool gloves, cotton cap, wool hood, cotton gloves, wool socks

2 tennis, jai alai, track, golf, kayak racing, hunting wild boars, baseball, football, swimming, fencing, bullfighting, climbing the Himalayas, basketball, skiing, soccer

5C Some of the following analyses are complete, including all main parts of the whole; for them write *C* in the blanks. Some are incomplete or include details illogically classified; for them mention one omitted subdivision or one misclassified detail.

EXAMPLE: Yucatan is not easy to reach. Native guides can find footpaths through the jungle, and it is possible to reach the country by boat.

by air

EXAMPLE: The tryptich told the story of the Crucifixion, the Last Supper in the left panel, the Resurrection on the right, and the Crucifixion itself in the center.

C

1 Prior to our ascent, only three routes up Mount Rykson had been negotiated successfully: up the east face, along the north saddle, and across Rykson Glacier.

2 The book is an analysis of the armed forces of the United States, the first part considering the army and the last discussing the air forces.

3 Among moving pictures, those dealing with travel have never achieved wide popularity. Love stories and adventure pictures have always been popular. Gangster films have gone out of fashion but detective stories are still popular. Musicals continue to be box-office attractions.

4 In the United States there are private colleges and universities, most of which were originally associated with churches, and newer institutions supported by municipalities.

5 The house commanded splendid prospects in all directions, north toward snow-capped Mount Algonquin, east up the gorge of the Black River, and west over the lake.

6 There are various ways to finish a room: you can plaster it and put wallpaper on the plaster; you can use one of the modern plaster boards and then wallpaper; if the wall is masonry, you can leave the masonry exposed; you can panel in wood, or you can use any of the plywood finishes, which can be waxed, varnished, or shellacked.

7 In recent national elections there have been two main parties, the Democrats and the Republicans; a few splinter parties like the Dixiecrats and the John Birch Society, most of which did not survive more than one or two elections; and a few minor parties like the Communists, Socialists, Prohibitionists, and Vegetarians, which never polled any large percentage of the vote.

8 An argument can be people trying to get in the last word first or people trying to make their first words last.

5D Following are groups of sentences taken from paragraphs on the history of the American colonies. In each group, one sentence states a topic on which the others present subordinate ideas. In the blanks write a *T* after the sentence presenting a topic and an *S* after sentences which are subordinate, that is, sentences which contribute to, but do not state, the topic.

EXAMPLE: First were the Scandinavians, mostly Danes, Norwegians, and Icelanders. *S*

Only the maritime European countries participated in the early exploration of the Americas. *T*

Some centuries later came the Spaniards, followed soon by Portuguese, Italians, Britons, and Frenchmen. *S*

1 Successive groups of Englishmen, Frenchmen, Germans, Scots, Irishmen, Dutchmen, Swedes, and many others came across the Atlantic in the eighteenth century. _____

Of necessity, colonial America was a projection of Europe. _____

These European colonists naturally attempted to plant their national habits and traditions in the new world. _____

2 It was the King who had agreed to establish colonies beyond the sea and the King who provided the colonies with governments. _____

That the King was equally a King of England and a King of Massachusetts the colonists agreed, but that the English Parliament had no more right to pass laws for Massachusetts than the Massachusetts legislature had to pass laws for England they also firmly insisted. _____

The American leaders argued that no "imperial" Parliament existed and that their only legal relations were with the Crown. _____

3 Settling in villages and towns around the harbors, New Englanders quickly adopted an urban existence. _____

Common pasture land and common woodlots served to satisfy the needs of townspeople who acquired small farms nearby. _____

Compactness made possible the village school, the village church, the common meeting, and frequent communication. _____

4 In Maryland the Calvert family sought to establish a refuge for Catholics in the new world. _____

Maryland settlers were also interested in creating estates which would bring them profit. _____

Religious as well as economic reasons led to the colonization of Maryland. _____

5 Support of the increased empire required money, and unless the taxpayer in England was to supply it all, the colonies would have to contribute. _____

Serious in its repercussions on the colonies was the financial policy of the British. _____

But revenue could be extracted from the colonies only through a strong central government, and this could be achieved only at the expense of colonial self-government. _____

5E In each of the following classifications, select the one item that has not been classified on the same basis as the others and write its number in the appropriate blank. The dictionary will provide help.

EXAMPLE: Buildings: (1) brick, (2) concrete, (3) office, (4) wood, (5) stone.   _(3)_

   1 Students: (1) the grind, (2) the apple-polisher, (3) the freshman, (4) the cheat, (5) the student who constantly asks questions in class.   _____

   2 Fish: (1) pike, (2) turbot, (3) fingerling, (4) trout, (5) catfish.   _____

   3 Roofs: (1) tile, (2) gable, (3) shingle, (4) slate, (5) canvas.   _____

   4 Novels: (1) realistic, (2) Victorian, (3) romantic, (4) picaresque, (5) sentimental.   _____

   5 Oysters: (1) scalloped, (2) stewed, (3) fried, (4) Eastern, (5) on the half-shell.   _____

   6 Governments: (1) monarchies, (2) republics, (3) oligarchies, (4) tyrannies, (5) democracies.   _____

   7 Subjects for study: (1) physics, (2) anthropology, (3) geology, (4) ontology, (5) zoology.   _____

   8 Photography: (1) testing the light, (2) adjusting the focus, (3) selecting the subject, (4) setting shutter speed, (5) making photography pay.   _____

   9 Military victory: (1) superior strategic skill, (2) better armaments, (3) more favorable geographical position, (4) psychological preparation, (5) requirement of reparations payment.   _____

   10 Good study habits: (1) allotting time on a schedule, (2) outlining and organizing complicated materials, (3) having a quiet room and good light, (4) keeping work up to date, (5) questioning oneself on important parts of the assignment.   _____

   11 Automobile drivers: (1) the overly cautious driver, (2) the speed demon, (3) the driver who enjoys the scenery, (4) the truck driver, (5) the sensible and careful driver.   _____

5F The following paragraph is less clear than it should be, largely because material has not been classified and presented in an organized pattern. Several bases for classification are possible, one of them suggested in the first sentence. Select a suitable basis, and then on separate paper list details used in the paragraph, grouping them into appropriate classes. Then rewrite the paragraph, using the system of classification you have worked out.

   Australia's three best known animals all have unusual characteristics. The long, powerful tail of the kangaroo is an example. Another is the curious duck bill of the platypus. The kangaroo can use its tail as a third support when sitting up. It carries its young in a pouch. The koala bear is also marsupial. The platypus, however, lays eggs and suckles its young, combining characteristics of animal, bird, and fish. The koala does not drink, but obtains all the moisture it needs from the juices of gum leaves. The kangaroo feeds principally on grass but has a taste for cultivated crops. The platypus has a six-inch tail not unlike that of a beaver, a furry body, a duck-like bill, and webbed feet ending in claws. The koala sleeps in a tree during the day and wakes as much as it ever does at night. Female koalas are habitual kidnappers and steal one another's babies whenever they can. The platypus hunts its food in rivers and creeks. The koala is a small, soft, furry bear, weighing only about twenty pounds.

PATTERNS OF ORGANIZATION: 6
THE OUTLINE

Objectives: (1) To put materials into an order suitable for the topic and the writer's purpose. (2) To make an outline that consistently reveals patterns of coordination and subordination.

Analysis, classification, coordination, and subordination establish much of the organization of a composition. In addition, however, the writer must decide on the order in which he will present his materials. Following are some of the commonest ways in which details can be ordered.

Chronological organization.   An obvious way to plan a paper is to put first things first, that is, to organize according to time. Order reveals a time relationship to the reader; the reader infers that what is set down first happened first. If we read:

The mouse began to nibble the cheese. The trap closed with a sharp click.

we assume something about the fate of the mouse. If we reverse the order of the sentences, the mouse has gained a reprieve. Order reveals so much about the sequence of events that chronological organization is usual for a record of happenings, a narrative.

Spatial organization.   A description of a scene is often clearest if the arrangement of details reflects their relationships in space. Details may be enumerated in the order in which they might meet an observer's eye, or as they relate to some fixed point near the scene.

Logical organization.   Details can be arranged so that their order reveals or enforces relationships of coordination and subordination. A composition advocating improved facilities for social activities for women students might present first the needs and then the possible methods for reform.

Ascending or descending order of importance.   Some material can best be ordered on the basis of importance. If a writer is trying to convince or impress his reader, he may wish to start with his weakest argument, with his least interesting details, and build up to his strongest evidence or his most startling facts. The reverse order also has its uses; newspaper accounts usually put the most newsworthy material first and grade down from what is called the "lead." Newspaper writers know that readers may start many items but finish few of them.

Cause to effect, effect to cause.   Often causes cannot be known, and effects may be difficult to identify. Doctors labor to discover the causes of diseases, but frequently they cannot. The results of lead poisoning or atomic exposure may not be known for decades or even centuries. But whenever cause-effect relationships can be known, they may provide the most revealing sort of organization.

6a Appropriate Organization   Org

Reexamine organization; be sure you have an orderly plan and follow it consistently.

Organizing is necessary in all stages of composition—in selecting and ordering material in the prewriting stages, in writing, and in revision. In all these processes, outlining can be a useful tool. Particularly as a way of checking on the consistency of a plan, it is useful to make an outline of a draft of the paper as it has turned out. The outline usually reveals any weaknesses in the organization of the paper and suggests ways of revising.

Making and Using Outlines

Outlines have two main uses. They may be used as a study technique. Many students have developed the habit of outlining their textbooks, and find that once they have outlined a chapter, they remember it. And if they have trouble recalling information, the outline gives them a start.

The other use is to provide a skeleton for a piece of writing, a plan to which the writer can add notes to himself, or an orderly summary to guide revision.

The readiest way to make an outline is to start jotting things down, random thoughts on a subject. Let us assume that a student has recently received a credit card from an oil company, and he thinks this is interesting enough to write about. He jots down the following notes:

> I just got a credit card from the Super Oil Company.
> I find I can use it at some motels, too.
> It is really a new kind of money.
> I hear there are other kinds of credit cards, but I don't know much about them.
> Mother had a credit card, one from a department store and probably some others.
> They allowed her to buy what she wanted to when she wanted to, whether she happened to have the money or not.
> I wonder what happens if you lose a credit card. Can people run up bills on it?

Looking back over this list the student realizes that he has three ideas here: (1) credit cards represent a new kind of money; (2) there are several kinds of credit cards; and (3) credit cards may have both advantages and disadvantages. Accordingly, he tries to arrange these ideas under three headings. He knows that the standard form for an outline is the following:

Title

Statement of main idea (see **2b**)

I. _____
   A. _____
      1. _____
      2. _____
   B. _____
II. _____
   A. _____
   B. _____

In this form the roman numerals (I and II) represent the principal subdivisions of the main idea, A and B are the results of analyzing I and II, and such headings as 1 and 2 are subdivisions of A and B.

Accordingly, the student now tries to fit his jottings into this pattern, leaving himself notes on omissions or inconsistencies. He improves the wording as he can and produces the following:

The New Money

Main Idea: Credit cards, the new money, have many conveniences, but they have some dangers, too.

  I. Credit cards are the new money.
 II. There must be various sorts of credit cards.
   A. Some companies issue credit cards.
     1. The most widely used are oil company cards.
       a. They can be used at any station representing that company.
       b. They have some other limited use.
     2. Various businesses like department stores issue credit cards good only at that store.
     (Find out about other sorts of cards.)
III. Credit cards are partly good, partly bad.
   A. They do have great convenience.
     1. One can buy what he wants when he wants it.
     2. He does not have to carry much money, thus avoiding loss, discouraging robberies, and the like.
     3. Oil credit cards can also be used for some motels.
   B. (Find out more about what happens if your credit cards are stolen.)

Looking back over his outline, the student notices several things. First, his number I says that credit cards are the new kind of money. The statement implies that there are older kinds of money. What are they? Similarly, for his number II he has only one subhead; but he must have missed important subdivisions. He has already noticed that his III, B needs development, and he notices now that his III, A, 3, about the oil credit cards being good for some motels, belongs somewhere else, probably under II, A, 1. Accordingly, he makes some inquiries and revises his outline so that it looks as follows:

The New Money

Main Idea: Credit cards, the new form of money, provide many conveniences, but involve some dangers.

Introduction: Perhaps start by describing my troubles when I got caught in a blizzard with very little money and had trouble getting any credit.

    I. Credit cards are becoming the modern money.

        A. Formerly, buying and selling was done by barter, then through cash as a medium.

        B. Checks and bank drafts greatly simplified financial exchanges.

        C. Now credit cards are replacing checks, and they may lead to credit systems relying on computers.

    II. Currently, credit cards are mainly of three sorts.

        A. Some credit cards can be used nationally, even internationally.

            1. These are cards like Diner's Club and American Express; the user must buy them.

            2. They account for only a small percentage of credit sales.

        B. The rapidly growing cards are free national cards like Bank-America and Master Charge.

        C. Some individual companies issue credit cards.

            1. The most widely used are the oil company cards.

                a. They are honored at any service station representing the company.

                b. They have other limited uses, at some motels, restaurants, and the like.

            2. Various businesses, including many department stores and chain stores, issue cards valid only at that store or chain.

   III. Credit cards are not an unmixed blessing.

        A. They offer many conveniences.

            1. The holder can buy what he wants when he wants it.

            2. He does not have to carry much money, thus avoiding loss, discouraging muggings, and the like.

            3. In emergencies credit cards even permit the card holder to borrow money quickly.

        B. They have their limitations.

            1. They are time-consuming; somebody has to make out the form.

            2. Some merchants resent credit cards because they become in effect a tax on business.

            3. Unless the card holder insures himself against loss, he can face big bills if his credit card is lost or stolen.

Formally, there are two kinds of outlines, the sentence outline and the word-and-phrase outline. Obviously, the outline just presented is a sentence outline; every entry is a complete sentence. It has the advantage of reflecting the writer's thinking rather accurately, of preserving phraseology he may want to use when he writes, and of providing quite a bit of detail. The word-and-phrase outline has the advantage of being briefer. The sentence outline, put into word-and-phrase form, would look something like the following:

Main Idea: Credit cards, the new form of money, provide many conveniences, but involve some dangers.

Introduction: Perhaps start by describing my troubles when I got caught in a blizzard with very little money and had trouble getting any credit.

I. Modern form of money
  A. First barter, then cash as medium of exchange
  B. Checks, bank drafts
  C. Credit cards; eventually systems based on computers

II. Three kinds of cards
  A. National and international pay cards
    1. Diner's Club, American Express, etc.
    2. Limited use.
  B. Free general cards: BankAmerica, Master Charge, etc.
  C. Cards issued by companies
    1. Oil company cards
      a. Honored at stations representing company
      b. Limited use at motels, etc.
    2. Others: department stores, chain stores, etc.

III. Advantages and disadvantages
  A. Many conveniences
    1. Buy any time, any place
    2. Carry less money—less mugging, loss, etc.
    3. Borrow money in emergencies
  B. Some limitations
    1. Delay, waiting for form to be made out
    2. Irritate some merchants, who refuse cards
    3. May lead to big bills if lost or stolen

An outline is not a work of art; it is a practical, useful tool to help writers and speakers. It need not be fixed up for display and need not always be as formal as the outlines we have presented here. For a brief piece a few headings will suffice. Furthermore, for most uses, a working outline need not be constructed with the care apparent in our examples. Attention to the machinery of outlining should not discourage the writer from using the outline as a practical aid.

6b   The Complete Outline   Out

Revise the outline—and hence the plan of any paper
based on it—by making it logical in its form.

Although informally listed headings are often sufficient, for a long paper or to insure more orderly thinking, an outline should follow either the topic or sentence pattern and should respect certain logical conventions. A good outline includes a statement of the main idea (see **2b**), suggestions for an introduction, main headings under the main idea, and subdivisions of the main head to give some indication of the details that will be used to develop the main idea. The headings should cover the subject and be as concrete and specific as possible. Logically, any heading that is divided must be divided into at least two; nothing can be divided and produce fewer than two. Thus heading A will be left without subdivision or will be divided into 1 and 2 or more. Classification within subdivisions should be on a consistent basis and coordinate items should be parallel in form in a topic outline.

6A   Following are some characteristics of a good working outline:

1. There is a tentative title and a carefully phrased main idea.
2. There is a suggestion for an introduction.
3. The subdivisions are adequate; no major headings are missing.
4. Details are logically classified under headings.
5. Material appears in an appropriate order.
6. Headings are inclusive, but phrased as concretely as the material warrants.

Below are two brief outlines, neither as good as it could be. In the blanks to the right, copy in the numbers of the six characteristics that suggest means of improvement. Then, in the blank space prepare an improved version of the outline. If the outline is vague, you may have to invent details:

A Fishing Trip

(Numbers) _____

    I. Preparations
   II. Getting there
  III. Getting back
      A. Getting out of gas
      B. Getting a farmer up at night
  IV. What we caught

Revised Outline:

TV Trends

Main Idea: To tell what the trends are in TV in this day and age.
Introduction: I would expect to tell how excited I used to be about
TV, and how I would rush home from school every day and watch it.
And I would go on watching it until my parents made me stop. I saved
up money to buy my own portable TV, but they wouldn't let me watch
that very long either. Finally I quit watching it so much and went out
with girls instead and played basketball. Then the other day, when I
went home for the weekend, I watched it again, and the programs
were all different. I didn't know hardly any of them.

  I. Programs I liked
    A. Space programs
    B. International spy intrigue programs
    C. FBI programs
 II. Programs I didn't like
    A. Doctors, nurses, and hospitals
    B. Westerns
III. Others

Revised Outline:

6B In the discussion you have been given several bases for organization that might be summarized as follows:

1. *Chronological*: events in the order of occurrence.
2. *Spatial*: organization by position, sequence, or space.
3. *Logical*: subordination, development, and the like.
4. *Importance*: either ascending or descending order of importance.
5. *Cause to effect or effect to cause.*
6. *Other*: many are possible, such as personal preference, humor, inconsistency, and the like.

The following are suggestions for possible brief papers. Consider how you might develop each; then write the corresponding number from the list of six bases, inserting it in the blank to the right. In the blank spaces, explain why you would consider this a good choice.

1 An editorial on population control, giving statistics revealing recent   _____
population growth, the apparent influence of family planning or the lack of it, and suggestions about what will happen if population cannot be controlled.

2 A reminiscence telling how you registered, the trouble you had, and   _____
what you learned about colleges and students while registering.

3 An argument intended to show that students should or should not have   _____
a larger part in drafting the regulations that govern the campus and in the daily administration of campus affairs at all levels.

6C Listed below are a series of possible notes for an outline for a theme. The topics, however, are not listed in any logical order and may not be as specific as they could be to be useful. In the space at the right organize these topics into a clear and consistent outline, supplying appropriate numbers or letters and rewriting topics that you are able to improve.

Personal Opinion in Newspaper Columns

Topic Statement: Discuss how personal opinion affects newspaper columns.

Introduction: Something on importance of personal opinion—compare with news stories.

1. Opinions on personalities of political figures
2. Personal opinions important in relaying society gossip
3. Interpretation of importance of social events
4. All-America teams
5. Columnists sometimes predict outcome of sports events
6. Interpretations of political motives
7. Columns interpreting news of national political affairs
8. Discussions of styles in clothes
9. Sports columns
10. Columnist relates current international events to other events
11. Biographical sketches of sports figures
12. Sometimes columnists are writing on society
13. Forecasts of sports scores
14. Personal views of international happenings
15. Predictions on horse racing
16. Discussions of ability of individual sports performers
17. Predictions of effects of international incidents
18. Some columns interpret current news, national, political, and international especially
19. Discussions of sports rules and regulations

*Objectives:　(1) To use devices like repetition, word
order, and transitional expressions to provide continuity.
(2) To write strong introductions and conclusions.*

Every piece of writing has to start, keep going for a while, and stop. If it is good writing, it starts in a way that leads quickly into the main development; the development is such that the reader acquires the information and has the experience necessary for the conclusion, and it stops in such a way that the writer has gained the effect he wants. All this is called coherence, tying a piece of writing together.

Examine the following comic strip:

GASOLINE ALLEY

A person today is so accustomed to following comic strips that he is likely to appreciate the joke almost immediately and not be aware of the machinery by which he did so. But there is continuity in the strip or he would not understand the joke. The viewer of a comic strip, or the reader of a piece of writing, need not consider coherence, but the cartoonist or the writer must.

Let us look at the strip from the cartoonist's point of view. The first frame is an introduction. It tells us who the actors are to be; Judy, a nice girl; Rufus, a moronic-looking man; and Kitty, his pet. The action is also given a place; we are in a cubbyhole in city hall, and some indication of Rufus's occupation is provided by a broom and a pail with something like soapy water in it. We suspect that Rufus is what is probably called "maintenance personnel," in older terminology, a janitor, but he is trying to ape the city bureaucrats by pretending to be busy and important.

The continuity is inconspicuous, but it is there. The vertical lines mark off four scenes, and we assume that these are in chronological order, an assumption that is confirmed by a continuing conversation and by such refer-

ences as *yesti'day* and *t'day*. If we have any doubt that this is routine activity
for Rufus, we have only to follow Kitty through the four pictures. The second
picture is tied to the first; Rufus has said he was busy (although apparently
he had been doing nothing). Now he refers to this pretense of his by telling
what he did yesterday, picking up the cat to go about his job, and looking
in the direction of Judy. The third scene is tied to the second by the same
relative position of the speakers, by *t'day*, and Kitty. It looks forward to the
last picture by Rufus's pointing with his thumb, and by the phrase *doin' th'
books*. The last picture is the conclusion, giving us the key to understand
the preceding pictures and complete the joke.

7a Continuity   **Con**

*Improve continuity by strengthening reference from
sentence to sentence, from paragraph to paragraph.*

Writing should hang together. Several means help. To cohere, writing
must have essential unity, a main idea, as we have seen in Chapter 1. A
clearly phrased topic or theme sentence can help; see Chapter 2. Writing
should have plan and order; see Chapter 6. But this plan should be made
apparent, and the writer will need to add any topical and transitional matter
necessary to make the whole clear.

A paragraph or a part of a piece of writing is usually tied to preceding
material through something in the topic sentence, usually a word or a few
words, a phrase, or a clause. Within a paragraph repeated words, synonyms,
or ideas may reinforce continuity. Notice the following; it is part of a book
about secret messages, *Cloak and Cipher*, by Dan Tyler Moore and Martha
Waller. The phrase in the topic sentence, "of this technique," refers to a
device for tricking censors by secreting information in an apparently innocent
letter.

A refinement of this technique was invented by an Armenian family which
had settled in Lebanon after the Revolution had driven them from their
home in Russia. The Communists used every sort of blandishment to induce
young men who were valuable as laborers to return. At last, three brothers
were talked into going back to Russia. They knew the Communists would
pressure them into sending for their families. Before leaving Turkey, they
agreed with their relatives that in their first letter they would send a snap-
shot of themselves. If the picture showed the group standing up, it would
mean that all was well, and that the family should start packing. But if
the picture showed them sitting down, the family was to understand that
the worker's paradise was not as advertised, and that it would be safer
to stay put.

At last the letter arrived, full of praise for the life in Communist
Armenia. Enclosed was the promised picture of the three young men—
lying flat on the ground.

The idea of the family is carried throughout, although broken into two parts, the "three young men" and the remainder of the family in Turkey. Other references abound. The idea of the *technique* is carried through the whole, along with the repressions and trickery of the Communists.

7b Transitions Trans

Improve continuity by adding or revising transitions.

We have seen in 7a that the essential unity of a piece of writing must be made apparent through devices that ensure continuity. Among these are transitions, references that remind the reader of what has come before or is about to follow and that suggest the relationship among the various parts of the composition. Most frequently, this transitional material is part of the topic sentence; see Chapter 2.

For example, notice the following pair of sentences:

> After months of indecision, I finally decided one night that I ought to go to college and get a degree.

This is the final sentence of an introductory paragraph. A new paragraph begins as follows:

> With my mind made up, I started feverishly examining every college or university catalog I could get my hands on.

Here the phrase "with my mind made up" is transitional. It links the new paragraph to the preceding one.

Most transitions can be brief, and some words serve mainly as transitions, such terms as *however, nevertheless, accordingly, thus, therefore, likewise, similarly*. They have different meanings, and since they carry a heavy burden they should be chosen with care. *Accordingly* introduces a result; *similarly* provides an additional example; *however* provides for an exception. Sometimes longer transitions may be required. A transitional sentence may be needed along with a topic sentence, and in more complex pieces of writing a transitional paragraph may lead the reader from one part of the composition to another. Transitions should be as brief as may be, considering the job to be done, but they should appear wherever needed.

7c Introductions Intro

Provide a more adequate introduction or an introduction more aptly suited to the composition.

Every piece of writing has to start, but a good introduction provides something more than a starting place. It leads the reader into the piece of writing, giving him something that will prepare him for the subsequent development and conclusion. In general, introductions should be short. A book may require an introductory chapter, and an article may need an introductory paragraph or several paragraphs, but for a short composition a carefully drawn theme sentence is usually enough.

Here are some things a good introduction can do:

1. It can state a proposition.
2. It can provide factual background.
3. It can isolate a problem, sometimes by asking questions.
4. It can provide analysis.
5. It can state a view to be opposed.
6. It can justify writing the paper.
7. It can provide a relevant incident, anecdote, or illustration.

Introductions, especially in popular and journalistic writing, may be used to attract the reader, to make him want to go on reading. For some writing such introductions are inappropriate. The author of an encyclopedia, for example, although he may need an introduction to explain how his book should be used, will not try to get anyone to read it. A scientist or scholar, writing a serious report for his fellow specialists, would consider a flashy introduction in bad taste.

7d Conclusions   Conc

Add a conclusion or strengthen the conclusion you have; consider making it shorter, more exact, more precisely applicable, or more vigorously and economically phrased.

Conclusions, if they are needed at all, should generally be short. The idea that emerges as the result of a brief piece of writing may be so obvious that the writer prefers not to insult his reader's intelligence by phrasing a conclusion for him. Paragraphs may have a concluding sentence, but more frequently they are left without formal conclusion. The writer assumes that the transition to the next paragraph will provide any conclusion that is needed. Most compositions of some length require some conclusion such as a sentence, a brief paragraph, or more. And since they represent the writer's final word to his reader, the end toward which he has been writing, they should be drafted with special care. Here are some things a conclusion can do:

1. It can restate the main idea, relying on the discussion.
2. It can add a supplementary comment.
3. It can stress the importance of the idea developed previously.
4. It can bring together the parts of a previous discussion.
5. It can be used to move the reader to action or to change his ideas.

A conclusion should not be long, rambling, or apologetic.

COHERENCE: CONTINUITY, INTRODUCTIONS, CONCLUSIONS   7

7A

OBJECTIVE: To identify and describe some means of promoting coherence.

INSTRUCTIONS: Examine the following comic strip carefully. Review the supposed devices for coherence enumerated earlier in the chapter. Notice the description of the comic strip at the beginning of the chapter. Record in the blank space below the comic strip any evidences you have discovered of devices for coherence.

EVIDENCE: The characters in the strip are Churchy La Femme, a turtle, and Howland Owl, a crackpot dreamer.

CONCLUSIONS: In the following space survey any evidences of coherence described in the preceding chapter and apparent in the comic strip. Then describe any devices you have discovered that seem not to be treated in the discussion in this chapter.

7B Following are groups of sentences from which transitional words or phrases have been omitted; omissions are marked by numbers. For each omission, write in the correspondingly numbered blank what seems to you an appropriate transitional expression.

Christianity has had many versions in America, many strange and eccentric variants. (1)—it has always been inherent in the American way of life, binding it together in subtle ways, even for Americans who do not actually profess it. The idea of perfectibility of man, (2)—, which gives Americans so much drive, is a Christian ideal. (3)—the democratic virtues, which have to do with the relation of one man to another, are essentially Christian virtues.

(1) _____ (2) _____ (3) _____

The history of the U.S.A. begins with a revolution. (4)—the merest glance at the fundamental documents of the time show that, in the eyes of its leaders, it was not merely a revolution against Britain but a revolution in human affairs. It had, (5)—, been in preparation for many hundreds of years; . . . .

(4) _____ (5) _____

Many Americans feel uncomfortable about restating an eighteenth-century proposition in so different a century, feeling that these ideas may in fact be dead, or if not dead, obsolete, or if not obsolete, doomed. (6)—, there are many dangers involved in this course. There is the danger, (7)—, of using the great thoughts of the founding fathers as a substitute for our own thoughts . . . .

(6) _____ (7) _____

The revolution of the individual can never become the status quo because the human spirit, as revealed in Palestine by the Founder of Christianity, is limitless. (8)—the task of the revolution, which is to make that spirit free on earth, can never be finished.

(8) _____

There is still one more social area that private parties are trying to do something about. This has to do with the business cycle. The question here, (9)—, is not the elimination of the cycle. (10)—, it is extremely doubtful whether it *can* be eliminated . . . .

(9) _____ (10) _____

How well American management has actually done by its employees is a question that leads to inevitable debate. The fact is incontestable, (11)—, that it has done better than management ever dreamed it could, under the old form of capitalism. The problem, (12)—, may be to prevent management from becoming overgenerous.

(11) _____ (12) _____

Many of the organizations in America are primarily social. Many (13)—, have other functions. There are, (14)—, the so-called "service" clubs, dedicated to the betterment of the community. (15)—, there are organizations that are mainly pressure groups.

(13) _____ (14) _____ (15) _____

7C As indicated in the text, continuity is often reinforced by sentence structure. Of the following pairs of sentences, the one in italics has been changed so that continuity is less clear than it was originally. In the spaces rewrite each of the italicized sentences, adding transitional expressions, changing order to continue a subject, repeating synonyms, or using other devices to improve coherence.

EXAMPLE: American labor is not "working-class conscious." *"Proletarian" does not describe it, and class war is not basic in its beliefs.*

Answer: It is not "proletarian" and does not believe in class war.

1 Twenty years ago it was easy to dismiss the peculiar characteristics of the American labor movement as signs of the "immaturity" of the American worker. *The U.S. may well be today the most unionized of the free countries.*

2 *Precedence is still given by many to the big, quick profit.* Many incline to regard the stockholder mainly as a convenient personification of the profit goal, labor as a lamentably sensitive kind of commodity, and the customer as the man who gets rolled.

3 The confidence that he is the equal of any man gives the American a certain ease of manner, even a brashness, which can be extremely irritating to those who have not been bred to "equality." *The American is a friendly fellow, on the other hand, partly because of it.*

4 Americans, indeed, have taken on the task of endowing man in this way with a certain positive attitude, as if it were their special cosmic assignment. *It is a belief and feeling they have that something important is being done by them.*

5 *Equality usually won the eventual compromise in a situation in which the right of the individual was chiefly a property right.* When a more abstract right was disputed, as in prohibition, the individual eventually won.

6 Because the American system is a fixed system, American society has a reputation for being fixed as well. *The actual workings of our constitutional machine reveal a situation in which this reputation is belied.*

7 Here was the principle of property ownership carried to its absurd conclusion, capitalism gone berserk. *The moral indignation of the American people was also here.*

8 For one thing, the scorn of some of the nation's most effective writers made preoccupation with moral issues unfashionable if not ludicrous. *Business seemed to be doing fine, for another thing, and seemed to deserve not reform but praise.*

9 *He has frequently begun at the bottom and often worked his way up by sheer merit.* Or more often he has been carefully chosen from a number of bright and appropriately educated young men.

10 Now the mere comprehension of a moral axiom, as all parents know, does not guarantee its observance. *A subject is more and more acutely aware of the importance of, and thus eventually is influenced by, the constant iteration of an axiom.*

11 There is still plenty of resistance by "polite society" to accepting the union leader. *He is hardly more strenuously resisted today than a newcomer always is.*

12 Only a positive acceptance of the American Proposition, a positive creed, will strengthen both American society and the American labor movement. *The union can be made an instrument for the worker's responsible citizenship in capitalist society rather than just a device for getting more from it only through positive policies.*

7D The following are final portions of introductory paragraphs that suggest the organization or outline of the themes to follow them. After each, write topic sentences that might serve to begin three key paragraphs of the theme, according to the plan suggested in the introduction.

1 ... The cabin was built like an L, with the long living room at one end, the sleeping quarters at the other, and the small kitchen between.

a

b

c

2 ... My father told me that jobs used to be rather easy to get, but the labor market is now worse, partly because institutions of higher learning are preparing many more trained applicants, labor-saving devices are replacing workers, and the city ghettos are producing great labor pools with too few sources of employment nearby.

a

b

c

3 ... Mainly, however, I wish to criticize the style of the novel—particularly the affected diction, the amateurish speech introductions, and the preponderance of clichés in the descriptive passages.

a

b

c

4 ... but for the beginning skier, at least three basic maneuvers are essential: walking, the snowplow, and the kick turn.

a

b

c

7E Think of possible ways of approaching a theme on quick-frozen foods, of possible attitudes you might take if you were writing about them. You might, for example, consider that they are good because they save time, and because they may allow a housewife to serve special dishes that she would not know how to prepare. Or, you might feel that they are bad because they make American women lazy and increase the budget for foods, or that freezing spoils the taste of vegetables and destroys the texture of meat. Then invent two different introductions, as indicated by the following, that you might use for this theme.

a An introduction stating the main idea or purpose of the theme.

b An introduction describing a happening or incident to illustrate the main idea of the theme.

Write two brief conclusions as specified by the following for the theme just suggested.

a A conclusion that summarizes the paper.

b A conclusion that requests a change in attitude or a specific action.

Objectives: *(1) To write paragraphs in the standard expository pattern. (2) To vary the pattern to fit varying purposes. (3) To use indentation conventionally, as in indicating dialogue.*

A piece of writing can be many things, depending on how one looks at it. It can be a series of words or a series of sentences. It can also be a series of ideas, and in Modern English, especially in expository and argumentative prose, the series of ideas may appear as a series of paragraphs, units of writing strung together. Formally, a paragraph is whatever appears between two indentations, but for a serious writer it is more than that. Notice the following:

> Although lower levels of usage may sometimes be interesting as items of linguistic curiosity, it is well to remember that social success in life is determined linguistically by standard English. Common sense, therefore, tells us not to use taboo words, vulgar words, slang, cant, argot, and so on. Socially it does not pay.
>
> ROBERT A. PETERS, *A Linguistic History of English*

This paragraph is made up of four main parts: (1) the first part of the first sentence, through the word *curiosity*, is transition from the preceding paragraph; (2) the remainder of the sentence is a topic sentence (see Chapter 2), introduced by the evaluative statement, "it is well to remember"; that is, the main idea of the paragraph is "social success in life is determined linguistically by standard English"; (3) the next sentence is development, enlarging this idea; (4) the last sentence is conclusion.

A Basic Pattern

This is what we shall call a *standard expository paragraph*. It can be highly varied in length, order, method of development, and the like, but the pattern is frequently a variation on the following:

1. *Transition.* This is usually brief, a word, a phrase, at most a sentence or so, showing how the paragraph is related to the preceding paragraph, a preceding section, or the whole composition. If these relationships are clear enough, there may be no transition.

2. *Topic sentence.* Typically, some topical material forecasts the paragraph. This "sentence" may in fact be a sentence, although for a long paragraph it may be punctuated as two sentences, or for a short paragraph it may be no more than a phrase or clause. In the Peters example it is a clause. Some paragraphs that are part of an idea need no topic sentence other than a transitional phrase or so, because topical material has appeared earlier and

carries over to the present paragraph. Topic sentences may appear anywhere, but they usually work best as the first sentence or part of it.

3. *Development.* Usually, development takes up most of the paragraph, particularly if a paragraph is adequately developed. Longer paragraphs usually reflect more than one method of development; see Chapter 3.

4. *Organization.* A paragraph should be consciously organized. Especially for brief paragraphs, the author may assume he can safely trust his reader to guess the organization. Even so, in much writing the reader can grasp the idea sooner and clearer if he knows the organization without having to guess at it. Some paragraphs break into two or more distinct parts; if so, the reader should be shown where these parts begin and end.

5. *Conclusion.* A paragraph may end with a conclusion. For many paragraphs the conclusion is obvious enough so that it can be left to the reader.

The following paragraph is the next after the passage quoted above; the numbers are not part of the original, but are inserted to aid discussion.

(1) A *dialect* is a regional or class variety of a language that differs from the standard language in features of phonology, morphology, syntax, and vocabulary. (2) As a variety of a language, each dialect differs from every other in some linguistic features. (3) For example, the Southern dialect of American English differs from the Northern dialect of American English in various linguistic features. (4) The Southern, Northern, and other regional American dialects, however, together make up or constitute American English. (5) Although the dialects of a language differ from each other, each contains features of the linguistic core or structure of the language. (6) If this were not so, speakers of different dialects would be unable to communicate with each other. (7) But, as we know, speakers of the different American dialects are able to communicate with each other, because each American dialect shares a sufficient number of common linguistic features intelligible to speakers of the other dialects. (8) For example, a Northerner may have some difficulty in understanding every phrase and expression a Southerner uses, but the linguistic difficulties he encounters are not so great as to make communication between the two speakers impossible.

The first sentence is the topic sentence; it explains that the paragraph will be a definition of *dialect*. Sentence 2 is what is sometimes called a subtopic sentence. It repeats the idea of the topic sentence, adding some details, and it serves as a sort of topic sentence for the first part of the paragraph, announcing that dialects differ. Sentence 3 starts the development, and we are warned by the transitional phrase, *for example*. That is, this part of the paragraph is to be developed at least in part by an example; the organization hinted at in sentence 2 is being made specific. Sentences 4 and 5 continue the example, the relationships among the three sentences being indicated through words like *however* and *although*. Sentence 6 is a conclusion for this first part of the paragraph. Sentence 7 is a subtopic sentence for the second part of the paragraph, the break signaled by the word *but*. We are warned that the second part of the paragraph will grow from the first, but that it will differ somewhat from it. We are also told what this difference will be; we have learned that dialects differ, but we are now being told that the differences are limited. Sentence 8 is development, and again the organization is made clear by the phrase *for example*. There is no conclusion. Peters might have written a ninth sentence, something like the following: "We can now see that dialects differ, but that they do not differ so much as do languages; the speaker of one dialect can understand a speaker of another dialect of the same language." Apparently, he thought this conclusion was obvious enough.

Paragraphs as Commitment and Response

Good paragraphs can be built in many ways, but one of the best grows from the suggestion made in Chapter 3 that writing can be thought of as commitment and response. The writer tries to decide what he wants to say and phrases this idea in a carefully drawn sentence. This is his commitment, what he is promising his reader he will do, and he can use it in his first draft as a topic sentence. He then responds to this commitment, giving an example, as Peters does in the last paragraph quoted from him, or he can list details, provide a logical discussion, or whatever. If he finds that his response will break into two or more parts, he can provide a commitment for each of these parts, in a subtopic sentence or in some briefer indication of the topic. That is, the body of the paragraph becomes a response to a topic sentence or to subsidiary ideas that have grown out of the topic sentence.

Variety is welcome in almost everything, and paragraphs are no exception. They can appropriately vary in length, organization, and method of development. Usually, however, the writer finds he needs to pay but little attention to paragraph variety. If he develops his ideas appropriately, variety comes naturally. In Peters' book, for example, the first paragraph quoted is short, three sentences. It is a conclusion, which as we have seen, can usually be short. The next paragraph quoted carries considerable detail, as do most paragraphs in the body of a work, and is accordingly much longer. It is broken into two parts, each developed with examples. Following is another brief paragraph, introductory to a chapter on writing and printing:

> We have also said that language and writing differ. We equated language with human speech and called writing a system of signs. Although both speech and writing are forms of human communication, the former is an oral system of signs, the latter a visual one. We hear speech, but we see writing.

Peters, like many orderly writers, produces one standard expository paragraph after another, but they vary naturally. This paragraph has the first sentence as its topic sentence, the final sentence is a conclusion, and the two intervening sentences provide development. But here the development comes through contrast. By suiting his methods of writing to his materials, Peters gains variety in length and in development, although he probably did not seek any such variety. Discussion requires detail, and a discussional paragraph, if it is adequately developed, will inevitably be rather long. But Peters is also concerned with economy, and beginnings and endings can usually be brief. As to methods, the paragraph on dialects cried out for examples; most people do not know much about dialects. On the other hand, a paragraph on writing and speaking requires no examples; everybody knows the difference, but the contrast could be made revealing.

8a The Standard Expository Paragraph ¶

Use standard paragraph patterns to replace short, choppy paragraphs, to develop isolated statements, or to order paragraphs lacking organization.

For the second paragraph quoted, Peters could have written many short paragraphs had he wished. If he had, the passage might have begun somewhat as follows:

> A dialect is one of the varieties of language.
> A dialect differs from the standard language in several ways. These varieties have a number of sorts of features. They include morphology and phonology. They also include syntax and vocabulary.
> Each dialect is different in some ways from every other. These differences appear in linguistic features.
> We can give an example of this.
> The first example makes use of the Southern dialect.

For some persons writing like this might be welcome. Children or feeble-minded adults, who cannot be expected to grasp or understand very much, might find it easier than the paragraph Peters wrote. Somebody has described a paragraph as a "mindfull," and some people have more capacious minds than have others. For literate adults, Peters's paragraph is obviously better. It is much briefer and reveals relationships more extensively.

8b Conventional Indentation: Dialogue ¶ Di

Revise paragraphing of dialogue so that indentation separates the words of each speaker.

Paragraph indentation is sometimes used formally rather than logically. Because newspaper columns are narrow, and journalists are interested in what they call *display*, newspapers use frequent indentations, allowing no paragraph to run for more than a few printed lines.

In other writing, paragraphs may serve formal purposes, of which the most common is the identification of various speakers in a dialogue. Notice the following:

> "And ain't it natural and right for a cat and a cow to talk different from us?"
> "Why, mos' sholy it is."
> "Well, then, why ain't it natural and right for a Frenchman to talk different from us? You answer me that."
>
> MARK TWAIN, *Huckleberry Finn*

The passage is printed in accordance with the standard practice of beginning the speech of each person with a paragraph indentation.

8A   Review the summary of the five sorts of things you may expect to find in a standard expository paragraph. Then analyze the following paragraphs, filling in the spaces provided. The first paragraph is from a popular article describing lightning.

> There are a number of different types of lightning. The most common, called intracloud lightning, occurs within the thundercloud itself. However, we will be mainly concerned here with another common type— cloud-to-ground lightning that carries a *negative* charge to the ground. Most of the available information on lightning relates to this variety, for it is the most amenable to photographic studies. Other, rarer types include ground-to-cloud lightning and cloud-to-ground lightning that carries a *positive* charge. Also, thunderclouds are not the only source of lightning. It can occur in snowstorms, sandstorms, near erupting volcanoes and nuclear explosions, and even on a clear day (thus the phrase "a bolt from the blue").

1   Is there any evidence of transition? If so, what is it? (The preceding paragraph ends, "His [Franklin's] work . . . made him the forerunner of modern lightning research.")

2   Is there a topic sentence? Copy it here:

3   What parts of the paragraph are devoted to development? Can you characterize any of this development (for types of development see Chapter 3)?

4   Is there evidence of organization? If so, copy out specific words that reveal this organization.

5   Is there a conclusion? If so, copy it here.

The next paragraph is from the diary of Anne Morrow Lindbergh written when, as a girl, she went to Mexico, where her father had become United States ambassador. Since this is a personal and emotional reaction, presumably written only for the author, evidences of organization may not be as clear as they were in the first paragraph, but attempt the analysis, using the five headings just listed.

This was to be an objective diary. It stops here! I don't care how much I rave if only I could get down to keep a *little* the feeling of what has happened this last week. I wish to heavens I had written it down as it happened, but I was too moved—and too ashamed of my emotion. It has to be written down, though. I must—I must remember. The trouble is that for the first time in my life I was not conscious of wanting to write it down—I have never felt so *completely* inarticulate. So often I have felt: I cannot express this delicate thing, my instruments are too clumsy, too thick. But here, now, all I can feel is: my instruments are too small, too inadequate, I have *nothing* to express this, no way to deal with it.

The best I can do is to piece together painstakingly the small superficial details, all—everything I can remember, everything no matter how little—and rather blindly hope that a miracle will happen, that this conglomerate, patched collection of fragments may ignite somehow—at least for me—and that some glimmering of the indescribable feeling may be relit in me.

1 Is there any evidence of transition? If so, what is it?

2 Is there a topic sentence? Copy it here:

3 What parts of the paragraph are devoted to development? Can you characterize any of this development (for types of development see Chapter 3)?

4 Is there evidence of organization? If so, copy out specific words that reveal this organization.

5 Is there a conclusion? If so, copy it here.

8B Following are a topic sentence and notes recording the materials used in a student paragraph. The notes are listed in the order in which they appeared in the original paragraph, but not in their original form, and some connectives have been omitted. From the notes, write a paragraph, combining, reordering, reworking in any way to produce a coherent paragraph. Your instructor can provide the original for comparison.

Angle, the college's first attempt at a student literary magazine, failed miserably, but for obvious reasons.

Published issues only partly written by students.

Dozen students in title-page list of editorial board.

Board members apathetic.

As a result faculty advisers had to do most of actual editing.

They also selected material.

Much nonstudent writing in magazines.

In one issue: two faculty articles, reprint of an old story by former student, poem by established writer.

Poem presumably included to give issue prestige.

First issues literary in only a limited sense.

Every issue had many reviews, editorials, articles adapted from classroom papers.

Fewer poems and short stories.

The failure of *Angle* does not prove that the campus will not support a good student literary magazine.

Has had no good literary magazine to support.

8C Following are topic sentences of paragraphs with notes on the details used by their authors to develop them. The details are not in the form of the original and are not necessarily in their original order. On separate paper use each topic sentence and the details provided to write a clear, well-organized paragraph. Your instructor can provide the original of each paragraph for comparison.

1 *Topic sentence*: The American farmer in the nineteenth century was subject to recurring periods of critical hardship.

Development: One basic cause soil exhaustion. Another cause vagaries of nature. By end of century dilemma of the farmer a major problem. Century had seen greatest agricultural expansion. Overproduction of staple crops a cause of problems. Also decline in self-sufficiency and lack of adequate legislative protection and aid caused problems. Cotton culture in South had exhausted soil. In West and on plains soil erosion and wind storms had caused trouble. Also in West insect pests had ravaged land. Southern tobacco growing had exhausted soil.

2 *Topic sentence*: At the gates of the national park the family meets its first Ranger.

Development: Rangers in parks all year around. Maintain and improve facilities. Protect fauna and flora from fire and other damage. Public servants in best and largest sense. Have charge of the parks. Cheerfully answer questions of tourists. Teacher, guide, and friend to the visiting family. Trained naturalists. Specialists in particularities of area. Conduct tours, lectures, exhibits.

3 *Topic sentence*: Winter and summer, then, were two hostile lives, and bred two separate natures.

Development: Winter requires effort to live. Summer offers tropical license. Winter and compulsory learning. In summer children rolled in the grass or waded in the brook and this was one aspect of sensual living in summer and country. Also in summer and country one sailed in the bay or fished for smelts in the creeks. Another example of how summer and country were sensual living was that one could net minnows in the salt marshes or take to the pinewoods and the granite quarries. One could chase muskrats and hunt snapping turtles in the swamps. One could hunt mushrooms or nuts in the autumn hills. Winter was school. Summer was the multiplicity of nature.

4 *Topic sentence*: The "American Way of Life" is a phrase that must be read in two different ways.

Development: Vast and complex network of human particulars is one aspect of phrase. Particulars characterize American society. "American Way of Life" animated by certain ideals. Ideals a second meaning of term. Particulars of society an aspect of the term not transferable. These particulars cannot be imagined as native to any other society on earth. Ideals of "American Way of Life" not peculiar to their existence. British way of life animated by ideals. Peculiarity of American ideals is to be found in the attitude that Americans entertain toward them. French way of life and Belgian way of life also animated by ideals. American ideals to a large extent replace conventional sense of nationality. Sometimes ideals even in conflict with conventional sense of nationality. American thinks of ideals as human ideals. He thinks of ideals as universals belonging to all mankind. He thinks of himself as in certain respects custodian of those ideals.

*Objectives: (1) To define terms and concepts accurately
and completely. (2) To use definition for developing ideas.*

The preceding chapter reprints a paragraph by Martin T. Uman about lightning, which the class may have concluded was developed by analysis. The same article begins as follows:

> We know today that lightning is nothing more than a giant electric spark, the big brother of the spark that jumps from your finger to the light switch after you shuffle across a nylon rug in winter, and that thunder is the noise created by the spark as its hot gasses expand against the surrounding air.

This sentence is definition, whatever else it may be. It tells us that lightning is a spark, an electric spark, but a spark so big that compared with other sparks it can be characterized as *giant*.

As Uman continues his article he uses definition for two purposes. He sometimes defines words he thinks we will not understand. He tells us that there are two kinds of lightning, *hot lightning* and *cold lightning*, and he assumes that many of his readers would not know the difference, because the two sorts of flashes develop the same temperature and may be more than five times as hot as the surface of the sun. But even as he defines the terms we might not otherwise understand, he is developing his essay. This is one of the virtues of definition as a means of development, particularly of the sorts of definition that rest upon the use of detail. The details complete the definition and at the same time clarify and order the entire composition.

9a   Definition as Organization or Development   Def

Make more use of definition for organization or development, or refine the definitions you have already used.

Definition, as the Uman essay illustrates, has at least three uses in writing. It is one of the devices for clarifying organization. Uman uses it for his introduction. Definition frequently works along with analysis to outline organization; the writer breaks down his subject into parts by analysis and then defines each of the parts. Definition is necessary to make unclear terms clear, especially terms used in a technical or specialized sense. Both arguments and misunderstandings frequently disappear as soon as terms are defined. Definition also provides material for development. As the following descriptions show, definition can take varying forms, any of which may be used to elaborate on a topic.

As with many other sorts of composition, writers are likely to sense intuitively when definition will provide good development, even though they are not much aware of definition as a way of writing. Some understanding of definition may help the writer to use it better. Here are some of the commonest sorts:

1. *Definition by identification.* A child, seeing a brilliant flash, might ask, "What's that?" An older person might reply, "That's lightning." Definition by identification is probably the commonest and certainly the simplest sort of definition, the equivalent of pointing. It is not very useful in writing. Unless the person needing the definition can see or taste or hear or smell or feel the object, definition by identification does little good. Of course, the writing can be supplemented with pictures; and dictionaries, especially elementary dictionaries, may rely on identification for definition: "This is a picture of a horse," "This is a picture of an ostrich."

2. *Formal or logical definition.* This sort of definition, described by the ancient Greeks, is still common, especially in science. It works by putting an object in a class and identifying it within that class. Uman, in the passage quoted in this chapter, is using formal or logical definition. He puts lightning in the class of sparks, and eliminates most other sparks, which are either not electrical or not gigantic. If these two restricting qualifications do not eliminate all sparks except lightning, Uman could have eliminated them by adding more restrictions—for example, that the sparks result from natural causes.

3. *Definition by description.* Formal description may isolate an object, but it may not make it very real or even recognizable. Most people would not recognize lightning if all they knew about it is that it is a big electrical spark. Hence we need not be surprised that Uman uses description, also, in his definition, describing a *stepped leader* in certain types of lightning, telling us how hot lightning is, how fast it moves, and the like.

4. *Definition by example.* Some ideas, especially relatively abstract ones, can be defined in part by giving an example. If one were trying to define *natural force*, he might find he could help his reader to understand the ideas by giving lightning as an example of a natural force. Since most adults have seen lightning, know it has killed people, and have even seen evidence of its power in blasted trees, and the like, an illustration may help make the idea vivid.

5. *Definition by significant detail.* Definition by detail is very much like definition by description. Description by detail is especially useful in making distinctions. For example, in another part of his book Uman distinguishes flashes of lightning from strokes by giving us significant details, the duration of each type of flash. He points out that an electrical discharge "on the order of 0.2 second is called a flash," whereas other types of discharge "which generally last less than one one-thousandth of a second, are called *strokes.*"

6. *Definition by content.* Definition can be promoted by telling what is in something, what it is made of. Uman establishes the source of electricity by describing what a thundercloud is made of electrically. He says that the top part of a thundercloud contains positive charges, and the lower part negative charges, except for the very bottom, which is again positive. Notice that these are also significant details, since they account for the electrical discharge.

7. *Definition by comparison.* Unfamiliar things become more familiar by being compared to something known. Uman helps us understand the nature of lightning, in the quotation above, by comparing the spark that is lightning to the spark that is generated in the human body "after you shuffle across a nylon rug in winter."

8. *Definition by contrast.* Contrast is comparison of different sorts of things, or a comparison that emphasizes a difference. For example, Uman defines hot and cold lightning by pointing out that although the two sorts are about the same temperature, hot lightning starts forest fires, but cold lightning does not.

9. *Definition by interpretation.* Interpretation may enhance definition. Uman recounts Benjamin Franklin's famous experiment with a key attached to the string of a kite, and by interpreting it can define it as the beginning of modern research into lightning.

10. *Definition by origin.* Origins may help to define. Uman helps us see the difference among different sorts of lightning by describing their different origins. Definition by origin is especially useful in defining organizations, institutions, principles, and the like. An athletic club may owe its origin to the belief of some students that athletics is not sufficiently supported, and the origin of the club may reveal its character, in effect, define it. Similarly, the origin of a club promoting zero population, or of a club that shows foreign moving pictures, may define it and its activities.

Fallacies in Definition

Definitions may be used improperly or inadequately or even misused. Following are some of the readiest pitfalls in definition:

1. *Misclassification.* In formal definition, the object to be defined must be put in the proper class. Aristotle failed to understand lightning in part because he misclassified it. He thought it was an exhalation of dry air that caught fire. More subtly, many people misunderstand because they misclassify, although they are not aware of making a formal definition when they do so. For example, some people think of a college or a university as a business—perhaps because institutions of higher learning require large budgets—and try to judge schooling on a campus on the basis of profit or loss.

2. *Inadequate differentiation.* Logically, a formal definition should include enough qualifications to eliminate all the other objects in a class. For instance, the definition of *standard poodle* must contain so many qualifications that other members of the family *Canidae*, both dogs and all other dog-like

creatures, are eliminated. This way of defining may become complex, and completeness often is not necessary in writing, but good formal definition requires enough qualifying details so that the definition is clear for the purposes in hand.

3. *Circular definition.* Usually, nothing can be well defined in terms of itself. To say that "a football is the ball used in a game called football" does not tell us much of what a football looks like. The Norsemen played a game after a battle that they called football. For it they are said to have used the severed heads of their fallen enemies. A definition that does not distinguish between a human head and an inflated, oblate, leather or plastic ball is not a very good definition.

4. *Definition too general.* Some definitions must be general, but usually a definition, like other sorts of writing, profits from being precise and exact. Particularly in definition by description, comparison, contrast, or interpretation, at least some details should be concrete and ·specific.

5. *Definition through faulty origin.* Origins may go far back, and may be unknown. Guessing at origins, or accepting other people's bad guesses, can lead to unsound definition. Aristotle, in the discussion referred to under Misclassification, thought that thunder was caused by the impact of escaping air on the surrounding clouds, and hence concluded that thunder preceded lightning. Considering the state of science in Aristotle's day, he was making a good guess, but he was misinformed about the origin of thunder and lightning, and partly as a consequence misdefined both of them.

6. *Confusion of analogy and example.* An analogy is a comparison of unlike things that have something in common. A basketball team is like an ant colony in the sense that various individuals in each are involved in different activities, but the two sorts of groups are so different that using one to define the other requires great caution.

7. *Failure to select significant details.* Given a dog and a cat, we might say that one is brown and the other black, that one weighs twice as much as the other, that one sleeps with its head between its paws and the other does not. But these are not very significant details for distinguishing between the two or defining either. With individual cats and dogs the details might as well be reversed. To define with details, the writer must choose significant details, details that differentiate or reveal essential characteristics.

9A For each of the following terms produce a logical definition, writing down first the general class into which you will place the term, then writing notes on how you will differentiate it from others in the class, then writing the definition as a statement. Use the dictionary when you need to.

1 Calumet

class

differentiae

definition

2 Pollution

class

differentiae

definition

3 Red

class

differentiae

definition

4 Political party

class

differentiae

definition

9B Evaluate the following formal definitions by writing in each blank one of the following numbers:

1, if the definition seems to you clear and adequate;
2, if what is to be defined is not clearly put into a class;
3, if differentiae are not sufficiently inclusive or exclusive;
4, if differentiae are not understandable in nontechnical writing;
5, if differentiae merely repeat what is to be defined.

1   Man is a two-legged carnivore without feathers.   _____

2   A cormorant has a long neck, a wedge-shaped tail, a hooked beak, and a patch of bare, often brightly colored skin under the mouth.   _____

3   Pachisi is a game played in India.   _____

4   A pipe organ is a wind musical instrument consisting of from one to many systems of pipes sounded by compressed air and played by means of one or more keyboards.   _____

5   A horseless carriage is a carriage propelled by means other than a horse.   _____

6   A sonnet is a poem with a division in the thought, usually after the first eight lines.   _____

7   A raphe is in anatropous ovules that part of the funicle adnate to the integument forming a ridge along the body of the ovule.   _____

8   An orator is a public speaker who can talk forever without saying anything.   _____

9   Philately is the collection and study of postage stamps.   _____

10   Freedom is the quality or state of being free.   _____

11   A metaphor is a figure of speech in which a name or descriptive term is transferred to some object to which it does not usually apply but with which it suggests a comparison or analogy.   _____

12   An empire is a group of nations or states under a single sovereign power.   _____

13   Induction is a process in logic by which a general principle is derived from particular instances.   _____

14   An albatross is a large sea bird.   _____

15   A grogshop is a shop that sells grog.   _____

16   An honest man is the noblest work of God.   _____

17   Tragedy is a type of drama in which somebody dies at the end.   _____

18   A line is length without breadth.   _____

19   Character traits are the basic continuum that, when operative in conjunction with surrounding conditions, provide the frame of reference indicative of the adaptation of emotional adjustment factors to life situations.   _____

20   Women are only children of a larger growth.   _____

21   Man is a tool-using animal; without tools he is feebler than a big cat, but with them he conquers the universe.   _____

22   *Abortive* describes an action or project that is unsuccessful because it miscarries at an early stage of its development, as in *an abortive revolution*.   _____

23   An unbridled tongue is the worst of diseases.   _____

24   A true mother is feminine, maternal, womanly, and above all motherly, the embodiment of the reproductive principle.   _____

25   A radical is a man with both feet firmly planted in the air.   _____

9C Review the ten types of definition on pages 68 and 69. Then study the following list of words. See if you can find one word or phrase that you can define in all ten ways. If not, come as close as you can to doing so.

freshman, dean, "mickey mouse" course, curriculum, campus leader, modern girl, hippie, drug addict, quiz, examination

1

2

3

4

5

6

7

8

9

10

9D The following paragraph is an extended definition of language. Study it and then list (a) the general class into which the term has been placed and (b) differentiae that distinguish it from other members of the class.

> The way is now cleared for a serviceable definition of language. Language is a purely human and noninstinctive method of communicating ideas, emotions, and desires by means of a system of voluntarily produced symbols. These symbols are, in the first instance, auditory and they are produced by the so-called "organs of speech." There is no discernible instinctive basis in human speech as such, however much instinctive expressions and the natural environment may serve as a stimulus for the development of certain elements of speech, however much instinctive tendencies, motor and other, may give a predetermined range or mold to linguistic expression. Such human or animal communication, if "communication" it may be called, as is brought about by involuntary, instinctive cries is not, in our sense, language at all.
>
> EDWARD SAPIR, *Language*

a *class*

b *differentiae*

9E Select one of the following terms and consider how you might plan an extended definition of it, using facts from a dictionary or reference book or developing your own ideas. Then list (a) a general class into which you might place what you are defining and (b) differentiae that might distinguish it adequately.

basketball, skiing, fashions, regulations, snobbery, courtesy, conservative, liberal, scientific method, sportsmanship

a *class*

b *differentiae*

*Objectives: (1) To distinguish between inductive and
deductive reasoning. (2) To make generalizations that
follow logically from evidence. (3) To provide evidence
that is adequate and relevant to support generalizations.*

Writing is a record of thinking. Much of the thinking that writing records can
be analyzed into two basic processes: (1) observing evidence and then coming
to some general conclusion about it, and (2) applying such generalizations to
other events or facts. The first of these is known as *inductive* thinking—
using evidence, facts, data, observation as the basis for generalizations. The
second is *deductive* thinking (see Chapter 11)—reasoning from such generalizations by applying them to specific instances.

These processes are fundamental to gaining knowledge, to making
simple decisions, or to thinking creatively. A child puts his finger in a candle
flame and feels pain. He touches a burning match with the same result. Then
he uses inductive thinking and makes a generalization from his specific experiences, that things like a candle or match flame hurt. This generalization
then becomes a useful tool to him for further thinking, for deductive thinking.
When he sees a flame on the gas stove, he remembers his generalization, applies it to this particular phenomenon, and avoids burning his hands. The
same processes allow more complex thinking. Louis Pasteur experimented,
observing specific cases, until he generalized that certain bacteria cause
fermentation and decay. He was then able to apply the result of this inductive
thinking deductively—to milk, for example—and conclude that certain bacteria cause fermentation in milk. He then went back to inductive thinking
and was able to generalize from observation that certain harmful bacteria in
fluids are destroyed at temperatures between 131° and 158°. He could then
proceed deductively toward a method of pasteurization.

The goal of writing, like the goal of thinking, is usually a generalization
—whether a personal opinion, that a particular course is of little value, or a
political belief, that the United States should cease all military aid to Asian
countries. In such writing, two operations are crucial: (1) the generalization
must be drawn with great care, and (2) the evidence from which it is drafted
must be adequate and appropriate.

10a Hasty Generalization   Gen

*Reexamine the generalization, being sure that it follows
from evidence and that it is carefully and conserva-
tively phrased, that it does not claim too much.*

As already discussed (see Chapter 2) a generalization frequently carries the main idea of a composition, the notion that gives the writing its individuality, its "idea." If the generalization cannot be supported with evidence, however, or if it is merely an unsupported judgment (see 3a), it is not likely to be very convincing. The most common difficulty with generalizations is perhaps the most easily corrected; the writer carelessly claims more than he can hope to support—and usually has no need for the excessive commitment. He asserts confidently "Everybody believes it is time for a change in the national government"; he could have been more accurate and more convincing by making his generalization less sweeping, "Recent polls indicate that a majority of voters want a change in the national government." Or compare the following:

HASTY GENERALIZATION: None of the courses given here are relevant.
REVISION: I do not see how my course in calculus will help me to become a television service man.

The revision is less inclusive, but evidence or arguments can be mustered to support it.

One kind of hasty generalization or unsupported judgment is namecalling, an easy substitute for logic and evidence. The device is especially common in irresponsible political dialogue or even news reporting. By putting a label like *liberal, conservative, radical, demagogue, communist, troublemaker*, or *agitator* on a person or by categorizing an event as *tragic, significant, trivial, progressive*, or *reactionary*, a writer can make a judgment indirectly. Such name-calling is usually the resort of a writer trying to persuade a reader too easily, an attempt to cover up a lack of real evidence.

10b Adequate and Reliable Evidence   Ev

*Supply additional evidence or revise writing so that
evidence is adequate and reliable.*

Evidence can be inadequate and untrustworthy in many ways, and the writer must be sure that he has enough evidence and that what he has is admissible and pertinent to his generalizations. The following eight tests identify some of the most common weaknesses in evidence.

1. *Is the evidence adequate?* Evidence must be extensive enough and typical enough to eliminate drawing conclusions from insufficient examples. Experience with two or three bad-tempered collies is not adequate evidence to conclude that all collies are bad tempered.

2. *Is the evidence relevant?* To be relevant, evidence must lead to the conclusion. The fact that traffic in marijuana has increased does not lead to the conclusion that an increase in juvenile delinquency results solely from drugs. Particularly useful for many questions are compiled statistics, because they provide so much concrete evidence; but unless they are relevant, they are of no use. And they seem to be so plausible and revealing that an unwary

person may readily accept them as relevant to a particular question when in reality they are not.

3. *Is the evidence typical?* Some evidence can be found for almost anything. Evidence can form the basis for reliable generalizations only if it is typical. A former popular magazine, the *Literary Digest*, died probably because it became a laughing stock, and it became a joke because it predicted on the basis of a supposedly scientific poll that Herbert Hoover would win overwhelmingly over Franklin Roosevelt. Roosevelt won by a landslide and the *Digest* went out of business. It had made the mistake of relying on evidence that was not typical. The people it polled were its subscribers and those who had telephones; they tended to be middle-class people, not typical of the mass of voters.

4. *Is the evidence up to date?* New evidence is appearing all the time; it may alter conclusions or even reverse them. Statements in print will seem to establish that London is the largest city in the world and that Pakistan is divided into East and West Pakistan—but the statements were probably written before Tokyo started to grow rapidly and Bangladesh became a nation. Even our concepts of things that have not changed may be altered by new evidence; presumably the structure of the moon has not recently changed, but descriptions of the moon that antedated space travel are now mostly obsolete.

5. *Is the evidence unprejudiced?* No one expects a campaign biography to be objective, and investigators like Ralph Nader have shown that even when testifying under oath the representatives of great corporations may alter the evidence to help the companies they represent. In fact, of course, unprejudiced evidence may be impossible to obtain. Even a trained judge, a scholar, or a scientist cannot be entirely without prejudice, especially in the areas in which he has not been specially trained; but the writer should try to use objective material when he can, and to allow for prejudice when he cannot.

6. *Does the evidence come from a capable witness?* A small boy who says that his father can lick anybody on earth probably believes what he says, but he may not know much about professional fighting.

7. *Is the evidence more than an illustrative analogy?* An analogy may be useful for explanation, but it cannot be used for evidence (see Chapter 9, fallacy 6). An analogy is a partial comparison of things essentially different. A duck and an airplane both fly, but a plane cannot run on angle-worms.

8. *Does the evidence show cause or only coincidence?* That one thing follows another does not necessarily mean that the first caused the second. People frequently eat breakfast just after getting up in the morning, but getting up is not the only cause of hunger. This sort of fallacy is very common, because we see so much of the world as sequences of causes and resulting effects. The sun rises and the heat increases; we never question that the sun causes the heat. A diner eats too much and feels discomfort; he may assume that the overeating caused the pain, and he will probably be right. But of course he may not be. He may have an inflamed appendix or diverticulitis or something else. Perhaps because this sort of fallacy is so common, it has

a special name, *post hoc, ergo propter hoc,* "after this, and hence because of this." Such thinking is often logical, but it is fallacious when no real causal connection exists.

Usually, faulty evidence is faulty in a number of ways at the same time. The little boy who thinks his father could trounce a professional boxer is probably prejudiced, is incompetent as a witness, is relying on inadequate evidence, and may even be mistaking an analogy for an example.

Name_____

10A Study the following table. Then consider the statements below it. In the blank space below each question, select the pertinent evidence, indicate if the evidence is in any way faulty or inadequate, and write *yes* in the space to the right if the generalization is justified on the basis of the evidence here presented, *no* if it is not.

BUSIEST WORLD AIRPORTS

Source: International Civil Aviation Organization
Airports are ranked here according to their total passenger traffic for 1969. Airport usage in the USSR is not included.

Airport	Passengers (in millions)	Airport	Passengers (in millions)	Airport	Passengers (in millions)	Airport	Passengers (in millions)
Chicago (O'Hare)	32.5	Paris (Orly)	8.9	Honolulu	5.5	Palma Mallorca	4.1
Los Angeles	21.3	Tokyo	7.6	Minneapolis	5.4	Kansas City	3.9
New York (JFK)	19.5	Frankfurt	7.5	Copenhagen	5.3	New Orleans	3.8
Atlanta	15.1	Detroit	7.4	Toronto	5.2	Zurich	3.8
San Francisco	14.5	New York		Cleveland	5.1	Sydney	3.8
London		(Newark)	7.1	Dallas	5.1	Madrid	3.7
(Heathrow)	14.1	Philadelphia	7.1	Seattle	4.8	Baltimore	3.1
New York		St. Louis	6.5	San Juan	4.6	Tampa	3.1
(La Guardia)	11.7	Osaka	6.4	Berlin		Las Vegas	3.0
Miami	10.6	Denver	6.0	(Tempelhof)	4.5	Memphis	3.0
Washington		Pittsburgh	5.8	Houston	4.5	Mexico City	3.0
(National)	9.9	Rome		Amsterdam	4.3	London	
Boston (Logan)	9.7	(2 airports)	5.7	Montreal	4.1	(Gatwick)	3.0

1 O'Hare airport in Chicago, usually called the largest in the world, accommodates more passengers than the five largest airports in Europe combined.   _____

2 Most air passengers in the United States use fewer than a dozen airports in a few great cities.   _____

3 Most of the biggest airports in the United States serve a few large communities.   _____

4 Except for adjacent islands, such as those of Japan, there are no great airports in four of the six continents; Africa, Asia, Australia, and South America.   _____

5 With only a few exceptions, the great airports in the United States are on or near the coast.   _____

10B   Read the paragraphs below. Ask yourself for each of them if induction is used in the development, write the answer *yes* or *no* in the space to the right, and explain your conclusion in the blank space below.

This open-mindedness could be one of the most important contributions the new voters might make to political life. It also makes political forecasting a cloudy business. By all accounts, the new voters favor the Democratic party over the Republican. In a poll he conducted for *Newsweek*, George Gallup reported that 48 per cent of the new voters would register as Democrats and only 22 per cent would go Republican. Frontlash, an organization whose aim is to register noncollege young voters, says its registrations are running 3 to 1 Democratic nationwide and close to 5 to 1 in parts of California. In New York City eighteen-to-twenty-year-olds have been registering Democratic by a nearly 6 to 1 margin. Yet among the new open-minded voters, registration hardly implies strict party loyalty. Only 38 per cent of those whom Gallup polled "considered themselves" Democrats. Only 18 per cent considered themselves Republicans. If you ask a new voter what he is, he's as likely to say "Capricorn" as anything else.

[The following paragraph contains no topic sentence, but one is implied in an earlier paragraph, that Tallulah Bankhead impressed her friends differently, that she was "seven different women, at least."]

That is why Alfred Hitchcock could call her "a woman without inhibitions," and her friend Eugenia Rawls describe her as "secretive." Vincent Price says: "She was magnificent. There ain't nobody like her. In her heyday nobody had a bigger ball." Virginia Graham believes "she had the honesty of the very rich. She just couldn't give a damn. She said it and she said it. She was a warm, sensitive, loving, emotional woman who put a slip cover on herself because she didn't want the world to know." Lee Strasberg found her "fascinating." Billy Rose: "I've staged shows that called for the management of a herd of buffalo, and I've shot actors out of cannons for fifty feet into the arms of an adagio dancer, but both of them were easier than saying 'good morning' to Miss Bankhead." "A wonderful human being," says Estelle Winwood. "She frightened the bejesus out of me," says Joan Crawford. "I think she was slightly insane," says Tamara Geva.

10C Comment on the adequacy of the following generalizations by writing in each blank at the right the number of at least one of the following criticisms (from material in Chapter 6) which would apply; then comment briefly on each generalization.

1. Inadequate evidence
2. Irrelevant evidence
3. Instances not typical
4. Outdated evidence
5. Prejudiced evidence
6. Incompetent evidence
7. Faulty analogy
8. Assumed causation

EXAMPLE: He is certainly a murderer; even the deaf old lady who lives down the street says he is always trying to shoot her.   *1, 6*

Answer: The evidence is inadequate and probably incompetent. What do the other neighbors say? The old lady may be a paranoiac; if she is deaf, how does she know he shoots; and if he is "always trying to shoot her," it is strange he has not hit her.

1 I've been driving fifteen years, and I can tell you that a woman driver never signals properly before she turns.   _____

2 You shouldn't change horses in midstream.   _____

3 According to a news magazine, "The average Yaleman, Class of '54, makes $25,111 a year." The figures are determined from questionnaires returned by members of the alumni association.   _____

4 I've known many politicians during my lifetime, and I know by now that politicians are never to be trusted.   _____

5 Comic books deal mainly with sex and crime. Four of the five books I found in my children's room last night were lurid crime stories.   _____

6 The youth of America are the hope of the world.   _____

7 At least for myself, I have determined scientifically the cause of hangovers. On Monday night I drank only whiskey and soda and had a hangover in the morning. Tuesday I had rum and soda with the same result. Wednesday I had only gin and soda, Thursday vodka and soda, and Friday brandy and soda, all followed by hangovers. Obviously I have to give up soda.

_____

8 All the girls in Winnemac University are snobs. Why I knew one of them, Jane Smith or Jones or something, who came from my home town, and every time I called her for a date she made some silly excuse and never would see me.

_____

9 Tuesday I argued with my instructor about my chemistry grade. Wednesday we had an examination. It's easy to see why I failed.

_____

10D Following are the topic sentence and the concluding sentence of a paragraph from a book on American history, along with a list of details that might be used in developing the topic. Some of the details listed are relevant, some are not. In the space at the end list numbers of the details that you consider relevant. Then on a separate sheet develop the topic sentence into a paragraph, using the details that you have considered relevant, combining and working them into sentences that reveal their relevance. For comparison, your instructor can supply the original paragraph.

Topic sentence: The main impulse of American energy, however, was westward. (1) New Englanders and Pennsylvanians moved into Ohio. (2) Virginians and Carolinians moved into Kentucky and Tennessee. (3) Freedom of speech had been guaranteed in the Constitution. (4) Industrialism had not yet developed in Virginia. (5) White-topped wagons of immigrant trains climbed the long slopes of the Alleghenies. (6) Buckskin-clad hunters moved into Kentucky. (7) The use of the rifle later became important to hunters. (8) Pioneers moved into Kentucky. (9) Pioneers took carts of furniture, seeds, simple farm implements. (10) Pioneers took domestic animals. (11) Scientific breeding had not yet improved many strains of domestic animals. (12) Frontier farmers began raising cabins of logs. (13) They chinked timbers with clay, covered roofs with oak staves. (14) Year by year more rafts and boats floated down the Mississippi. (15) They went to New Orleans. (16) They carried grain, salt meat, and potash. (17) Year by year, western towns grew more important. (18) Governmental systems in western towns were often primitive. (19) Wild animals, disease, and other perils and hardships had to be faced. (20) Ten thousand rivulets of settlements, nevertheless, spilled into the wilderness. _Concluding sentence_: The keynote of an earlier day—"Westward the course of empire takes its way"—was still the watchword.
Relevant details:

Objectives: (1) To reason deductively, avoiding logical fallacies. (2) To recognize the assumptions behind a statement and avoid unwarranted assumptions.

Most users of this book have never seen a *pinus binata*, and would not recognize one coming down the street, or even know whether it customarily wanders down streets. As soon as a reader knows that it is a Monterey Pine, however, he may know a great deal about it at once; he may have seen such pines making handsome silhouettes along the southern California coast. But even if he knows only that it is a pine tree—which means at least two things, that it is a tree and that it is a needled evergreen—he will know something about it.

He will know, for example, that it stays in one place, that it does not go hopping about like a gazelle. He will know that it has nothing we would call a brain, that it can neither read nor write checks against a bank account. He will know that it does not suckle its young as mammals do, that it reproduces itself by bearing cones that contain seeds. He will know that it has a strong, resilient stem, that it is either alive or dead, that if it is alive it is growing and that if it is dead it is decaying. This is only the beginning of all he would assume, once he knows that *pinus binata* is a plant, the kind of plant we call a tree, and the particular sort of tree we call a pine.

As we have seen in Chapter 10, this is one of the complementary ways we have of knowing things. By induction we examine evidence and draw general conclusions: a plant is a living thing that has roots and characteristically attaches its roots to something, most frequently to the ground; a tree is a plant, taller than a bush, with a strong, woody stem; and so on. As soon as we have established such categories, we can classify particular objects within them, and know a great deal about the objects. This is what we call deduction, and it is one of the basic ways of knowing. The word may be easier to remember if one knows the word *deduce; deduction* is *deducing* information about something because one already knows the class to which it belongs.

And since knowing is closely related to writing, it provides a basic device in writing. Part of what we know we can infer because we have already built up generalizations by induction. Once we have made such generalizations we can write in particular because we can relate particular things to this generalization. But there are pitfalls, ways we can go wrong in trying to use logic, and at least two of them are so common that we should consider them here.

Revise the deductive sequence to make it valid, with the middle term "distributed" at least once and stable in meaning.

Deduction works generally because we can relate two ideas through something they have in common. A statement like "The tree I have ordered from the nursery will have needles because it is a pine tree" depends on a common idea in the statement and in the generalization behind it. The statement can be detailed in a sequence: "Pine trees have needles. The tree I have ordered is a pine tree. Therefore the tree will have needles." The two ideas leading to the conclusion have the pine tree in common. In a deductive sequence this common element is known as the middle term.

This kind of logical sequence, called a syllogism in formal logic, works only when the middle term is "distributed"—that is, phrased so that it includes or excludes the entire class to which it refers—"all pine trees" or "no pine trees." If the first statement of the sequence were "Some pine trees have needles," the conclusion would not necessarily be valid. The middle term would not be distributed. For a similar reason the conclusion would not be valid if the sequence were "All pine trees have needles. The tree I have ordered has needles. The tree I have ordered is a pine tree." The term "all pine trees" is distributed, but it is not the middle term. The middle term is "has needles," and it is not distributed. The tree might be a spruce.

Or consider another statement that involves an undistributed middle term: "Since a considerable proportion of marijuana users eventually turn to heroin, he is certain to become a heroin addict because he smokes marijuana." Reduced to a syllogism, the sequence would be: "A considerable proportion of marijuana users turn to heroin. He is a marijuana user. Therefore, he will take up heroin." The conclusion is not valid, because the middle "marijuana users" is not distributed, does not include all marijuana users.

Similarly, the middle term must not shift in meaning if the deductive sequence is to be valid. In an earlier chapter we encountered the cartoon character Rufus, a kindly, stupid fellow who likes to appear important. He tells people that he is one of the directors. His statement sounds as though he is a member of the board of directors, an executive, probably a wealthy financier. Actually, Rufus, a janitor, means that he is one of several people who give directions to strangers, such as how to find the men's room. Rufus's claim implies a syllogism like the following: "Directors are wealthy business men. Rufus is a director. Rufus is a wealthy business man." "Director" is the middle term and it is distributed in the first statement, but the word has quite different meanings in Rufus's usage from the usage in the first statement. It is an example of a sliding middle term. Or consider an absurd example: "Heels, since they aid walking, are very useful. This murderer is a heel. This murderer is very useful." Obviously, the middle term, "heel," slides considerably. The sliding middle term is useful as the basis for jokes, but it can also distort serious arguments. Consider the following: "It is criminal to destroy the means of industrial production. Strikes, by shutting down machines, destroy the means of industrial production. Therefore strikes are criminal." The middle term, "to destroy the means of industrial production," shifts in meaning from the first to the second statement; the sequence is an example of the logical fallacy known as equivocation.

Assumptions and How to Use Them

We live by assumptions, more than most people understand. But the word *assumption* has acquired a bad odor. We say, "That is a mere assumption," as though all assumptions were bad, or at best not very good. Presumably the implication is that assumptions are less reliable than fact, or evidence, or something objectively known.

The distinction is more apparent than real. As we have seen, supposed "facts" are more or less factual, and supposed "evidence" may or may not be reliable. On the other hand, most assumptions are relatively reliable because they are based on well-known facts, on carefully controlled and sifted evidence. Assumptions are unreliable if the evidence on which they are founded is unreliable. Men once believed that the earth was flat; they thought they had evidence, since it looked flat and people did not fall off it. We now assume it is roughly spherical. Few people know from experience that the earth is a sphere flattened somewhat at either end; probably nobody has ever flown around the earth following the equator and also by crossing over both poles, and then has measured the degree of flatness at the poles. But all educated people believe they have evidence for these supposed facts, and consequently we believe so much that the earth is a sphere that we assume it is a sphere. An astronaut, planning to orbit the earth, assumes it is a sphere—although this would be a "mere assumption." He does not even consider the possibility that the earth was a sphere last year but may be a flat square this year, and that he may bump into it if he moves in an orbit about a center.

An assumption, then, is a belief, presumably founded on fact, and so familiar to us that we accept it without serious question. We rise in the morning assuming that we are still alive, not dead and gone to heaven. We go about our business without forcing ourselves to breathe; we assume that our intercostal muscles, our diaphragms, and our lungs will take care of normal breathing. We assume that the sun will come up, or if it seems already to have done so, we assume that the sun still exists, that what we see is not an optical illusion that will soon wink out, leaving all inhabitants of the earth to perish from cold.

These are, of course, pretty safe assumptions. They are founded on events that have occurred so regularly that we assume they approach eternal truth. We remain pretty much unaware of them. This ready acceptance works if the assumption is well founded—and in toto, most assumptions are—but as we have seen, some assumptions are not. Since, like the supposed flatness of the earth, they are unsound, being based on unreliable evidence, they can become the basis for irrational, unreasonable, or unwarranted action.

Reexamine writing for illogical conclusions, especially for those arising from unsound assumptions.

Particularly dangerous are unphrased assumptions. Consider the following:

This dictionary must be very valuable; it is so old it is yellowed with age.

Many people would accept this statement without a second thought, but the fact is that it rests on a series of assumptions, several of which are invalid, and hence the observation is nonsense. One assumption is that anything that is old must be valuable. On the contrary, although some old things are very valuable, most old things are worthless or nearly so. Another more particular assumption is that old dictionaries are valuable; most of them are worthless. Another assumption is that old books turn yellow; quite the contrary is true. Very old books were printed on rag paper, which never turns yellow. Another assumption is that paper turns yellow from age; much more, it turns yellow from light. A newspaper, printed on newsprint, will start turning yellow within hours if exposed to sunlight. Thus the fact that the book is turning yellow means not that it is old but that it was printed on cheap paper.

All of the following sentences are illogical in one way or another. Some rest upon unsound assumption; some involve sliding middle terms, and some are illogical for some other reason—for example, that the writer has not examined his terms carefully, or that the negative of a proposition is not necessarily true. If the sentence contains a sliding middle term, write *sliding* in the blank to the right and in the space below the sentence identify the term. If the sentence relies on an unsound assumption, write *unsound* in the blank to the right, and state the assumption in the space below. If the sentence is illogical for some other reason, write *other* in the blank to the right and try to explain the illogicality in the space below. Some sentences may be illogical in more than one way; you need identify no more than one illogicality for each.

1 Aunt Phyllis ran into the garage door. What can you expect? She's a woman driver.   _____

2 It is probably true that cleanliness is next to godliness, because for my little brother keeping clean is next to impossible.   _____

3 Tarheels have better taste than any other cigarette because the greatest quarterback of all times smokes them.   _____

4 Karen is majoring in art, but she has no taste; she smokes Tarheels, and they have no taste at all.   _____

5 Senator Fence-mender should not be reelected; he has never had to meet a payroll in his life.   _____

6 We should pay no attention to what Myron says, because constructive criticisms are valuable and his are not constructive.   _____

7 Martin should be the best chairman of the Safety Committee; he got a medal for shooting down a MIG over Vietnam.   _____

8 The referee who called a foul on me was wrong, but I suppose you can't blame him. Nobody can see everything.   _____

9 They should not execute Trigger-happy Harry. After all, evolution requires the survival of the fittest, and Harry was the only one of the highjackers to survive.

_____

10 Since opposites cancel out each other, and science and religion are opposites, you cannot expect any minister to accept science.

_____

11 The painting he bought was junk; you couldn't recognize a thing in it.

_____

12 Mr. Heinrich is a good teacher because he is interested in his students.

_____

13 Cooperation is the basis of modern society but the administration of this school will not cooperate; they refused all of our non-negotiable demands.

_____

14 All schools should be required by federal law to require driver education, because all modern people have to drive.

_____

15 Homer must be an atheist; he has not gone to church for years.

_____

16 Cats catch mice, so our Scotch terrier, which catches mice, must be a cat at heart.

_____

17 Man is a rational animal, but Louise is not a man so she is not likely to listen to reason.

_____

18 A good husband loves his wife, and Sultan Sufi must be a very good husband because he loves all of his two hundred wives.

_____

19 Ignorant people are superstitious; Margy never walks under a ladder, so she must be ignorant.

_____

20 Industry is the foundation of modern American business; my client is the most industrious man I know, so it would be a crime against society to convict him.

_____

Karen
Ral

*Objectives: (1) To distinguish and be able to write
examples of basic sentence patterns. (2) To recognize
basic patterns in complex sentences. (3) To begin
learning purposes for which each different pattern is most
useful. (4) To avoid unintentional use of sentence fragments.*

The following chapters treat the rhetoric of the sentence. That is, they consider ways of constructing sentences so that they do the jobs for which they are intended. Or, to put it another way, sentence rhetoric tells how to make choices among the available grammatical devices. Sentence rhetoric is thus different from grammar, but it depends on some knowledge of grammar.

Grammar is a study of how words work together in sentences, how they are related. A detailed grammar, explaining all the ways in which sentences can be produced, is complex and difficult; several different sorts of modern grammars have been developed for such full descriptions. But the basic characteristics of English sentences, the grammar necessary for sentence rhetoric, are not difficult to understand.

Sentence Patterns

A major characteristic of sentences is that they all, in English, turn about a few simple basic patterns. Even the most complex and lengthy sentences in English can be viewed as expansions of or variations on the subject-verb-complement (SVC) pattern. Following are the basic patterns:

	Subject	*Verb*	*Complement*
1. SV	Birds	sing.	
2. SVO	The dogs	chewed	the bones. (*direct object*)
	The dogs	gave	their master trouble. (*double objects*)
3. SLVN	Knowledge	is (*linking verb*)	power. (*predicate nominative*)
4. SLVadj	Advice	is (*linking verb*)	cheap. (*adjective*)
	SLVadj	The dogs	smell (*linking verb*)	bad. (*adjective*)
5. SLVadv	The answer	is	here. (*adverb of place*)

The *Subject* is usually the first word in a sentence that can function as subject—that is, the first word not shown by function words or meaning to be a word having some other use, such as a verb or modifier or part of one. The *Verb* occupies the second position in the pattern, showing that the subject acts or exists or links the subject to a noun or a modifier. The *Complement* may be a *direct object* (*bones, trouble* in pattern 2), an indirect object (*master* in pattern 2), a predicate nominative (*power* in pattern 3), a predicate adjective (*cheap, bad* in pattern 4) or an adverb of place (*here* in pattern 5).

Unexpanded, these simple patterns are seldom adequate for complex communication; the patterns may be augmented in the following ways:

1. *Using word groups.* A word group rather than a single word may function as subject, verb, or especially as complement:

> The dogs liked *chasing cars.* Everyone suspected *that Oliver had taken the money.* A new car was *what he wanted. What they demanded* was *out of the question.*

2. *Compounding or coordination.* Words or word groups may be combined or coordinated to serve as any of the main parts of the pattern.

> The *owl* and the *pussycat* went to sea. He was *eager* to swim but *afraid* of the water. They knew *what they wanted* but not *what they deserved.*

3. *Modification.* Any part of the pattern, or the entire pattern, can be modified by words or word groups subordinated to it (see Chapter 16):

> The *huge* dogs *that my uncle kept for hunting always* barked *at the children playing outside the fence.*

The pattern 1 basic sentence, "The dogs barked," is expanded with modifiers for both the subject and the verb.

12a The Complete Sentence   Frag

Revise the sentence so that it contains at least one independent basic pattern.

In conversation and sometimes for stylistic reasons in writing, incomplete patterns may be effective; missing parts can be supplied or understood from context. Unless there are reasons for variation, however, most prose is written in complete sentences—sentences that contain at least one independent basic pattern, one that is not transformed, usually with a function word like *before* or *after* or *that*, to function as part of another pattern or a modifier. Usually a fragment can be combined with another sentence.

ORIGINAL: For one important reason fraternities have failed to fulfill their obligations as educational institutions. This reason being their emphasis on social rather than academic interests.

REVISION: Fraternities have failed to fulfill their obligations as educational institutions mainly because they have emphasized social rather than academic interests.

ORIGINAL: Western movies are still profitable for producers. Although plot and characterization have become monotonously standardized.

REVISION: Western movies are still profitable for producers, although plot and characterization have become monotonously standardized.

12A In the blanks write the verb of the main independent pattern of each sentence and the complement of the pattern, if there is one.

	Verb	*Complement*
EXAMPLE: I have heard with admiring submission the experience of the lady who declared that the sense of being perfectly well-dressed gives a feeling of inward tranquility that religion is powerless to bestow.	*have heard*	*experience*
1 A large ostrich walked calmly into the living room.		
2 No one can buy happiness, even if he is a millionaire.		
3 She wore a gown of crimson velvet ornamented only by three heavy gold buttons.		
4 When Helen turned the corner, she could see the two men swinging onto the rear platform of the moving streetcar.		
5 Although the legend of Barbara Allen originated in Great Britain, it has had a new growth in American folklore.		
6 After Jake had cleaned the trout, he packed it carefully in his creel, protecting the meat with bunches of aromatic grass that he found along the stream.		
7 Six-mile Creek ran through a narrow canyon, the walls of which were green with thick grass and moss.		
8 Although the high school was only six years old, students were already crowding it beyond capacity.		
9 The story of the flood, best known to us in the Old Testament, appears in different forms in the legends of many peoples.		
10 Sack, a white wine usually imported from Spain or the Canary Islands, was the favorite drink of Falstaff, a character in Shakespeare's *Henry IV*.		
11 Edward Jenner, the pioneer of vaccination, first developed vaccine from cowpox in 1796, reporting his findings in a paper published in 1800.		
12 Reading the poetry of William Wordsworth helped John Stuart Mill in his recovery from a crisis in his life.		

12B Combine each of the following pairs of sentences, rewriting the first of each pair for insertion into the second so that it can serve as subject or complement of the new sentence. Then in the blank write the first three words of the first sentence as you would change it to be subject or complement.

EXAMPLE: Everybody favored cleaning up the campus. Alfred thought this.

Alfred thought that

[Alfred thought that everybody favored cleaning up the campus.]

EXAMPLE: Somebody washes the dishes. This is Claudine's job.

Washing the dishes

[Washing the dishes is Claudine's job.]

1 John could win the mile run if he practiced. The coach believed that he could. _____

2 The janitor was afraid to go outside the building at night. The janitor explained this. _____

3 The river widens into a deep pool full of trout. My brother knows the place. _____

4 Mr. Jordan learned the names of all his students the first day. I did not know how he did this. _____

5 Somebody feeds the chickens every evening. This was my first job.

_____

6 Someone burned all the records in the registrar's office. He must have had a key to the building. _____

7 Somebody put the pictures on the bulletin board. He must have left in a hurry. _____

8 Somebody tore down all the election posters. I did not know who had done so. _____

9 Jerry sang some of his own songs. Everybody wanted him to.

_____

10 Nobody had reported the accident to the police. The judge wondered why not. _____

11 Somebody argued with the umpire. This was a mistake.

_____

12 Old bottles should be collected for recycling. The club plans to do this.

_____

12C Rewrite each of the following passages, combining whenever possible and eliminating any fragments.

1 A girl can get along in college with a limited wardrobe. If it is well selected. Two pairs of slacks and two blouses. Two street dresses or a skirt and blouse. And one good dinner dress.

2 Surrealism was not just a fad. Although it has lost much of its popularity. Writers and painters being sincere in their attempts at symbolic expression. That is, those who were serious about surrealism.

3 I have never been very fond of chickens. Mostly because they are stupid. For example, the way they huddle together in the rain instead of using shelter that is near them. Or scratching their food out of the feed trays and then working doubly hard to get it off the ground.

4 Wolfe in the days just before the Battle of Quebec looked little like a hero. Haggard with disease and drawn with pain, helpless in bed. In spite of all this his mind dwelling constantly on capture of the city.

5   The Boston Massacre being not entirely the fault of the British soldiers. There being, possibly, an organized effort by agitators to goad the Boston mob into an attack. Certainly, loitering groups in Boston did a good deal to provoke the "lobsters" and "bloodybacks" before some unknown person gave the order to fire.

6   Spanish-American music has become very popular in America. Played frequently at dances and on radio and television programs. Partly because of the interest in dances like the tango. Also the rhumba and the samba. The mambo, too.

7   I was alone much of the time when I was a child. Having, therefore, to create many of my own games. Such as playing I was an Indian chief. Or racing through the woods back of our house. Sometimes stopping to pick up a stick and pretending it was my favorite Indian pony.

8   Theatre-in-the-round or central staging as a practical medium for little theatres. Economic because of little scenery. Effective because of intimacy with the audience.

Objectives: (1) To use the most appropriate
sentence pattern. (2) To choose sentence subjects that
lead to the most useful sentence patterns. (3) To
recognize and revise sentences that rely on misleading
predication or illogical equation.

As we have seen in Chapter 12, English relies upon relatively few basic structures. Each of these, however, has its uses, and works best when it is employed for what it is best adapted to do, not when it is misused for something else. The five basic patterns serve three rhetorical uses, as follows:

1. Pattern 1, if the writer wishes only to name an actor and report his action.

2. Pattern 2, if the writer wishes to say that somebody or something acted, and that this action had results.

3. Patterns 3–5, if the writer wishes to say something about the relationships between or among persons or things.

Clearly, the second of these patterns is the most used, although each has its uses. Our world is a world of action, and actions have results. Most of the time a writer wants to say that something acted, and that the action involved somebody or something else: boy meets girl, John Barth wrote a novel, Becky hates hamburgers.

Pattern 1 serves best as a structural frame for modifiers. If the writer wants to observe an actor and his action, and one or both of these are complicated enough so that he needs many modifiers, pattern 1, with no complement, provides an economical structure. The pattern frequently records a customary or continuing action: "The committee meets on Thursdays." "Dogs bark at night." "She always arrives just before lunch."

Patterns 3–5 are quite different and are suited to different uses. They do not involve action. They are static and concern relationships. We need such structures; sometimes a writer needs to relate things without concern for action. But if the writer uses a static structure when he is writing about action, he weakens his prose and may trick himself into well-meant blunders.

Controlling Sentence Patterns

The following sentence fits regular grammatical patterns and at first glance seems to make a kind of sense:

> The education picture in America, which is extremely unsatisfactory, will not disappear until salaries for teachers increase.

On closer examination, the meaning of the sentence seems either unclear or unlikely. The writer probably did not mean to say what the basic pattern of the sentence says, and the difficulty appears if the key words in the pattern are isolated: "picture will not disappear." The parts of the core of the sentence do not work together. The writer probably intended to say either that the picture will not improve or that the inadequacies in education will not disappear. The sentence needs a more accurate predication in the main pattern:

> Education in America, which is unsatisfactory, will not improve until teachers' salaries increase.

Predication refers to the relationship of subject, verb, and complement. If predication is to be clear, these parts of the main pattern must be selected so that they are compatible in meaning, so that they work together to say what the writer intends.

13a Choosing Sentence Subjects   Subj
Select a new subject and revise the sentence.

Since the subject is the first word in a standard predication, its choice is crucial to the success of the sentence. A writer, for example, is working on a paper about humor in Shakespeare's plays and wants to say something about how Sir Andrew Aguecheek's use of pantomime and his stupidity both contribute to the liveliness of *Twelfth Night*. He could begin with any of several subjects: *pantomime, stupidity, contribution, liveliness, Sir Andrew,* or perhaps others. He might begin: "The most important contribution to the liveliness of *Twelfth Night....*" By choosing *contribution* as subject, the writer limits himself to choosing as a verb something that contribution can "do." In the context the contribution cannot "do" anything, and only a linking verb is possible. The writer resorts to it and easily slips into using an inappropriate complement:

> The most important contribution to the liveliness of *Twelfth Night* is the scenes in which Sir Andrew Aguecheek produces clever pantomime as well as getting fun with his stupidity.

The sentence slides into wordy collapse for a number of reasons, but the choice of subject starts the skid. Another possible choice would lead to similar results: "The reason for much of the liveliness in *Twelfth Night* is the...." The choice of *pantomime* is also risky: "The clever pantomime of Sir Andrew Aguecheek as well as his amusing stupidity produces the source of much of the liveliness of *Twelfth Night*." The writer could, of course, have written much better sentences with these subjects by choosing verbs and complements that can work with them; in fact, in some contexts or for special emphasis, one of these subjects might have been the best one.

Usually, however, the writer runs least risk of illogical predication when he chooses for his subject the name of something or somebody that can do something—in this case the actor:

Sir Andrew Aguecheek enlivens *Twelfth Night* with his pantomime and his amusing stupidity.

And frequently an unclear sentence is best revised by choosing a new subject and writing a new basic pattern:

ORIGINAL: The reason for Angela's wanting to transfer to the state university was because it is coeducational.

REVISION: Angela wanted to transfer to the state university because it is coeducational.

One common variety of indirect predication combines failure to pick the right subject with a vague use of the pronoun *it* (see also **17e**). The writer makes a false start in his sentence, sometimes burying his most likely candidate for a subject in a modifier, and then attempts to disguise the illogical predication by using *it* as a dummy subject. Consider the following:

When there are constant arguments over trivial matters, it makes constructive discussion impossible.

The general meaning is probably clear, but the sentence is wordy and indirect. A revision using a direct pattern 2 construction is sharper:

Constant arguments over trivial matters prevent constructive discussion.

Sometimes when a writer resorts to the vague *it*, a likely subject gets pushed to a complement position:

If attendance records of congressmen were published more widely, it would make it possible for voters to act more intelligently.

The dummy subject only clutters the main part of the sentence, and revision mainly involves cutting to allow the logical subject to work:

If attendance records of congressmen were published more widely, voters could act more intelligently.

Or consider another example in which the dummy subject is even more obviously unnecessary:

With the cash actually in his hand, it made buying the car only a matter of a few minutes.

Revision requires supplying a subject:

With the cash actually in his hand, he bought the car in only a few minutes.

13b Logical Predication   **Pred**

Revise so that subject, verb, and complement can work together.

The following sentence is muddy because the subject and verb of the main pattern do not fit logically together:

The tennis court, which was full of sticks and stones, meant that the match had to be canceled by the coaches.

Although a kind of sense lurks in this sentence, the sense is not precise. The court did not mean; if anything meant, the sticks and stones did. As usually, however, the best revision selects a new subject, the actor.

> The coaches had to cancel the matches because the tennis court was full of sticks and stones.

The writer of the following sentence probably had a subject in mind different from the one that appeared in his sentence.

> Once these weaknesses are removed, they will allow the new sports program to develop rapidly.

They refers to *weaknesses*, and the sentence turns out to be nonsense, saying that the weaknesses will allow the program to develop. The writer probably meant something like:

> Once these weaknesses are removed, the new sports program will develop rapidly.

Program becomes the subject. In the following sentence the writer starts well, but by the time he gets to his second clause he chooses a verb that cannot work with his new subject:

> The administration proposed three compromises, which we could not do.

Such a sentence can be revised in several ways, provided the subject is followed by a predicate that can work with it:

> The administration proposed three compromises that we could not accept.
> The administration proposed three compromises, but we refused to compromise.

We cannot work with *do* in this context, but can work with either *accept* or *refuse*.

13c Logical Equation with *To Be*   Eq

*Revise to correct an implausible equation of subject and
subject complement, usually by shifting the sentence
to a pattern not using* to be.

Sentences that turn on a linking verb usually express a kind of equation —that something is something else or is like something else. The verb *to be,* the most common verb in such sentences, has many meanings, but often it has almost the force of an equals sign in mathematics. When it does, the sentence works only if the subject and complement can be plausibly considered equal in meaning. When they do not equate, the effect is a little like saying $2 + 2 = 5$. Consider the following:

> The first powerful action of the government after the election was its position regarding price controls.

The sentence is presumably pattern 3, subject-verb-predicate nominative, "the action was the position." The writer probably did not mean to equate *action* and *position*, which make no logical sense linked by *was*. The writer can say what he probably intends by revising into a different pattern, without the linking verb.

> In its first powerful action after the election, the government modified price controls.

An equation is also awkward if it attempts to link a singular with a plural.

ORIGINAL: A notable weakness of the architect's plan was the two doors side by side in the kitchen.

REVISION: The architect's plan was notably weak because it placed two doors side by side in the kitchen.

REVISION: The position of the kitchen doors weakened the architect's plan.

The first revision shifts the sentence from pattern 4 to pattern 3, subject-verb-predicate adjective; but the most direct revision, the second, shifts to pattern 2, subject-verb-object.

Perhaps the most subtle confusions with equations develop when word groups appear as modifiers in complement positions. In pattern 5, the verb *to be* does not work as an equals sign as it does in 3 and 4. In "The children are in the park," *to be* is much like the verb in a pattern 1 sentence, meaning something like "exist," and *in the park* is an adverbial modifier. This pattern works only when the modifier locates, indicates a place. But modifiers look so much alike that meanings can become confused. Technically, even the following sentence could be taken in two ways, although meaning makes its intent clear: "The new rock group was out of this world." The sentence obviously intended to follow pattern 4, with *out of this world* functioning as an adjective modifying *group*. Literally, however, the modifier could be considered an adverb of place, and the sentence could be interpreted as pattern 5, locating the rock group in space or on Mars. Or consider the following:

> The device for taking baggage off the ship was by means of a large net.

The sentence looks like pattern 5, similar to "The device was on the deck"; but "by means of a large net" does not indicate place. The sentence does not fit any of the standard patterns, but it could be revised. Grammatically, pattern 3 would work: "The device for taking baggage off the ship was a large net." The sentence is clumsy, however, because it says so little of what the writer meant; he probably was not much concerned with saying that "the device was a net." He had to deal with an action, and he had better use pattern 2, which provides an actor as subject, an action, and an object: "The longshoremen, using a large net, took the baggage off the ship."

Constructions with *is-because, is-when*, and *is-where*, although common colloquially, illustrate the same sort of problem of equation. Consider:

> The reason I failed is because I never had time to study.

Because, like *when* and *where*, normally introduces a modifier, not a word group that can serve as predicate nominative in a pattern 3 sentence. *That* is conventionally used when a word group like the above fills an equation: "The reason I failed is *that* I never had time to study." Usually, however, a change to pattern 1 or 2, with the subject the actor, revises more economically: "I failed because I never had time to study."

13d Consistency in Structure, Shifts   Shift

Revise to avoid either shifts in construction within basic patterns or illogical shifts from one pattern to another.

Shifts in construction may occur because a writer starts a long sentence with one pattern in mind, forgets, and proceeds with some other scheme. Consider the following:

> For any advice about selecting a good guitar may usually be supplied more reliably by an experienced player than by a music store salesman.

The sentence becomes confused because the writer has apparently forgotten that he opened with a modifier and finishes the sentence as if *advice* were the subject. Complete revision, with a new subject, works best:

> An experienced player can usually supply more reliable information about selecting a guitar than can a music store salesman.

For shifts in point of view—person, number, tense—see Chapter 21.

13A   Rewrite the following paragraph sentence by sentence. Choose as the subject of your first sentence *Cardano*. Keep this same idea as the subject of subsequent sentences; that is, as subject use *Cardano, he, this sixteenth-century scholar*, or some appropriate synonym.

1   As part of the heritage that has been handed down to us from the sixteenth century, I have just been reading about the way science and mathematics were promoted by a physician who was the most fashionable one of his day named Cardano.

2   Being a man of skeptical mind, many customs of the day were attacked by him, including the use of perfumes by almost everybody to cover up the fact that what was needed was a bath.

3   Among the principal factors in the admiration we can have today for Cardano was the fact that the first essay on the theory of probability was written by him, and the theory of probability is now made use of in modern higher mathematics.

4   Only recently has credit been given where credit was due in the matter of recognizing the many-sided nature of Cardano.

5 Along with such side issues as dabbling in spiritualism, thinking he had a personal devil, casting a horoscope for Christ, the following factors are among those which make Cardano rate the title *great*: taking up alchemy, contributing to philosophy, while recognizing that asthma is an allergy and he was still the first as a physician to provide a good description of typhus fever.

13B The following sentences are a distortion of the opening of Lord Raglan's *The Hero*. Basic patterns have been changed, and the whole passage is less effective than the original. Revise each sentence, choosing a new subject for the main pattern; then write in each blank the subject you have selected for your revision.

1 The habit of taking an objective view of the past is a quality acquired by only the smallest fraction of the human race.

2 A prologue to the present is what the past is for most people, even most educated people, not merely without interest insofar as it is independent of the present, but simply inconceivable except in terms of the present.

3 Our memories of the events of our own past life are not as they seemed to us at the time, but merely as incidents leading up to our present situation.

4 Persuading ourselves is impossible, in fact is not attempted by us, that undertakings which ended in failure or fiasco were entered upon with just as much forethought and optimism as those which have profoundly affected our lives.

5 Our beliefs and mental processes are supposed by us to have been ever the same as they now are, and the story of our lives is regarded by us not as a cross-country walk upon which we are still engaged, but as a path, cut deliberately by fate and ourselves, to the positions which we now occupy.

6 Our consideration of the story of others is where our minds work in the same way.

7 Every event is judged by us by its consequences, and that these consequences must have seemed just as inevitable to those who took part in it as they do to ourselves is assumed.

8 There is a difficulty found by us in believing that when the ship went down those who were to be drowned felt just the same as those who were to be saved.

9 It is said by us that coming events cast their shadows before them, but what we really mean is that later events cast their shadows back over earlier ones.

13C Predication is illogical in the following sentences. On separate paper revise each sentence by selecting a more logical and more appropriate subject, usually the name of the actor, and using it to govern an active verb. Often the revision requires subordinating one part of the original (see example). Then in the specified blank write the subject and verb of each of your new sentences.

	Subject	Verb
EXAMPLE: The lack of enthusiasm among the students meant the abandonment by the Dean of his plans for a spring study week. [Because of the students' lack of enthusiasm, the Dean abandoned plans for a spring study week.]	*Dean*	*abandoned*

1 The many unsuitable friends he made came about because of the depressing environment in which he grew up.

2 The unexpectedly large number at the try-out meant that another reading had to be scheduled by the director.

3 A new way basketball plays can be taught by a coach means putting them on the blackboard.

4 The preparation of the meal by the girls caused us to be ravenously hungry because it was lots.

5 Teachers' positions are being replaced in many areas by half-educated nincompoops.

6 The wing dams in the Mississippi River means the growing importance to transportation of barge lines.

7 The setting of the story takes place in the mountains of Mexico.

8 The men with masks over their faces made it so grandfather couldn't identify them.

9 Everywhere we looked made us see evidences of the storm all around us.

10 The very appropriate name of one of the characters, Doll Tearsheet, has one of the play's most amusing roles.

11 The situation of Alfred entering professional prize fighting took place for the reason that he desperately needed money.

12 A president in conflict with his board of directors usually produces chaos in a company.

13D   The sentences below contain inaccurate equations linked by forms of the verb *to be*. In each sentence, underline the subject and the complement, if there is one. Some may have no complement. Then revise each sentence by using a subject and a complement that fit together, or by supplying a new verb, or both. Write the subject and verb of your revision in the blanks.

	Subject	Verb
EXAMPLE: A foul is when the referee catches a player hacking. [The referee calls a foul when he catches a player hacking.]	*referee*	*calls*

1   An allegory is when abstract ideas are represented by characters.

2   One other example of Chaucer's humor in his characters was that of the Wife of Bath.

3   To be termed a tragedy, the ending is not, as is a popular conception, the deciding factor.

4   Using the poise gained in speech class is an advantage in any social circumstances.

5   Acquiring leadership in campus activities is a basic factor in the future of any student.

6   A crisis is where an irresistible force meets an immovable object.

7   His reputation was the best farmer in this section of the country.

8   The only way of curing the evils of government in business is more businessmen in government jobs.

9   Getting up a charivaree used to be quite an event when we were children.

10   The picture is how the hero and his girl keep the villain from getting the little black box.

11   The point of the story is no longer about his drifting off to dreamland.

12   The reason for the senator not including the fee in his income tax is because of suspicion there is graft.

13   Happiness is a category to which I always thought Evangeline belonged.

14   The first thing to be considered by the new consul is the rifles being smuggled across the border.

15   The source of my information on the subject is from a large number of recent books.

VARIATIONS IN PATTERNS: 14
EXPLETIVE, PASSIVE

*Objectives: (1) To use passive and expletive con-
structions for special purposes. (2) To revise sentences
having these patterns when they are inappropriate.*

Most sentences in modern prose are expansions of the five basic patterns
described in Chapter 12, following subject-verb-complement order. For special purposes, however, variations on these patterns have developed in the
language. The first of the following nonsense sequences follows regular
pattern 2 order, but the others vary the pattern:

The wogs brattled the mindle.

1. Did the wogs brattle the mindle?
2. Brattle the mindle.
3. There are wogs brattling the mindle.
4. It was wogs that brattled the mindle.
5. The mindle was brattled by the wogs.

The first familiar variation moves part of the verb (supplying *did* in this
example) to the beginning of the sentence to ask a question. The second
omits the subject, *you* understood, for a command. Neither of these variations
presents rhetorical problems. The remaining examples, however, which likewise have developed for specific purposes, cause trouble if they are used when
regular patterns would serve better. Examples 3 and 4 illustrate the variation
that postpones the subject, placing it after the verb and using *there* or *it,*
called expletives in this function, in the subject slot. Example 5 illustrates the
passive variation, in which the object of a pattern 2 sentence is moved to the
subject slot.

14a Postponed Subject, Expletives   Expl

*Revise the sentence by removing expletives and using
subject-verb order.*

With a few exceptions *to be* works in English only as a linking verb; that
is, it must have a complement after it that is linked to a subject. The language
therefore has no ready way to indicate mere existence through the regular patterns; it is not idiomatic to say "Objections to the proposal will be." By
using *there* or *it* as an introductory word, as an expletive, we can postpone the
subject, locating it after the verb, and say "There will be objections to the
proposal." The variation has three main uses:

1. *To assert simple existence.* When the information necessary to complete a regular pattern is unknown or not to be expressed, the expletive pattern serves:

> There is only one solution. It is too early to tell.
> There will be trouble when his mother hears about this.

2. *To provide special emphasis dictated by context.* Sometimes, even when a regular pattern is possible, an expletive sentence may be useful. Consider, for example:

> The city council heard complaints about the holes in the streets after the hard winter and about the lack of summer recreational programs for children. It was the rough pavement, however, that got immediate attention.

A regular pattern would work for the second sentence and might be equally effective—"The rough pavement got immediate attention"—but a writer might want the special emphasis provided by the expletive variation.

Except for these special purposes, regular patterns almost always are more efficient. Compare the following:

ORIGINAL: There were two speeches at the conference that emphasized that there were many advantages to training in ballet.

REVISION: Two speeches at the conference emphasized the advantages of training in ballet.

The framework in the original is useless; the revision is briefer and stronger. Or compare:

ORIGINAL: It was when she heard I had a new dress that Janet decided not to go to the party.

REVISION: When she heard I had a new dress, Janet decided not to go to the party.

If the context warrants special attention to the time, the roundabout original might be preferable; usually the more direct revision would work better.

3. *To simplify modification or reference.* Usually, expletives only complicate structure, but occasionally they can be used to simplify it. In English, appositives and long modifiers follow nouns; if a subject that opens a sentence is extensively modified, the verb may be postponed too long. By using an expletive construction the subject idea can be moved to the predicate, where it can serve easily as a head word.

ORIGINAL: Several proposals, to reduce Black Week to a few days, to combine it with Chicano Day, or to develop one week for all ethnic groups, were considered.

REVISION: There were several proposals, to reduce Black Week to a few days, to combine it with Chicano Day, or to develop one week for all ethnic groups.

14b The Passive **Pass**

Change the sentence from a passive to a regular pattern with an active verb.

In the passive variation an expression that would function as an object in a pattern 2 sentence is made the subject, and *to be* is used as an auxiliary to the verb, directing the action of the verb toward the subject. Compare:

PATTERN 2:   The ghosts ate asphodel.
PASSIVE: Asphodel was eaten by the ghosts.

Like other variations, the passive pattern is appropriate in special situations.

1. *When the subject for an SVC pattern is not known or the actor is to be omitted.*   In "The building was not finished in time for classes in the fall," naming whoever was responsible for delaying the finishing would probably be impossible or perhaps impolitic. Or consider the following:

The book was published just before Christmas. The car had been looted before it was found. The stadium was filled before noon.

Specifying who published the book or found the car or filled the stadium would be impractical. Notice that the last example illustrates how the passive pattern is often much like pattern 4, subject-linking verb-adjective.

2. *When context warrants special emphasis on the receiver of the action or requires the passive for continuity.*   Consider the following:

The students requested a complete revision of the grading system, but only minor changes were authorized by the faculty committee.

The first pattern in the sentence suggests the special emphasis on *minor changes* provided by the passive pattern that follows. In the following the passive improves continuity:

The children arrived on buses early in the morning. They were assigned to tents by the counselors. They started quarreling almost at once.

Using the passive for the second sentence allows the writer to continue the same subject through this part of his paragraph. In the following sentence the passive construction is useful for both emphasis and continuity:

Immediate withdrawal of all troops was specified by the framers of the bill, and the provision antagonized many members of both houses.

The passive in the first part of the sentence puts emphasis on the provision, the main concern of the sentence, and allows the writer to use the same subject in both clauses.

3. *When an active pattern would widely separate subject and verb.* Compare:

ACTIVE: My youngest brother, who had served as a cook in the navy, who had made an extensive collection of gourmet recipes, and who had a knack for predicting what would appeal to varying tastes, prepared the dinner.

PASSIVE: The dinner was prepared by my youngest brother, who had served as a cook in the navy, who had made an extensive collection of gourmet recipes, and who had a knack for predicting what would appeal to varying tastes.

The passive avoids putting the modifiers between the subject and the verb.

Except for such special purposes, active patterns are more direct and usually clearer. Compare:

ORIGINAL: The inability of the bill to be passed by the legislature was caused by a few influential clergyman.

REVISION: A few influential clergymen kept the bill from passing in the legislature.

ORIGINAL: It is possible for passing work to be done by any student who is conscientious.

REVISION: Any conscientious student can do passing work.

When all the elements for an SVC sentence are available, the actor usually is the best subject.

14A   *There* or *it* and a form of *to be* at the beginning of a sentence can have different meanings; for example *there* can be an adverb or an expletive. For each of the following sentences frame a parallel sentence that uses the opening words with the same meaning.

EXAMPLE: There are no rotten apples in that crate.
PARALLEL: There are no lazy students in that class.

1   There is a cockroach in the bathroom.

2   There is a fly in the ointment.

3   There is the fly in the ointment.

4   There is the source of the trouble.

5   It is impossible to read his handwriting.

6   There will be no laughter in this courtroom.

7   There is the one man who could perform the operation.

8   There is a unicorn eating grass in the garden.

10   There are too many generals in this army.

14B In the following sentences at least one subject is postponed by the use of an introductory word. Consider how you would revise each sentence into actor-action order; then in the blanks at the right record the subject and verb of each sentence as you revise it.

	Subject	Verb
EXAMPLE: There was a giraffe calmly munching on her hat.	*giraffe*	*munched*

1 There were an expensive-looking mink coat and a silk evening gown lying in a heap in the corner.

2 There were hundreds of students who had made long trips at their own expense to join the march.

3 It was because of the fact that they had more experience that the sophomore team won.

4 There were twelve large oysters which floated in the broth.

5 There were several ragged children who were standing around the gate.

6 There were two problems in the examination which I could not finish.

7 It was because he was afraid that George ran away from the policeman.

8 It was obvious that both men could not pitch the opening game of the series.

9 It was after breakfast that we decided to change our plans and try skiing down the old trail.

10 There was only ignorance behind the decision to abandon the city.

11 There were a leaky boat and a single oar lying on the beach.

12 It was her selfishness which kept her silent when the dean asked for information.

13 There were two guards on duty, but the money disappeared.

14 There is nobody who can help her now that she has rejected all her friends.

15 There is great probability that Mary knew of Bothwell's plot against Darnley.

16 It would not be impossible for the play to be presented successfully by good actors.

17 It is a fact that it would be embarrassing to present an apology now.

18 There were three long delays in the negotiations which showed that the general did not wish to compromise.

14C In the following sentences the actor has a subordinate position, and the verb is in the passive voice. Consider how you might revise each sentence to fit the actor-action pattern with an active verb. Then write in the blanks the subject and active verb that would appear in the revised sentence.

	Subject	Verb
EXAMPLE: The new magazine was read by Mother as soon as it arrived.	*Mother*	*read*

1 After he finished barber college, all the hair in the fraternity was cut by Alfred.
_____ _____

2 The elevated train schedule was ordered to be revised by the director of transportation.
_____ _____

3 The wrong note had been played by the girl who had just joined the orchestra.
_____ _____

4 An application was submitted by me during the first week of the semester.
_____ _____

5 After presenting more than a dozen arguments, a constitution was proposed by the dean.
_____ _____

6 Her first painting was bought by the president of the art society.
_____ _____

7 The tree was cut down by the young man with the new hatchet.
_____ _____

8 Mrs. Tompkin's house was painted inside and out by the children of the neighborhood.
_____ _____

9 Before the race, the sled runners were heated by Jim with a blow torch.
_____ _____

10 There was an order of the city council by which the paving of the streets was stopped.
_____ _____

11 Early in the winter of 1916, the house had been destroyed by a tornado.
_____ _____

12 The main weaknesses of the curriculum were outlined by the committee in a long report.
_____ _____

13 No time was lost by the jeep squadron in starting the search for the missing plane.
_____ _____

14 When a faculty adviser lived in the house, more was accomplished by the fraternity.
_____ _____

15 Having slipped from the hands of the batter, his teeth were knocked out by the flying baseball bat.
_____ _____

16 By the machine gun fire the attacking force was divided into two groups.
_____ _____

14D Revise the following sentences by changing passive verbs to active verbs and using actor-action order. Write the active verbs in the blanks at the right and the revised sentences in the space provided.

1 The reason for the first witness's lying was shown by the attorneys to have been that he was bribed by the company.   _____

2 Of the Armada there were fifteen ships taken and destroyed by the English fleet in the Channel.   _____

3 No arrangements for guests having been made by the proprietor, our bags were left by the taxi driver in a corner of the large hall.   _____

4 There is much ridicule accomplished of the late eighteenth-century tales of romance and terror by Jane Austen's novel *Northanger Abbey.*   _____

5 Immunity against poisons was, according to legend, achieved by Mithridates by constantly using various poisons as antidotes.   _____

6 There is a possibility that the accomplishment of the passage of the bill will be when a compromise is arrived at by the representatives from the northern part of the state.   _____

7 The purpose of the meeting was explained by the chairman to be to decide how community organizations could cooperate to sponsor a juvenile detention home.   _____

14E Unjustified variations in sentence patterns often cause tangled, wordy writing; usually meaning can be clarified by putting sentences into actor-action order. For each of the following sentences choose a good subject and write it in the blank at the right; then rewrite the sentence with the subject, using a verb in the active voice and making other revisions or omissions that will improve it.

EXAMPLE: The reason for all the noise that was noticed in our history class was that for certain students there was no real interest in the subject matter and so their main occupation was talking.

class

Answer: Our history class was noisy because certain students were not interested in the subject and spent the hour talking.

1 Among the American heroines is Betsy Ross and the reason is because everybody remembers that the first American flag was made by her from an old petticoat.

_____

2 There is an old saying that you should plant corn when the oak leaves are as big as squirrels' ears, and that was always when Father did it.

_____

3 That was the corkscrew he was very proud of, with a kind of double action to pull the longest cork, and which he had brought back from Italy.

_____

4 In the first place, there is no reason to think it was a good thing for the quarterback to call for a line buck when it was obvious that the opposing backfield was all ready for it.

_____

5 There was a great deal of fun to be had if you went to the native market where any tourist was sure to find things of interest to him, and this was the way we spent a lot of time.

_____

6   That is one of the things about a bed of pansies that if they are started in the summer from seed you are likely to find in many climates blooms can be picked from it every month of the year.   _____

7   It was when we were just in process of gaining altitude for the purpose of passing over Mount Monadnock that the storm was encountered, thus causing me to lose my dinner.   _____

8   That was where I could have been found almost any day in the summer, sitting on the banks of the Ohio River, although it was true that I got more mosquito bites than there were fish bites, that was when I learned the rudiments of the gentle art that is now my hobby, fishing.   _____

9   Those were the ones which he did not like because it was one of his theories that no trailers which were any good were not made in California on account of not needing insulation in temperate climates.   _____

10   It was when they were in the middle of the lunch she had invited him to and she had made her famous clam sandwich spread that she thought she could recognize the first gleam of matrimony in his eye.   _____

Objectives: *(1) To use coordination to expand patterns and show how ideas are related. (2) To make coordinate sentence elements parallel in form.*

Grammatical devices allow us to relate ideas. One of these devices, useful in expanding basic patterns (see Chapter 12), is coordination. Coordination links two or more ideas so that they have equal rank or so that they function in the same way in the sentence. That is, coordinate elements relate in the same way to other elements in a sentence, perform the same grammatical function. Coordination is signaled by position and commonly by *and, or, but*, or other function words joining the coordinate elements. (For punctuation to clarify coordination, see **25b–25d**.) In "Ham and eggs are good," for example, *ham* and *eggs* both occupy the subject position in the pattern and are joined by *and* to signal that they are coordinate. They are presented in this way to fulfill the writer's particular purpose at the moment, not because of anything inherent in their meaning. For a different purpose the writer might not have coordinated: "The eggs on the ham were rotten." The writer in this sentence wants to talk mainly about the eggs and puts *ham* in a modifying or subordinate position, only to locate or identify the eggs.

The following sentences make more complex use of coordination:

> The strike had begun in the first week of November, and it ended in the first week in March, when the faculty accepted a settlement offered by the trustees. Students and teachers alike, we were physically and spiritually depleted, and many of us had to borrow money on which to live. And so we had given in, in order to survive, with or without dignity.
>
> KAY BOYLE, *The Long Walk at San Francisco State*

In the first sentence, two complete patterns are coordinated, joined by *and*: "The strike ... of November" and "it ended ... in March." The second sentence opens with coordinate appositive modifiers of the subject, *students* and *teachers*. It employs coordinated modifiers of *depleted* in *physically* and *spiritually*, and includes two coordinate complete patterns: "we were ... depleted" and "many ... to live." In the third sentence two function words, *with* and *without*, are coordinate, joined by *or* as alternatives.

Coordination can be thought of as an economy device for combining what might otherwise have to be more than one separate pattern. The process is like the simple formula: if *A* does *C* and *B* does *C*, then *A* and *B* do *C*. Consider the following series of simple patterns:

> I bought jade earrings. I bought a green leather bag. I bought white linen shoes. They could be dyed green. Then I bought a green belt. I bought a perky green hat. I had an ensemble.

Five of the sentences have the same subject and verb, *I bought*, which is like *C* of the formula. They can be combined by coordinating:

> I bought an ensemble of jade earrings, a green leather bag, a green belt, a perky green hat, and white linen shoes which could be dyed green.

In the revision, the final pattern of the original has been incorporated into the main pattern and the fourth has been subordinated.

15a Coordination and Parallel Structure   **Paral**

Make coordinate elements parallel in form, or revise
to correct illogical or unintended coordination.

Coordination is clear only when items in coordinate positions are parallel, in sense and in grammatical form. A sentence like the following probably represents only a slip that a writer should have caught in revision: "As a basketball player he was clever on offense and excellent skill defensively." *Clever* is an adjective and *skill* a noun, and the two elements are not parallel. Revision makes the coordination clear: "As a basketball player he was clever on offense and skillful on defense." Or consider the following, in which the violation of parallel structure is less obvious:

> She was so eager to wear the dress that she tried exercise, steam baths, and even was taking diet pills.

The final part of the sentence is patterned—by order and with the comma and *and*—to coordinate three items as joint objects of the verb *tried*:

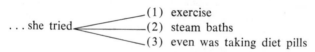

Obviously, the third item is not parallel grammatically; it does not even have a form that will fit after *tried* and probably appears only because the first two intervening items have blunted the writer's memory of his pattern. It can be made parallel easily by omitting some unnecessary details:

> She was so eager to wear the dress that she tried exercise, steam baths, and even diet pills.

Or take a more complicated sentence:

> Some hill-country moonshiners, realizing that their still was exposed and revenue officers being active in the area, put on old army uniforms and said they "were doing secret work for the Pentagon."

Two sets of items are set in different patterns of coordination:

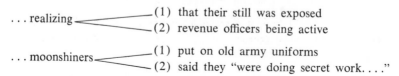

The second two are grammatically parallel, but the first two are not; *revenue officers being active* contains no complete verb and does not make up a clause parallel to the first one. The sentence needs revision:

> Some hill-country moonshiners, realizing that their still was exposed and that revenue officers were active in the area, put on old army uniforms and said they "were doing secret work for the Pentagon."

Another common difficulty with coordination occurs when elements are unintentionally coordinated, usually because an *and* is omitted.

> They produced plays by Shakespeare, Shaw, and musical comedies.

The sentence is constructed so that three items are coordinate after *plays by*; but obviously musical comedies did not write plays. Two coordinate patterns were probably intended.

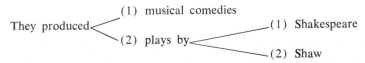

Revision might include reordering as well as adding an *and*.

> They produced musical comedies and plays by Shakespeare and Shaw.

Sometimes coordination is obscured by so simple a lapse as omission of a function word needed to make the elements parallel:

ORIGINAL: She finally found the new dress, snakeskin shoes, and the nylon sweater stuffed in a corner of her roommate's closet.

REVISION: She finally found the new dress, the snakeskin shoes, and the nylon sweater stuffed in a corner of her roommate's closet.

Repetition of the article, *the* shows that items are coordinate.

15b Completing Parallel Patterns   Inc
Supply words needed to complete a parallel pattern.

As indicated, coordination works because the common element of two basic patterns can be omitted and the patterns combined. "He decided that he should stop wasting time and prepare for his examinations" combines "*He decided that he should* stop wasting time" and "*He decided that he should* prepare for his examinations." The common element, "He decided that he should," need not be repeated in the coordinate pattern. Even when the common element requires a change in form, clear coordination may be possible: "He wanted to win and he did." The common element is expressed as *to win* in the first element and understood as only *win* in the second, but there is no confusion. Sometimes, however, clarity requires filling the pattern.

ORIGINAL: The people were all paying customers but told they had to leave.

REVISION: The people were all paying customers but were told they had to leave.

ORIGINAL: I wish to announce that the new dictator has arrived and the people accepted him.

REVISION: I wish to announce that the new dictator has arrived and the people have accepted him.

Especially when a function word is part of a coordinate element, clarity may require that it be repeated.

ORIGINAL: Mary was both interested and clever at sewing.

REVISION: Mary was both interested in and clever at sewing.

REVISION: Mary was interested in sewing and clever at it.

In the original the pattern assumes that *at* be understood after *interested,* but it does not work there idiomatically.

15c Patterns of Comparison   **Comp**

Revise to make elements parallel in form and comparable in meaning.

Comparisons employ coordination in a number of patterns, involving omission of whatever is common to both elements: "The new law was more practical than the old (law was practical)." Since the coordinate elements in comparison patterns are not always side by side—as when elements are joined by *and*—care is needed to preserve parallelism. The following illustrate some of the most common difficulties.

ORIGINAL: In the new factory they found the ways of operating the machines more complicated than those manufactured earlier.

REVISION: In the new factory they found the machines more complicated than those manufactured earlier.

The original compares *ways* with *those*, which refers to *machines*. The writer apparently became confused as his sentence progressed, starting with the notion of comparing difficulties of operation but ending with the notion of comparing machines. The revision accomplishes the second task.

ORIGINAL: As a minister his salary was even less than a teacher.

REVISION: As a minister he received even less salary than a teacher.

ORIGINAL: The antics of Danny Kaye are very much like Jerry Lewis.

REVISION: The antics of Danny Kaye are very much like those of Jerry Lewis.

In both originals the items put in coordinate position are probably not those the writer intended to compare—*salary* with *teacher* and *antics* with *Jerry Lewis*. Another kind of difficulty occurs when one element of the comparison is so abbreviated that meaning is unclear.

ORIGINAL: I liked her better than Alice.

REVISION: I liked her better than Alice did. I liked her better than I liked Alice.

Either of the two revisions could be taken as the meaning of the original. In the following the meaning is probably clear but imprecise.

ORIGINAL: It was the best concert.

REVISION: It was a good concert. It was the best concert I had ever heard.

The original starts a comparison but does not finish it.

15A Combine each of the following groups of sentences into a single sentence by using coordination and avoiding repetition of common elements. Sometimes more than one coordinate pattern will be required in the combined sentence, and sometimes elements will need to be changed in form to make them parallel.

EXAMPLE: At the end of the game we were tired. At the end of the game we were hungry. At the end of the game we wanted to go home.

COMBINED: At the end of the game we were tired and hungry and wanted to go home.
OR: At the end of the game we were tired, hungry, and ready to go home.

   1 Gwendolyn wanted to play the clarinet. Or Gwendolyn wanted to play the violin. Or Gwendolyn wanted to sing.

   2 Knowing that life is hazardous, Mr. Pintz decided to live in a cave. Knowing of man's being treacherous, Mr. Pintz decided to live in a cave.

   3 Jeff's familiarity with various ethnic groups influenced the committee. Jeff was an able speaker, which influenced the selection committee.

   4 The dormitory regulations seemed reasonable. They seemed fair. However, enforcing them seemed difficult.

   5 My Uncle Sid lacked incentive. He also lacked energy. He quickly lost his job.

6 The candidates spoke at length about unemployment. They spoke at length also about the way food prices were inflated.

7 A student needs a dictionary to check spellings. He also needs it for finding the meanings of unfamiliar words. He needs it also because he can learn there how to pronounce words.

8 Sir Patrick Spens died at sea. The sea also claimed the lives of all his sailors.

9 In her first job Anita taught dramatics. She also had the job of teaching journalism. She also supervised the school newspaper.

10 The costumes were colorful. They also had brightness. They were not, however, appropriate to the period they were to represent.

11 Men with long hair were not allowed to buy tickets. Men not having ties were not allowed to buy tickets.

12 The camp specialized in horseback riding. Hiking was also one of its specialties. However, it had no swimming pool.

CONCLUSIONS: In a sentence, summarize your observation about the uses of coordination and the problems involved in controlling parallel structures.

15B Underline in each sentence expressions that violate parallelism and write in the appropriate blank a substitute expression that would produce clear parallel structure.

EXAMPLE: A recently invented clock tells the time on both the earth and <u>for Martians.</u>   _____*Mars*_____

1   In the summer she liked to play tennis, field hockey, golf, and to swim.   _____

2   After two weeks I decided that the summer recreation program was both worthwhile and a necessity.   _____

3   First take stock of your abilities and then you should decide what you want to accomplish in life.   _____

4   He was not allowed to join the club because of his smoking and he uses profane language.   _____

5   They broke either the bindings on their skis or got so cold they could hardly move their legs.   _____

6   I much prefer watching moving pictures on our television rather than go to a public theatre.   _____

7   Her job consisted of displaying sale items, planning and arranging window displays, and help for the salesgirls at rush hours.   _____

8   Ostrich parents divide the duty of egg-sitting, she sitting by day and he is the sitter at night.   _____

9   To err is human, but there is a divine aspect about forgiving other people.   _____

10   He could shoot, dribble, pivot, and handling the ball as if it were glued to his hand.   _____

11   The jumping jerboa has rodent teeth and leaflike ears, and some species in North Africa having stiff hairs to act like antiskid chains on the desert floor.   _____

12   Either the men talked so long that nothing could be decided or compromised on a decision so general that it had no meaning.   _____

13   She was not only lazy but also was characterized by stupidity.   _____

14   After one year in charge of the bank he had earned the admiration of the community, the respect of other businessmen, and his employees loved him.   _____

15   The law largely failed of its purpose, both as far as satisfying American farmers was concerned and in helping foreign nations to pay their debts.   _____

16   The echidna is an Australian animal somewhat larger than a hedgehog, with spines on the upper part of the body, a toothless mouth, and its snout being long and tapering.   _____

15C The following sentences contain comparisons that are unclear because they are not logically parallel. Clarify them by (1) crossing out an expression to be deleted and writing a substitute in the appropriate blank; or (2) inserting a caret (∧) in the sentence where an addition is needed and writing the addition in the blank.

1 Janet came home from the store with the loveliest hat.

2 She told me that she liked Toscanini better than any conductor.

3 The definition of my German binoculars is sharper than any American glasses I have seen.

4 Charles gave the new president a warmer welcome than the secretary.

5 The schedule for the basketball team next year is much harder than the football team.

6 To my childish eyes the puppy's ears seemed as long and pointed as a rabbit.

7 The Dean had tea more often with his new secretary than the President.

8 Washing her feet in the cool spray from the fountain was the most beautiful girl.

9 The girl he took to the dance was as old if not older than his mother.

10 Education is as well developed in the United States as any other country.

11 She found the fragrance of the rose more attractive than the lily of the valley.

12 The newspaper reporter seemed more interested in Mr. Capone's swimming pool than Mr. Capone.

13 In some districts the new attitude toward forests was much more advanced than the Congressman in his speech.

14 Although some people do not agree with me, I like Faulkner's style better than most books I have read.

15 One of the laborers testified to the committee that his job required much more training than a foreman.

16 Some said that they preferred doing their own work rather than to pay the high costs of labor.

17 The new assignment was as long if not longer than the one we had had the first week.

18 When we lived in the old part of town, all the neighbors were so thoughtful.

19 He had always thought of his life as like a nineteenth-century British clergyman.

20 The book on reserve says much more about friends of Marlowe than Marlowe.

122

15D Each of the following sentences could be improved by adding an expression to complete its pattern—a part of a verb or a needed function word. Place a caret (∧) in the sentence where you would make the addition, and write in the blank the expression to be inserted.

EXAMPLE: We visited Central Park∧ ∧ the Bronx Zoo, and took a helicopter ride out over the harbor. *and*

EXAMPLE: Many people had ∧ and continue to be impressed by Iago's "honesty." *been*

1 The furniture was old, inappropriate, and threw the room into confusion because it was all jumbled together in one corner. _____

2 To make her costumes harmonize with the colors in the stage set, Jean had to find a blue, chartreuse, or turquoise dress for the second act. _____

3 I took Aunt Louise, Uncle David, George, and Father took the others in the rented car. _____

4 I was afraid that someone would tell my mother and she would get the wrong impression about the club. _____

5 He had neither objections nor admiration for the new low-waisted gowns. _____

6 My family always has and always will be opposed to any attempt to cut down the orchard. _____

7 Did you sell tickets for the alumni banquet to more people than George and Anita? _____

8 Although John is on the varsity team, he is not a good swimmer but praised for his diving. _____

9 The old gilt frames added rather than detracted from the effectiveness of the paintings. _____

10 She displayed great interest but absolutely no talent for playing the piano. _____

11 The difficulty was his wife refused to give up custody of the children. _____

12 Joan was afraid but also excited by the sound of the drums pounding in the distance. _____

13 In the first meeting of the steering committee the senator had urged the bill should be passed. _____

14 The table was overturned in the middle of the floor and the chairs piled on top of it. _____

15 She had only fifteen minutes to clear the table, dust the furniture and to sweep the floor. _____

16 Karl knew that he was playing the most difficult program he had ever attempted and the audience would notice the slightest error. _____

17 All college students should study history, government, and get a reading knowledge of at least one foreign language. _____

18 He was immediately attracted by the strange pale color of her hair and her long, expressive fingers.

_____

19 After her death he took up drinking, gambling, and finally killed a child in an automobile accident.

_____

20 He told the committee that he would not be a candidate for any office, he would not run if nominated, and that he would not serve if elected.

_____

21 She stopped at the grocery store to cash a check, buying a bottle of milk, and to find out whether she had won anything on the weekly raffle.

_____

22 There were many reasons for distrusting the motives of the messengers but no way to find out the truth.

_____

23 I do not know what the party will be like, but my husband says he will go if you are.

_____

15E The following paragraph could be improved by more use of parallel structure. In each numbered sentence cross out one expression that might be improved and write in the corresponding blank a substitute expression that would make co-ordination clearer.

EXAMPLE: According to a Rhode Island court, marriage is a discipline as well as being delightful.

a delight

(1) A certain Frenchman made himself famous by rising during a discussion of the difference between the sexes and he gave a shout. "Vive la différence!" There are differences. (2) A Detroit judge ruled that a boss who kisses an employee is guilty of assault and battery, but in Chicago a judge said a man kissing his secretary is not guilty of disorderly conduct. (3) Statistics show that most British girls marry somebody who lives or has the place he works within a thousand feet of her. (4) The American girl, according to the Institute of Family Relations, meets an average of only 3.29 "possible husbands" before she selects one, but what a man has to do or what kind of man he ought to be to become "possible" is not entirely clear. (5) As for courting customs, an engaged woman in Oregon who resigned her job was given unemployment benefits, the commission arguing that her hours had been irregular and a woman is entitled to a reasonable opportunity to be properly courted. (6) But everybody prefers marriage to having people getting divorced. (7) Citizens of Reno and Las Vegas, divorce centers, are proud that their cities have two or three times as many couples getting married as divorces. (8) A St. Paul woman complained in 1953 that her husband deserted her, alleging that he had gone to Shelby, Montana, to see the Dempsey-Gibbons fight in 1923, not returning since. (9) It has been said that there are three kinds of people who get married, those who are determined to marry, those who want to marry, and some are willing to marry. (10) There are, however, only two kinds of people who get divorces, those who dislike their husbands, some, of course, not liking their wives.

1. _____

2. _____

3. _____

4. _____

5. _____

6. _____

7. _____

8. _____

9. _____

10. _____

SUBORDINATION: 16
MODIFICATION

*Objectives: (1) To use subordination to expand
patterns and relate ideas. (2) To distinguish adjective
and adverb forms and use them appropriately. (3) To use
word order to make modification clear and to recognize
and revise unclear modification patterns.*

Coordination allows a writer to present ideas as equal in rank; subordination allows him to express even more complicated relationships (see **5b, 6a**). By using devices for subordination, a writer can make one idea dependent on another in various ways—for example, as a modifier, a qualifier, an illustration, or a specification. Consider the following sentence patterns:

> He [Frederic the Great] might rob a neighbor. He had promised to defend the neighbor. Black men fought. They fought on the coast of Coromandel. Red men scalped each other. They did this by the Great Lakes. The Great Lakes are in North America.

Macaulay, using the ideas, employed subordination to write the following:

> In order that he might rob a neighbor whom he had promised to defend, black men fought on the coast of Coromandel, and red men scalped each other by the Great Lakes of North America.

Two of the patterns are coordinated—"black men fought" and "red men scalped each other"—but the other patterns are subordinated. The subordination is indicated by position and by function words (see pages **135–136**).

16a Adequate Subordination   Sub

*Revise, using subordination to correct clumsy repetitions,
strings of short, choppy sentences, or strings of clauses
joined by* and *or with vague* this *or* that *as subjects.*

The following sentences are reasonably clear, but they have an amateurish, childish ring:

> Providing space for recreation is becoming increasingly difficult. This is especially true in the large cities. It is in the cities that every square foot of space is being gobbled up by greedy land speculators. These people are taking advantage of rapidly growing populations.

The sentences readily combine, with the opening sentence as the main pattern and the following sentences subordinated as modifiers.

> Providing space for recreation is becoming increasingly difficult, especially in the large cities where greedy land speculators, taking advantage of rapidly growing populations, are gobbling up every square foot of space.

Subordination is frequently the solution for a variety of writing ailments, especially for choppy, repetitious sentences that do not relate ideas. Compare the following:

ORIGINAL: When Shelley was at Oxford, he published "The Necessity of Atheism." It was a pamphlet. This was in 1811, and he was dismissed.

REVISION: In 1811 Shelley was dismissed from Oxford for publishing a pamphlet, "The Necessity of Atheism."

ORIGINAL: I can read rapidly. I sometimes do not know what I have read, however.

REVISION: Although I can read rapidly, I sometimes do not know what I have read.

Notice that subordination can be used as the writer needs it. The last sentence might have been written with the emphasis reversed for a different effect.

> Although I sometimes do not know what I have read, I can read very rapidly.

16b Forms of Modifiers: Adjective and Adverb   Adj, Adv

Change to an adjective or adverb form as the context requires.

Modifiers can be classified on the basis of their use: as adjectives, which modify nouns or pronouns, and adverbs, which modify other expressions. Single words that can function as adverbs are usually distinguished from adjectives by an *-ly* ending (*happy*, adjective; *happily* adverb); but some adverbs do not end in *-ly* (*very, slow*), and a few adjectives do (*homely, silly, lovely*). Furthermore, a few modifiers are enough alike that they are frequently confused:

ADJECTIVES	ADVERBS
good (kind, agreeable, satisfactory)	*well* (satisfactory, in a pleasing, desirable, or acceptable manner)
well (fortunate, fitting, in good health)	
real (authentic, genuine)	*really* (actually, in a real manner)
sure (firm, secure, dependable)	*surely* (certainly)
some (in an indefinite amount)	*somewhat* (to a certain degree)

Standard usage preserves a distinction between adjective and adverb forms:

> He did *well* (not *good*) on the examination. The first team won *easily* (not *easy*). The doctor came *quickly* (not *real quick*).

Confusion sometimes occurs when the modifier occurs after a verb that may or may not function as a linking verb; an adjective or adverb form is required depending on the meaning intended. For example, in "The girl looked pleasant," *pleasant* works as an adjective modifying *girl*, with *looked* as a linking verb; in "The girl looked pleasantly at the judge," *pleasantly* is an adverb modifying *looked*, which does not function as a linking verb. In "The dog smells good," *smells* is a linking verb and *good* an adjective; the sentence suggests that the dog needs a bath. "The dog smells well," with *well* as an adverb modifying *smells*, labels the dog as a good tracker. "I feel good this morning," indicates general contentedness. "I feel well this morning," indicates that the speaker is in good health. Or it could suggest that he has sensitive fingers, if *well* is an adverb and *feel* not a linking verb.

16c Degree of Modification: Comparative and Superlative Degree

Revise to make the degree of modification logical and appropriate.

Modifiers can be varied to indicate the degree to which the quality they represent is to be attributed to whatever is modified. That is, we may speak of a "*happy* person" with the positive degree, of a "*happiest* person" in the superlative. Most brief modifiers are compared by adding -*er* for the comparative and -*est* for the superlative (*long, longer, longest*); most modifiers of more than two syllables are compared by a preceding *more* or *most* (*dutiful, more dutiful, most dutiful*). Two-syllable modifiers may be compared using either system. One degree marker is sufficient: "Wilfred's playing was *better than* (not *more better than*) his singing." A few modifiers are irregular.

good	better	best	much	more	most
well	better	best	many	more	most
bad	worse	worst	far	farther	farthest
little	less	least		further	furthest

Logically some modifiers have meanings not subject to comparison; *dead* is dead, *waterproof* is waterproof, and *perfect* is perfect. *Unique* means "single" or "sole" and *fatal* refers to an absolute state. In practice, however, the comparative and superlative degrees of these so-called absolutes are usually taken to mean something like "more nearly" or "most nearly" in expressions like "a more perfect union" or "He has the fullest glass." Excessive superlatives do more to clutter than to strengthen prose, "He was the *outstanding* (not *most outstanding*) senior in school."

16d Position of Modifiers Mod

Revise to place modifiers so that the reader can readily understand what they modify.

Consider the following absurdity: "He is asking his reader to adopt his philosophy as well as the lady to whom the poem is addressed." With the final modifying clause located after *to adopt*, the sentence seems to say that "he is asking his reader to adopt . . . . the lady"—probably not the intended meaning. A change in order clarifies: "He is asking both the reader and the lady to whom the poem is addressed to adopt his philosophy."

In English, modification is signaled primarily by word order. A single-word adjective usually precedes the noun it modifies; an adjective clause or phrase usually follows. Adverbial modifiers are more flexible in their positions, but they can distort meaning if they are slipped into positions when they provide unintended modification. Compare, for example:

With her field glasses she could see the Martians filing out of the saucer.
She could see the Martians filing out of the saucer with her field glasses.

The position of "with her field glasses" obviously makes a considerable difference in meaning. The following are less obvious distortions:

ORIGINAL: In an effort to make all his guests happy, the hotel manager investigated *their* sources of discontent.

REVISION: In an effort to make all his guests happy, the hotel manager investigated the sources of *their* discontent.

ORIGINAL: I promised her at the end of the dance I would go.

REVISION: At the end of the dance, I promised her I would go.

REVISION: I promised her I would go at the end of the dance.

At the end of the dance is a so-called "squinting" modifier in the original, allowing the interpretation of either revision.

16e "Dangling" Modifiers   DM

Reword a "dangling" modifier or revise the main sentence so that modification is clear.

When an introductory modifier, especially a verbal modifier, does not include a subject, the reader automatically supplies either the subject of the sentence or the noun nearest the modifier. If this subject or noun does not fit with the modifier, the modifier is said to "dangle," without anything to which it can attach itself. Consider the following:

ORIGINAL: Assured of the votes of the outlying districts, victory banquets were arranged by the state committee as soon as the city returns were tabulated.

REVISION: Assured of the votes of the outlying districts, the state committee arranged victory banquets as soon as the city returns were tabulated.

The reader, because of the pressure of word order, tends to supply *banquets* as the subject of *assured* in the original. But, obviously the committee was assured, not the banquets. The cure for this error, as for many others, is to put the sentence into actor-action goal order, as in the revision.

16f "Split" Constructions   Split

Revise to avoid a "split" construction.

Although the split infinitive, contrary to an old rule, sometimes appears in good written English, usually separation of *to* from the remainder of an infinitive or separation of any closely related sentence elements is awkward, giving the inserted material unwarranted emphasis.

ORIGINAL: The nurse promised to *with the greatest care* insert the needle in my arm.

REVISION: The nurse promised to insert the needle in my arm *with the greatest care.*

16A   Rewrite each of the following groups of sentences by combining them into a single sentence, using one subject-verb pattern as a main clause and subordinating all other material. Write the revised sentences on a separate sheet of paper, and after each group write in the blank marked *S* the subject of the main clause of your new sentence and in the blank marked *V* the verb.

EXAMPLE: (a) Camille Pissarro was a painter. (b) He was French. (c) He flourished in the late nineteenth century. (d) He was an impressionist.

S *Pissarro*
V *flourished*

Answer: Camille Pissarro, a French impressionist painter, flourished in the late nineteenth century.

1   (a) Skiing is growing in popularity. (b) People like the fact that it is exhilarating. (c) It can be easily learned. (d) It can, that is, if one starts young enough.

S _____
V _____

2   (a) There are floods on the Missouri River. (b) The floods come in the spring. (c) Sometimes they inundate the lowlands. (d) Sometimes they cut new channels for the river. (e) Sometimes they get out of control.

S _____
V _____

3   (a) I was born in Brooklyn. (b) I have not seen Brooklyn for years. (c) I still think of our apartment as home. (d) It is in a part of Brooklyn called Brooklyn Heights.

S _____
V _____

4   (a) Hairs grow about a thousand to the square inch. (b) This applies to the human scalp. (c) It is true if the scalp is an average one. (d) This is on the authority of a New York tonsorial expert.

S _____
V _____

5   (a) The Pittsburgh police had a lineup of suspects. (b) Forty victims of a holdup could not identify any of them. (c) One of the suspects was obliging. (d) He identified three of the victims. (e) They were men, and he had robbed them.

S _____
V _____

6   (a) Adrian Holcomb was justice of the peace. (b) He lived in Des Moines, Iowa. (c) He made a ruling about horses. (d) He said it was illegal to ride them at night without lights. (e) This applied if they were ridden on the street.

S _____
V _____

7   (a) An old woman in Sidcup, England, died. (b) She bequeathed her bathtub to a plumber. (c) He was also a friendly person. (d) He had done her plumbing for twenty-five years. (e) He did it free.

S _____
V _____

8 (a) Dr. Leo Kaplan teaches at Southern Illinois University. (b) He made a statement about hay fever victims. (c) They would suffer less if their housekeeping were better. (d) Then certain molds would not be floating around their houses. (e) Molds can be irritating.

S _____

V _____

9 (a) Plants were no longer microscopic algae. (b) They progressed from this state. (c) They did this until they became seaweeds. (d) These seaweeds were branched and curiously fruiting. (e) They swayed with the tides. (f) Also they were plucked from the coastal rocks by the surf. (g) They were cast adrift.

S _____

V _____

10 (a) Uncle Harry is a law-abiding citizen. (b) He had to get a special identification card. (c) He looked very much like a picture. (d) This picture was of a criminal and it was on the bulletin board of the post office. (e) The card was to keep him from being arrested.

S _____

V _____

16B In each of the following sentences one independent clause could be reduced to a much shorter subordinate expression, often a single word or a short phrase. Other parts of the sentence, of course, might need to be revised to make the new subordinate expression fit. Decide how you could revise each sentence, underline the clause you would reduce to a subordinate expression, and then write in the blank the subordinate expression you would use in your revision.

EXAMPLE: On the first day the instructor assigned twenty problems in algebra, and these problems were difficult.

difficult

Answer: On the first day the instructor assigned twenty difficult problems in algebra.

1 The crowds had filled all the camping places a day before the festival was to begin, and these areas were all tiny.

_____

2 A small, ragged girl was coming slowly up the steps toward the cabin, and she ate turnips as she came.

_____

3 Buildings in this section of the city will be razed, but it is the condemned buildings that must go.

_____

4 Anteaters have a protruding, narrow snout and a tongue with which they pick up ants, and this tongue is very long.

_____

5 The room was cold, and Mary shivered when she came into this room where the meeting was scheduled.

_____

6 The mantis uses its forelegs to hold the other insects it uses for food; these legs are strong.

_____

7 The siren blared out chasing everyone from his bed, and this took place at a time early in the morning.

_____

8 Jane thought of how the others would worry when they found the notes, and she smiled to herself as she did so.

_____

16C Each of the following sentences contains a modifier, in italics, which is placed so that it modifies unclearly or obscures the intent of the sentence. Consider where you might move each modifier, and then write in each blank the two words that would immediately follow the modifier in its new position.

EXAMPLE: The children were so hungry that they *almost* ate all the cookies.   *all the*

1 A farm is a good place for a boy who likes animals to *live*. _____

2 Just ahead of us was an old man with an umbrella *walking through the traffic.* _____

3 He promised to *as soon as possible* sign the documents and walked out of the room. _____

4 After waiting for an hour outside the theater, we began to worry *with only our light coats.* _____

5 He kept a record of all the girls he had known *in a little green notebook.* _____

6 Mary decided that she would not marry him at *the last possible moment.* _____

7 He gave Salome, his pig, to a boy I know *with a drooping belly and a corkscrew tail.* _____

8 I *only* tasted the milk on the table; I drank none of the supply in the refrigerator. _____

9 The general showed how battles are often lost *in a series of lectures.* _____

10 I chose the white horse for my brother *with the good temper and the shaggy mane.* _____

11 The children were all convinced of the reality of the scene; the adults were not gullible, *however.* _____

12 She had two large albums showing pictures of her children *hidden in the attic.* _____

13 The coach showed us how most football plays are planned *in five minutes.* _____

14 I told her that I did not want to talk *in the first place.* _____

15 There was one course that showed students how to set off crude bombs *at the university.* _____

16 He ran up to her and asked her for the next dance *waving his program in the air.* _____

17 We never tried to decide what to do *until my mother had made up her mind.* _____

18 All through the meal he studied the woman who sat at the next table *secretly.* _____

19 I asked him to *after the class was over* lend me his notes. _____

20 The next act, a tap dance by the hostess's rhythm-deaf daughter, finished the program *practically.* _____

21 The play told the *typical* story of an American soldier. _____

22 The old man found a green toad *searching in the grass for his spectacles.* _____

16D Consider how each of the following independent clauses should be revised if the suggested introductory modifier were to be joined to it. Then write the first three words of the revised independent clause in the blank.

EXAMPLE: (Begin with *Playing ball in the park*) Her left ankle was sprained. *she sprained her*

1 (Begin with *When only an infant*) Two large serpents were crushed by Hercules with his bare hands. _____

2 (Begin with *To do good cabinet work*) Precise and well-kept tools are needed by a carpenter. _____

3 (Begin with *Never having seen a city*) It was natural that Freda should be impressed by the tall buildings. _____

4 (Begin with *Certain of victory*) No campaign was conducted by the Democratic candidate. _____

5 (Begin with *Having stolen a box of apples*) An old barrel was used as a hiding place by the boys. _____

6 (Begin with *Unable to pay its debts*) Bankruptcy proceedings were initiated by the store. _____

7 (Begin with *Sitting on the bridge*) The old clock could be watched by me without moving. _____

8 (Begin with *While still in prison*) The governor was written a letter by the gangster revealing where the money was hidden. _____

9 (Begin with *On finding a pertinent paragraph*) A complete transcription was made by the investigator. _____

10 (Begin with *While playing ball with the children*) The frames of George's glasses were broken. _____

11 (Begin with *By swimming an hour every day*) Jane's weight was reduced from 120 to 110 pounds. _____

12 (Begin with *Wandering carelessly across the street*) Mud got splashed on her new shoes. _____

13 (Begin with *Unable to get wood*) New plastic tables were developed by my uncle. _____

14 (Begin with *To win consistently at tennis*) Speed and accuracy must be cultivated by the player. _____

15 (Begin with *After hiking vigorously all afternoon*) The chicken and biscuits were certainly something we could enjoy. _____

16 (Begin with *Having been distributed widely*) Many of the young girls in the seminary were impressed by the Communist propaganda. _____

17 (Begin with *To produce outstanding work*) Good equipment is needed by the artist. _____

18 (Begin with *Entering the cabin*) A dirty table with a cracked mirror over it were all I could see. _____

19 (Begin with *Never having seen a flea circus before*) It was natural for me to want to stay in the tent as long as possible. _____

16E The following passage contains alternate modifiers numbered in parentheses. From each pair select the modifier appropriate in formal English and write it in the correspondingly numbered blank.

Some wills are so ¹(odd, unique) that they invite collection. One of the ²(amusingest, most amusing) is that of the South African woman who bequeathed seven pet lizards $560 each for ³(them, their) having amused her. When the ⁴(latter, last) of the lizards died, her husband was to have the remaining money, provided he treated the lizards ⁵(well, good) in the meantime and fed them ⁶(regular, regularly). ⁷(Similar, similarly) to this will in consideration for man's ⁸(dumber, dumbest) companions was that of the Chicago woman who ⁹(kindly, kindlily) willed $5000 to feed the birds because they seemed ¹⁰(hungry, hungrily). So much for the women. The men seem more ¹¹(thoughtful, thoughtfully) of human beings —at least they have sometimes provided for them more ¹²(thoughtful, thoughtfully). A London man bequeathed $14,000 to a woman who had ¹³(unceasing, unceasingly) urged him to play ping-pong, which game he said had kept him ¹⁴(unusual, unusually) well for his years, and thus he felt quite ¹⁵(spry, spryly). His wife got fifty dollars. Another Briton left one of the ¹⁶(oddest, most odd) provisions for his own funeral. He required as his ¹⁷(most absolute, absolute) injunction that the men keep their hats off only very ¹⁸(brief, briefly). They might ¹⁹(easy, easily) catch cold with their hats off, for he had himself caught his ²⁰(deadly, most deadly) cold with his hat off at a funeral.

1. _____
2. _____
3. _____
4. _____
5. _____
6. _____
7. _____
8. _____
9. _____
10. _____
11. _____
12. _____
13. _____
14. _____
15. _____
16. _____
17. _____
18. _____
19. _____
20. _____

16F For each of the following sentences select the appropriate one of the two words in parentheses, adjective or adverb, and write it in the blank at the right.

1 The children felt (strange, strangely) after eating the rice pudding.

_____

2 The new students studied (hard, hardly).

_____

3 John went alone because he drove so (reckless, recklessly).

_____

4 Marian felt (stupid, stupidly) wearing a fur coat in July.

5 The fresh peaches tasted (good, well).

_____

6 The car did not run (good, well) after the wreck.

_____

7 Grandmother could not see (good, well) with her smoked glasses.

_____

16G Following is an open sentence and then a series of facts and comments used in the opening paragraphs of an article "The Fragile Climate of Spaceship Earth." Using the material, try writing the passage, using subordination and coordination to relate the ideas and organize them into coherent sentences. Your instructor can supply the original for comparison.

OPENING SENTENCE: Perhaps the most significant lesson to be learned from the long history of our planet is that during more than 90 per cent of this 550-million-year period the earth was free of polar ice.

1   In a sense, we live in an ice age.
2   The late Paleozoic period was 250 to 300 million years ago.
3   An ice age occurred then. It lasted 30 to 50 million years.
4   After this was a long period without any polar ice.
5   After this was a gradual cooling.
6   This cooling brought the beginning of the present Antarctic glaciers.
7   These developed during the Pliocene period.
8   This period was about 5 million years ago.
9   Some glaciers appeared much later in the Northern Hemisphere.
10   They began first in the Sierra Nevada. This was in California.
11   They began also in Iceland.
12   These glaciers appeared about 2.5 million years ago.
13   We find ourselves in a phase of glaciation now.
14   There have been several periods in this phase.
15   We define these periods as the Pleistocene.
16   During this period large ice sheets formed over the North American and European continents.
17   These ice sheets have retreated. They are Pleistocene ice sheets.
18   They retreated only 8,000 to 16,000 years ago.
19   This retreat is so recent that its effects on the rocks and the distribution of soil are still clearly visible. This retreat was relatively abrupt.
20   The abruptness was a remarkable feature of the retreat.
21   The Greenland ice sheet has persisted.
22   This ice sheet has preserved the record.
23   The record is preserved in the layers of snow.
24   These have accumulated each year.
25   The evidence from this ice sheet suggests a rapid increase of the mean temperature.
26   This occurred during a period of about 1000 years at the end of the last ice age. It was by several degrees centigrade.
27   More recently the temperature has been relatively constant.
28   This constancy is in comparison with the earlier dramatic change.
29   This constancy has been during the last 10,000 years.
30   It is indicated by the Greenland snow.
31   There have, however, been many smaller fluctuations.
32   These have been significant.
33   An example is the cold period in the seventeenth century.
34   This has been called "the little ice age."

*Objectives: (1) To use function words so that they
distinguish relationships accurately. (2) To use pronouns
and other reference words so that they refer clearly
to their antecedents. (3) To make verbs agree with
their subjects and pronouns with their antecedents.*

The grammar of Modern English depends heavily on function words, expressions that may or may not carry much meaning but show how other words in the sentence function, how they relate to one another. In "The lions have eaten," *have* has lost its meaning involving possession, becoming part of the verb *have eaten*, showing how *eat* functions. In "He was a man of principle," *of* carries little meaning but shows how *principle* is related to *man*, as a modifier. The following principles suggest how function words and pronouns, which serve partly as function words, contribute to coherence in the sentence.

17a Coordinating Conjunctions   Conj C

*Make coordinating conjunctions show accurately
how sentence elements are related.*

Coordinating conjunctions join like or parallel elements; conventionally, *and, or, nor, for,* and *but,* and usually *so* and *yet,* are considered conjunctions. *And* usually signals the addition of a parallel idea; *but* emphasizes a contrast; *or* offers a choice. Compare:

ORIGINAL: The student committee voted to abolish grades, *while* the dean wanted to make grading more rigid.

REVISIONS: The student committee voted to abolish grades, *but* the dean wanted to make grading more rigid. *Although* the student committee voted to abolish grades, the dean wanted to make grading more rigid.

While emphasizes a time relationship which is probably not intended here; *but* or *although* defines the relationship more accurately.

17b Conjunctive Adverbs   Conj Adv

*Omit unnecessary conjunctive adverbs or substitute
less formal connectives.*

Like coordinating conjunctions, conjunctive adverbs link parallel elements, but they also function as modifiers and usually mark a relatively formal transition, as in the following:

I admire Flora's wit; *however,* I could never tolerate her as a friend.

Often a less pretentious conjunction works better in such a sentence:

> I admire Flora's wit, *but* I could never tolerate her as a friend.
> *Although* I admire Flora's wit, I could never tolerate her as a friend.

Conjunctive adverbs include *thus, then, nevertheless, nonetheless, moreover, likewise, also, furthermore, therefore, consequently, hence*, and *besides*.

17c Subordinating Conjunctions   Conj S

Choose a more accurate or more appropriate subordinating conjunction.

Subordinating conjunctions—words like *when, if, while, although, because, since, as, so that, whereas, before, after*—are used mainly to make a sequence of words into a clause that can function as part of another pattern. Thus *after*, preceding "The dance was over," turns the pattern into a clause that can work only as part of another sentence: "After the dance was over, we went out for hamburgers." Words like *that, how, what, whoever* signal that the clauses they introduce can function as nouns. Accurate use of subordinating conjunctions makes relationships clear, for example:

> He did not doubt *that* (not *but that*) Arthur had spread the rumor. *Although* (not *while* or *as*) we were expecting a dull concert, we decided to use our tickets.

17d Prepositions   Prep

Use prepositions idiomatically.

Prepositions may determine shades of meaning; compare *agree to, agree with, agree about, agree on*. Sometimes differences are only matters of custom: in America one book is different *from* another, in England it may be different *to* another. Sometimes differences reflect usage preferences; *in regards to* is a slip for the standard *in regard to*, and *on the part of* is often only a wordy substitute for *by*.

> He was unaware *of* (not *about* or *to*) their fears.
> The academy taught *obedience to and respect for* (not *obedience and respect for*) law and order.

17e Pronoun Reference   Ref

Make pronouns refer clearly to their antecedents.

Many words, especially pronouns, have dual uses: they convey meaning by standing for an idea expressed elsewhere and they aid coherence by linking ideas in a sentence.

A reader can relate a pronoun to its antecedent and accordingly can understand its meaning partly by word order and partly by distinctions in pronoun form (see pages 265–266). In general, a personal pronoun refers to either a preceding noun used as subject of a clause or a noun in a position parallel to the pronoun. A relative pronoun—*who, whom, that, which*—usually refers to the preceding noun nearest it. Pronouns like *this, that, it*, and *which* may be used to refer generally to an idea that has preceded them but is not expressed in a single antecedent: "The play failed miserably, but *that* is what we had all expected." Whenever reference is not clear, however, whenever the meaning for which the pronoun stands cannot be immediately and precisely determined, clarity suffers. Compare:

ORIGINAL: The purpose of the bill was unclear because *it* had been presented so late in the session.

REVISION: Because the new bill had been presented so late in the session, *its* purpose was not clear.

In the original *it* is intended to refer to *bill*, but *bill* is only part of a modifier and the reader tends to connect it with the subject of the sentence, *purpose*. The logical antecedent appears in the original, but order does not make the reference clear. In the following, no likely antecedent even appears:

ORIGINAL: We considered the gas consumption of the two cars, their mechanical condition, and the tires, and because of *this*, we decided to buy the sedan.

REVISION: In spite of its relatively high gas consumption, we decided to buy the sedan because it had new tires and was in excellent mechanical condition.

Reference is so vague in the original that one cannot be sure of the intended meaning; the revision, avoiding the pronoun construction, presents only one possible meaning. Notice that in this sentence an expansion of *this* to *these things* or even *these characteristics* would only add to the confusion.

17f   Word Reference   **W Ref**

Make reference words reflect the meanings of their antecedents.

In English many words function much as pronouns do, referring to an antecedent that clarifies or specifies their meaning. For example, *do* may substitute for a verb, acting as an auxiliary with the main part of its verb understood from a previous appearance: "The voters know more than you *do*." *Do* carries the meaning of *know*, abbreviating *do know*. Or a relatively general word may be used to restate or summarize preceding ideas, usually to avoid repetition; "The general finally agreed to send for reinforcements, and his decision shortened the war." *Decision* refers to the act of the first clause, refining the meaning. Reference of this sort is clear, however, only when the reference word accurately reflects the concept of its antecedent. Compare:

ORIGINAL: When he had time for studying, he tried to *do so*.

REVISION: When he had time, he tried to study.

Do will not work as a substitute in the original because it is not parallel in form; if the first clause were "When he had time to study," *study* would carry over to work with *do*. In the following, meanings are not compatible:

ORIGINAL: Many people believed that industrial pollution should be outlawed, and my brother was in that *category*.

REVISION: Many people, including my brother, believed that industrial pollution should be outlawed.

ORIGINAL: Of all the arguments for physical education, I was annoyed most by having to get up early in the morning.

REVISION: I was annoyed most by the argument that physical education was good because it forced me to get up early in the morning.

Both originals have examples of unclear reference. In the first, no category is specified, although the sentence rests on the assumption that there is a category of people who believe that pollution should be outlawed. In the second "having to get up early" is not an argument.

17g Agreement or Concord   Agr

Make verbs agree with their subjects in person and number and pronouns agree with their antecedents in person, number, and gender.

The few inflections or form changes that survive in English strengthen coherence by helping to establish the connection between a subject and verb and between a pronoun and its antecedent.

In the present tense, when the subject of a verb is a noun or *he, she*, or *it*, the verb form with the *-s* ending is used: "He doesn't believe in compromise"; and forms of *to be* are chosen to fit their subjects: "I *am* flying. The dogs *were* barking."

Pronouns also have different forms to correspond with the antecedent in number (*I, we*), person (*I, you, it*), and gender (*he, she, it*). Another distinction in pronoun form, to indicate case or function (*he, him, they, them*), does not depend on agreement but on the pronoun's use (see Chapter 27).

Difficulties with agreement occur when the number of the subject or antecedent is not readily determinable or when subject or antecedent occurs in an unusual position. Following are examples:

Corn and beans *are* (not *is*) the ingredients of succotash. Everybody *is* (not *are*) expected to do *his* (not *their*) duty. The committee *differ* (not *differs*, presumably the sense is plural—committee members) in *their* (not *its*) opinions. He was one of the children who *were* (not *was*) too tired to go on. A crate of spoiled oranges *was* (not *were*) behind the door. There *are* (not *is*) many opportunities for good workers. Just outside *were* (not *was*) my brother and the sheriff. If one studies the report, *one* (or *he*, not *you* or *they*) can understand it. Neither glory nor reward *interests* (not *interest*) him.

The number of the subject may be obscured by material that appears between it and the verb. Following are examples:

Josie, with all her sisters, *was* (not *were*) marching up the walk. Identify three aspects of modern music that *give* (not *gives*) it a special flavor.

17A Without changing their order, combine each of the following pairs of sentences into four single sentences, using different function words to produce different meanings. Write the sentences on separate paper if you wish. Then write in the blanks the connective you use.

EXAMPLE: He liked most modern art. He disliked my painting.

Answer: Sentences on separate paper: **a** Although he liked most modern art, he disliked my painting. **b** He liked most modern art, but he disliked my painting. **c** Since he liked most modern art, he disliked my painting. **d** He liked most modern art; therefore, he disliked my painting.

a *Although*   b *but*   c *Since*   d *therefore*

1   The music was difficult. The director held a short rehearsal.

a _____   b _____   c _____   d _____

2   She wanted Chinese food. We went to the new restaurant.

a _____   b _____   c _____   d _____

3   I had seen Paris. I did not want to live in a city.

a _____   b _____   c _____   d _____

4   I saw a man looking in the window. I decided to go to bed.

a _____   b _____   c _____   d _____

5   We pried off the molding. We could not open the door.

a _____   b _____   c _____   d _____

6   I hear church bells. I think of my sister's wedding.

a _____   b _____   c _____   d _____

7   The traffic noises stopped. I was able to concentrate on the test.

a _____   b _____   c _____   d _____

8   The car swerves around the corner. The tires squeal loudly.

a _____   b _____   c _____   d _____

9   He favors desegregation. I will vote for him.

a _____   b _____   c _____   d _____

10   The fence was broken. The boys could see the game.

a _____   b _____   c _____   d _____

17B In the following passage, choose the more appropriate of the function words in parentheses and write it in the correspondingly numbered blank to the right.

[1](While, Although) conservationists watch our dwindling water supplies, scientists are looking [2](in, into) our most crucial potential shortage, water. [3](While, Although) important steps have been taken to bring available water [4](in, into) line with apparent needs, our consumption of water goes up [5](while, since, because) our water table goes down. [6](In, During, Among) some areas in Texas and California the water table has dropped as much as forty feet in a few years, [7](and, but) in Arizona it is dropping as much as five feet per year. There are three main users of water, [8](namely, for example), farmers, homeowners, and manufacturers, [9](and, but) at the moment the manufacturers present the most difficulty [10](because, although) they have recently become the largest users of controlled water, [11](even, nevertheless) passing the farmers. To manufacture an automobile requires 15,000 gallons of water, [12](and, or) enough to fill a small swimming pool, [13](and, or) to manufacture a ton of synthetic rubber requires 6,000,000 gallons [14](around, about) enough to fill a small lake. [15](Although, Since) this consumption is expected to double in a decade or two [16](and, but) [17](although, since, however) we consume more than 200 billion gallons a day, statisticians [18](now, nevertheless) predict that [19](in, by) 1975 we shall need some 400 billion gallons [20](if, unless) we can find some way to reduce our consumption. [21](Meanwhile, Nevertheless) some of our available water is being polluted by industry, [22](in spite of, because of) legislation designed to protect water resources, [23](and, but, while) meteorologists warn us that, [24](even though, whatever) we may hope to the contrary, our water supply from rain has remained relatively constant for many years at approximately 1300 billion gallons a day, [25](and, but, or) that we cannot expect to capture more than a third of this for practical purposes [26](even though, if) we adopt the most approved methods [27](along with, except for) the most modern techniques. The most hopeful prospect is [28](that, since) some practical method of purifying sea water may develop [29](although, whereas) existing systems all seem so costly [30](that, as) they provide little hope for immediate relief from shortages.

1. _____
2. _____
3. _____
4. _____
5. _____
6. _____
7. _____
8. _____
9. _____
10. _____
11. _____
12. _____
13. _____
14. _____
15. _____
16. _____
17. _____
18. _____
19. _____
20. _____
21. _____
22. _____
23. _____
24. _____
25. _____
26. _____
27. _____
28. _____
29. _____
30. _____

17C In the following sentences *this* is used to refer more or less generally to an idea that has preceded it. Sometimes the reference is clear, but in each instance the writing could be improved by subordination (see Chapter 16). Consider how the sentences could be combined, with *this* eliminated and one sentence converted into a subordinate part of the other. Then put a caret (∧) where you would insert the new subordinate element, and write in the space after each pair the new subordinate element you have created.

EXAMPLE: ∧ Kansas continued to enforce Prohibition. This, however, was not the case in some neighboring states where liquor was sold legally.

Answer: Although liquor was sold legally in some neighboring states.

1 *A Midsummer Night's Dream* is popular with summer theater groups. This is for the reason that it can be effectively produced outdoors.

2 The queen of the fairies showed how completely confused she was. This was by sitting and caressing the head of the donkey.

3 Finally Miss Heppletree began pushing the chairs into the swimming pool. This was after she had tried her sixth glass of punch.

4 Joseph studied German for six years. After this he felt confident in using the language when he went abroad.

5 I realize that education costs money. This is the reason for the fact that I contribute regularly to the scholarship fund.

6 Someone had let the air out of his tires. In spite of this, however, Grandfather arrived at the race on time.

7 Wordsworth and Coleridge received even more unfavorable criticism with the publication of a preface to the second edition of *The Lyrical Ballads*. This was in 1800.

8 We tried to tame the woodchuck. This was the one John had found under the house.

9 Public speaking courses provide training in the organization of ideas. This is the kind of training that is valuable.

17D In the following sentences *it* refers loosely to the whole idea of a preceding dependent clause. The pattern is common colloquially and sometimes the meaning is clear, but all the sentences could be made more precise. Consider how you would revise each to eliminate the pronoun, sometimes by supplying a new subject for the main clause, sometimes by combining the clauses, sometimes in other ways. Then write in the blank marked S the subject of your new main clause and in the blank marked V the verb.

EXAMPLE: When censorship of books and magazines was discontinued, it made pornography less attractive.

S *Discontinuing*
V *made*

Answer: Discontinuing censorship of books and magazines made pornography less attractive.

EXAMPLE: If all countries adopted the same language, it would be simpler.

S *Communication*
V *would be*

Answer: If all countries adopted the same language, communication would be simpler.

1 When there was a new law on pollution passed by the state legislature, it forced industries to install filtering systems.

S _____
V _____

2 When there is constant confusion in the classroom, it discourages students.

S _____
V _____

3 If everyone would follow the Golden Rule, it would make the world more pleasant.

S _____
V _____

4 If I can learn typing and shorthand, it will mean I can get a better job.

S _____
V _____

5 Whenever a criminal escapes punishment, it causes him to go on to his next crime with more confidence.

S _____
V _____

6 If Shirley goes to the dance alone, it will make everyone think her engagement has been broken.

S _____
V _____

7 If there are any factual errors in the report, it will weaken the committee's position.

S _____
V _____

8 When the instructor begins to play with his glasses, it means that there will be trouble for someone.

S _____
V _____

9 Whenever she thought about her husband's final words, it made her want to start for Reno.

S _____
V _____

10 Since cats express their emotions through their tails, it allows Aldous Huxley to say that a Manx cat is the equivalent of a dumb man.

S _____
V _____

11 If a student never learns to concentrate when he studies, it makes him get lower grades.

S _____
V _____

12 Because the saguaro has a large stem that can store water, it allows the plant to survive in the desert.

S _____
V _____

17E In the following passage select the appropriate form of the verb in parentheses and write it into the corresponding blank to the right.

EXAMPLE: The class of small children ¹(to be) being reorganized.

1. _*was*_

Father ¹(to be) one of those men who ²(to be) always anticipating the troubles of the future, and accordingly he early ³(become) concerned with the water problem. Neither he nor Uncle John, who ⁴(live) with us for years, ⁵(to be) much of an organizer, but soon the two of them ⁶(to drive) about the country and there ⁷(to be) water users' associations where none ⁸(to be) known before. The most active group ⁹(to be) the Red Horse Valley Rainmakers, whose first project, seeding clouds, ¹⁰(to be) put into the hands of one Tex Riley. Tex and his hedgehopping plane ¹¹(to be) to be paid twenty-five dollars an hour for seeding clouds with a certain chemical. Tex is a member of a group of former Marines who ¹²(to call, present tense) this chemical *goop*. Mother, who ¹³(to be) one of those women who ¹⁴(to be) not educated by the Marine Corps, ¹⁵(to call) it table salt.

The first sequence of cloud seedings, whatever ¹⁶(to be) the secret formulae supposedly concealed in *goop,* ¹⁷(to be) a tremendous success. Tex and his buddies ¹⁸(to say, present tense) the motto of the group is "When we sprinkle, it ¹⁹(to pour)," and it did. Everybody in the county ²⁰(to be) there to watch the flight, and within minutes after Tex took off there ²¹(to be) such pouring, hailing, snowing, and blowing as the Red Horse County Historical Association ²²(to have) not seen, and ²³(to have) not seen to this day. Father's winter wheat, the new shoots nicely above the ground, ²⁴(to be) washed out, and two goats, a pig, a cow, and my Maltese cat ²⁵(to be) drowned in a flash flood that swept our neighbor's house into the lake, where it, along with most of our farm machinery, ²⁶(to be) still sitting. Next summer, after some months of snowless winter, during which Tex and his plane ²⁷(to be) busy spewing table salt, ²⁸(to be) our time of disasters. We had one of those droughts that ²⁹(to turn) a farming valley into a dust bowl, and soon our family, burned out, ³⁰(to be) on the way to California.

1. _____
2. _____
3. _____
4. _____
5. _____
6. _____
7. _____
8. _____
9. _____
10. _____
11. _____
12. _____
13. _____
14. _____
15. _____
16. _____
17. _____
18. _____
19. _____
20. _____
21. _____
22. _____
23. _____
24. _____
25. _____
26. _____
27. _____
28. _____
29. _____
30. _____

17F In the following sentences underline expressions that should refer logically, but do not, because no clear antecedent is expressed or because they seem to refer to an antecedent not compatible in meaning. Then on another sheet of paper revise each sentence so that it is clear.

EXAMPLE: Since most of my friends play canasta, I am glad I fall into *that class.*

Possible Revision: Since most of my friends play canasta, I am glad that I also enjoy the game.

  1 In this camp, all the girls were looked on as a sister.

  2 One of the most important moments in a boy's life, including myself, is his first job.

  3 They were always telling stories to show that they were better than other families, a characteristic I have never admired.

  4 Most of us who are industrious and honest can build a successful future, and I am glad that I share this quality.

  5 Agnes was lacking in frankness, which annoyed me.

  6 A knowledge of past events is essential to understand the world today because they allow us to predict the future.

  7 I wish to question the validity of this statement, but I realize that you must have had just cause in doing so.

  8 In Houston, everytime a new oil well comes in, it is another millionaire.

  9 Children believe that if an adult says something it must be right, for they are older and have more authority.

  10 The man who will rule our country for four years after an election should be well qualified for that important task.

  11 He finally found the vacancy he had been looking for, an instructor in a small boy's school.

  12 A social worker must be patient, self-sacrificing, and tactful, qualities that I have always admired.

  13 Although there are many problems in the adaptation of atomic power to locomotives, designers believed the problems were not difficult enough to make it an unprofitable change.

  14 On inspecting the field of forest utilization, you will find that many useful discoveries are being brought forward by these imaginative technicians.

  15 I believe that the topic of my paper, which is offshore oil, is one of America's greatest remaining natural resources.

  16 You are likely to get more sunshine in the country than in the city because it doesn't have as many impurities which have to be filtered through.

  17 The other men in the service station conspired to give me the dirtiest jobs, aspects I had not anticipated.

  18 Fraternity or sorority life, the world dreamed about by so many high school students, did not live up to my expectations.

  19 Her reward was the life she was best suited for, a loving, understanding mother.

  20 All these men were given licenses, the only stipulation being that they had to be working as an architect at the time the bill was passed.

*Objective: To vary sentence length and order to
promote suitable emphasis.*

By using devices for emphasis, putting stress on certain ideas rather than
others, the writer manipulates the reader's attention. Emphasis is a broad
concept, and in some ways almost every characteristic of a sentence contributes to it; but the following three stylistic devices are associated especially
with emphasis.

1. *Length and variety.*   An obvious difference among sentences is that
some are longer or shorter than others. There is no inherent virtue in either
length or brevity in sentences; well-constructed long sentences may be clearer
than short ones. In fact, broad advice arbitrarily "to vary sentence length" or
to "use short concise sentences" is likely to be more misleading than helpful.
The writer can use sentence length, however, as a way of achieving different
kinds of emphasis. Compare, for example, the following two versions of the
opening of a famous essay by Robert Louis Stevenson:

> The changes wrought by death are in themselves so sharp and final, and so
> terrible and melancholy in their consequences, that the thing stands alone
> in man's experience, outdoes all other accidents because it is the last one,
> and has no parallel on earth.

> The changes wrought by death are in themselves so sharp and final, and so
> terrible and melancholy in their consequences, that the thing stands alone
> in man's experience, and has no parallel upon earth. It outdoes all other
> accidents because it is the last of them.

Either version is clear, but Stevenson wrote it the second way, in two sentences. The difference between the two is that the notion of death as the final
accident appears in Stevenson's version with more emphasis. In the shorter
separate sentence it stands out as a kind of summary of his comment about
death.

2. *Sentence rhythm and emphasis.*   Although most modern prose is
read silently, the reader is always conscious of the sound patterns behind
the prose, both the phonetic qualities and the patterns of accent. The following is from John Lyly's *Euphues*, written in the sixteenth century, and illustrates extreme self-consciousness in the use of devices of sound for emphasis
in prose.

> As therefore the sweetest rose hath his prickle, the finest velvet his brack,
> the fairest flower his bran, so the sharpest wit hath his wanton will and
> the holiest head his wicked way.

The alliterative repetition of sounds (*fairest flower, holiest head*) and the repeated rhythms seem artificial to the modern reader, but the sentence illustrates how much sound can do to affect emphasis even for silent reading. Most prose does not make such obvious use of sound, but in any passage the rhythmic qualities affect emphasis to some degree.

3. *Periodic and cumulative structure.* Although English sentences develop from a relatively small number of basic patterns (see Chapter 12), expansions of those patterns through subordination vary emphasis, mainly in two ways. In one, which produces the periodic sentence, modification is added at the beginning or somewhere within so that some part of the basic SVC pattern is left for the end of the sentence. In the other type of expanded sentence, the cumulative sentence, the SVC pattern is completed early in the sentence and modification is "cumulated" at the end. Compare the following:

> To the man with an ear for verbal delicacies—the man who searches painfully for the perfect word, and puts the way of saying a thing above the thing said—there is in writing the constant joy of sudden discovery, or happy accident.
>
> H. L. MENCKEN

> Women have served all these centuries as looking-glasses possessing the magic and delicious power of reflecting the figure of man at twice its natural size.
>
> VIRGINIA WOOLF

In the first, the main pattern, "there is joy," is withheld to produce a kind of climax at the end. This sort of movement, building to emphasis at the end on the central pattern, is characteristic of the periodic sentence and frequently of formal or oratorical styles. The second is cumulative, beginning with the subject and verb, "women have served," and concluding with a series of modifiers. Modern prose, especially in fiction, relies heavily on cumulative movement.

4. *Emphasis by subordination.* One of the most useful devices for emphasis has been discussed in Chapter 16 on subordination. In a broad way, one idea can be emphasized by reducing everything else to a subordinate grammatical status. Notice the following:

> The next day, because somebody had discovered that years before I had been paid as a ski instructor, the committee took my gold medal away from me.

Here the prominent fact, the one that stands out, is that the winner lost his gold medal. It gains its emphasis because the other details are subordinated —the time, the discovery of new evidence, the old evidence itself. Subordinating different details would shift the emphasis:

> The next day, as evidence for which the committee took my gold medal, somebody discovered that years before I had been paid as a ski instructor.

Shifting the subordination throws more emphasis on the discovery.

This device does not work, however, with the kind of frame sentence in which the main subject and verb are a formula like *It is said, Thus we can see*, or *She reminded me*. Notice the following:

Thinking back over what I had done, I had to conclude that I was a coward.

Here *I was a coward* retains main emphasis even though technically it is not the main clause but is subordinated as a complement, direct object of *conclude*.

18a Emphasis Through Structure   Em

Revise structure to make emphasis appropriate.

Both periodic and cumulative sentences, and various combinations of them, are useful in modern prose, and obviously no rule favoring one over the other is defensible. In general, however, the dramatic effects of the periodic sentence are less frequently warranted in expository prose than the more matter-of-fact effects of the cumulative. Compare:

PERIODIC: Only when it was presented with respect—even diffidence—and only when it did nothing to threaten the basic sanctity of the status quo, was student opinion tolerated.

CUMULATIVE: Student opinion was tolerated only when it was presented with respect—even diffidence—and only when it did nothing to threaten the basic sanctity of the status quo.

Both sentences are clear enough, but in most contexts the second would be less likely to sound too dramatic or even false in its emphasis.

18b Emphasis by Inversion   F Em

*Revise to avoid false emphasis produced by
unjustified inversion or artificial devices.*

A speaker may gain emphasis in ways that are almost denied to the writer. He may shout, or he may gesture, pointing his finger in his listener's face. He may use his facial muscles and his eyes. A writer may attempt similar effects by varying from standard patterns. He may shift word order—"Came the dawn"—or try for effects with rhetorical questions. He may insert nudges with words like *yes, now, well*. He may even rely on mechanical tricks like underlining words or using capital letters or sprinkling exclamation points about. For most prose, such relatively artificial devices are likely to have a false ring, suggesting that the writer is pushing too obviously for his emphasis. Consider the following examples:

I woke up early, anticipating a day of leisure. Little did I know what was really in store for me. (The inverted opening of the second sentence is trite, but it also overdramatizes the sense of the comment.)

After I had read the court decision, I had only two choices. What were those choices? (The rhetorical question is sometimes useful, but here it is repetitious and probably overemphatic.)

I decided to try to do something nice for everybody. Yes, I would get breakfast for the whole family. (Words like *yes, no, well, indeed*, inserted between sentences, often seem to emphasize insignificant parts of the writing; usually they are best omitted.)

Similarly, a writer is not likely to gain much emphasis by telling his reader that something is important. If he says only once, "Now I want to emphasize that this is important," he may be listened to, but if he keeps insisting direction on the value of what he is saying, he only discredits himself. Many zealous advocates have alienated readers or listeners by urging too frequently that their subject is important.

18A   Some of the following sentences from the opening of John Hersey's *Hiroshima* have been altered, mainly by moving modifying material so that the progress of the sentences is more nearly periodic than cumulative. In the blank after each sentence write *Rev* if you think the emphasis of the sentence could be improved by changing the order of modification; write *No change* if you think emphasis is best as the sentence stands. Then for those for which you suggest revision, underline modifying material that you think should be moved and indicate with a caret (∧) where it should be inserted.

1   At exactly fifteen minutes past eight in the morning, on August 6, 1945, Japanese time, at the moment when the atomic bomb flashed over Hiroshima, turning her head to speak to the girl at the next desk, a clerk in the personnel department of the East Asia Tin Works, Miss Toshiko Sasaki, had just sat down at her place in the plant office.   _____

2   At that same moment, on the porch of his private hospital, overhanging one of the seven deltaic rivers which divide Hiroshima, Dr. Masakazu Fujii was settling down cross-legged to read the Osaka *Asahi*.   _____

3   Watching a neighbor tearing down his house because it lay in the path of an air-raid-defense fire lane, Mrs. Hatsuyo Nakamura, a tailor's widow, stood by the window of her kitchen.   _____

4   On a cot on the top floor of his order's three-story mission house, reading a Jesuit magazine, *Stimmen der Zeit*, Father Wilhelm Kleinsorge, a German priest of the Society of Jesus, reclined in his underwear.   _____

5   With a blood specimen for a Wassermann test in his hand, a young member of the surgical staff of the city's large, modern Red Cross Hospital, Dr. Terufumi Sasaki, walked along one of the hospital corridors.   _____

6   At the door of a rich man's house in Koi, the city's western suburb, the Reverend Mr. Kiyoshi Tanomoto, pastor of the Hiroshima Methodist Church, paused and prepared to unload a handcart full of things he had evacuated from town in fear of the massive B-29 raid which everyone expected Hiroshima to suffer.   _____

7   A hundred thousand people were killed by the atomic bomb, and these six were among the survivors.   _____

8   When so many others died, they still wonder why they lived.   _____

9   And now each knows that in the act of survival he lived a dozen lives and saw more death than he ever thought he would see.   _____

18B Wolcott Gibbs in *The New Yorker* in 1936 wrote a criticism of *Time* magazine in which he parodied the style of *Time*. Following are some sentences from his parody-review. In the blanks rewrite each sentence, using standard word order and making any other changes you think might improve the sentences.

1 Yet to suggest itself as a rational method of communication, of infuriating readers into buying the magazine, was strange inverted *Time* style.

2 Backward ran sentences until reeled the mind.

3 Puny in spite of these preparations, prosy in spite of the contributions of Yale poets Archibald MacLeish & John Farrar, was the first issue of *Time* on March 3, 1923.

4 Always mentioned as William Randolph Hearst's "great & good friend" was Cinemactress Marion Davies, stressed was the bastardy of Ramsay MacDonald, the "cozy hospitality" of Mae West.

18C Writing styles in English have obviously changed since the appearance of the King James Bible in the early seventeenth century. Following is an episode from the Book of Joshua, Chapter 6. On separate paper retell the story in Modern English, then compare your version with the original, especially to see whether you have introduced any economies in the sentence structure and whether the changes have shifted emphasis.

2. And the Lord said unto Joshua, See, I have given into thine hand Jericho, and the king thereof, and the mighty men of valour. 3. And ye, shall compass the city, all ye men of war, and go round about the city once. Thus shalt thou do six days. 4. And seven priests shall bear before the ark seven trumpets of rams' horns: and the seventh day ye shall compass the city seven times, and the priests shall blow with the trumpets. 5. And it shall come to pass that when they make a long blast with the ram's horn, and when ye hear the sound of the trumpet, all the people shall shout with a great shout; and the wall of the city shall fall down flat, and the people shall ascend up every man straight before him. 6. And Joshua the son of Nun called the priests, and said unto them, Take up the ark of the covenant, and let seven priests bear seven trumpets of rams' horns before the ark of the Lord. 8. And it came to pass, when Joshua had spoken unto the people, that the seven priests bearing the seven trumpets of rams' horns passed on before the Lord, and blew with the trumpets: and the ark of the covenant of the Lord followed them. 9. And the armed men went before the priests that blew with the trumpets, and the rereward came after the ark, the priests going on, and blowing with the trumpets. 10. And Joshua had commanded the people, saying, Ye shall not shout, nor make any noise with your voice, neither shall any word proceed out of your mouth, until the day I bid you shout; then shall ye shout. 11. So the ark of the Lord compassed the city, going about it once: and they came into the camp, and lodged in the camp. 12. And Joshua rose early in the morning, and the priests took up the ark of the Lord. 13. And seven priests bearing seven trumpets of rams' horns before the ark of the Lord went on continually and blew with the trumpets: and the armed men went before them; but the rereward came after the ark of the Lord, the priests going on, and blowing with the trumpets. 14. And the second day they compassed the city once, and returned into the camp; so they did six days. 15. And it came to pass on the seventh day, that they rose early about the dawning of the day, and compassed the city after the same manner seven times: only on that day they compassed the city seven times. 16. And it came to pass at the seventh time, when the priests blew with the trumpets, Joshua said unto the people, Shout; for the Lord hath given you the city. . . . 20. So the people shouted when the priests blew with the trumpets; and it came to pass, when the people heard the sound of the trumpet, and the people shouted with a great shout, that the wall fell down flat, so that the people went up into the city, every man straight before him, and they took the city.

18D Read the following paragraph. It describes the engagement at Lexington and Concord, which did much to precipitate the conflict that Americans call The Revolution. The first sentence, the topic sentence, involves a figure of speech that in context can be seen to mean that after a long, threatening period, fighting broke out. The "Gage" mentioned in the passage is General Thomas Gage, who was at the time military governor of Boston. The numbers before sentences are not in the original.

(1) At last the thunder-cloud broke, and flash after flash lit up the gloom which overhung the land. (2) Gage, rather because he was expected to take some forward step, than because he saw clearly where to go, conceived the idea of destroying the stores which had been collected at Concord. (3) The force told off for this service, according to a faulty practice of those times, consisted of detachments from many regiments; and the officer in charge of the whole was incompetent. (4) The troops started before midnight. (5) At four in the morning, just as an April day was breaking, they reached the village of Lexington, and found sixty or seventy of the local militia waiting for them on the common. (6) Firing ensued, and the Americans were dispersed, leaving seven of their number dead or dying. (7) It was a chilly and a depressing prologue to a mighty drama. (8) The British advanced to Concord, where they spoiled some flour, knocked the trunnions off three iron guns, burned a heap of wooden spoons and trenchers, and cut down a Liberty pole. (9) In order to cover these trumpery operations a party of a hundred infantry had been stationed at a bridge over the neighbouring river, and towards ten o'clock they were attacked by about thrice as many provincials, who came resolutely on. (10) After two or three had fallen on either side, the regulars gave way and retreated in confusion upon their main body in the centre of the town.

GEORGE C TTC TREVELYAN, *The American Revolution*

Arbitrarily, consider any sentence of twenty or fewer words "short," and any longer sentence "long." In the blank to the right copy the numbers of the "short" sentences.

_____

In the space below, write two sentences in which you try to describe what, in this paragraph, Trevelyan uses short sentences for, and what he uses long sentences for.

a (short)

b (long)

On a separate sheet of paper, rewrite the paragraph, making what are now "short" sentences into parts of "long" sentences and reducing at least three of what are now "long" sentences to "short" ones. Be ready to comment on the effect of this revision on emphasis in the paragraph.

Objective: To understand basic facts of the development of English and of word formation and to use this knowledge as one way of increasing vocabulary.

John Ruskin, in *Sesame and Lilies*, urges that anyone educated "is learned in the *peerage* of words, knows the words of true descent and ancient blood, . . . remembers all their ancestry, their intermarriages, distant relationships, and the extent to which they were admitted, and offices they held, among the national *noblesse* of words at any time and in any country." Minimal communication requires no such extensive knowledge of the backgrounds of words as this passage commends, but Ruskin is surely right that knowledge about how words develop, about their origins, can promote precision in both reading and writing. The more a writer knows about his tools, the better he can use them. Particularly, some knowledge of where words come from can aid vocabulary building.

In general, the vocabulary of the English language, which now includes more than half a million words, has developed in three ways: (1) by descent from parent languages; (2) by borrowing from other languages; and (3) by creation of new words, usually from existing words.

Language by Descent

English can be traced to a now extinct language called Indo-European, which scholars have reconstructed by studying existing languages that grew from it. Most of the languages of Europe, and some Asiatic languages, have grown over the centuries from Indo-European. Languages as different as English, Persian, Latin, Lithuanian, and Celtic still carry signs of their common ancestry, such as words that are cognates, which had a common origin in Indo-European. In the following table, the common origin of a number of cognates is apparent:

English	Lithuanian	Celtic	Latin	Greek	Persian	Sanskrit
three	tri	tri	tres	treis	thri	tri
seven	septyni	secht	septem	hepta	hapta	sapta
me	manen	me	me	me	me	me
mother	moter	mathair	mater	meter	matar	matar
brother	brolis	brathair	frater	phrater	bratar	bhratar
night	naktis	mocht	noctis	nuktos		nakta

Working with similarities like these, linguists have been able to reconstruct ancient languages that have long disappeared from use. The Indo-European base from which *mother* and *mater* evolved, for instance, was **mater* (the asterisk marks a reconstructed word). The Indo-European base *peter, through a series of evolutionary changes, ultimately produced father, Vater in German, and pater in Latin. Many of these changes followed discernible patterns. For example, the initial sound /p/ was preserved in the languages that developed into Latin (pater), but changed to /f/ in Germanic languages (father). Indo-European *ped- produced Latin pes, pedis but German Fuss and English foot.

The branch of Indo-European known as Germanic fathered a number of languages, including the speech of the Angles and Saxons, Germanic tribes that settled in England after the Romans left the island about 400 A.D. Anglo-Saxon, now usually called Old English, is the ancestor of Modern English. To a modern user of English, however, Old English looks like a foreign language, because English, like all language, has been undergoing constant change since the eighth or ninth century. Consider the following Old English version of a verse from the New Testament:

> Eadige synd ða ðe for rihtwisnesse hingriaþ and þyrstaþ, forþam ðe hi beoþ gefyllede.
> Blessed are they that for righteousness hunger and thirst, for that they will be filled.

Some of the Old English words (eadige and synd and the letters ð and þ) have disappeared, although sind remains in modern German; but most of them have remained, changed in ways that make the older forms almost unrecognizable. In Modern English most of the commonest words, including the structure words, are native, descendants from Old English.

Borrowing and Vocabulary

Although the most common words in English are native—basic words for the universe and living in it like sun, moon, live, die, child, house, bed, hunt, fish, plow—many words needed for modern communication did not exist in Old English. Furthermore, every kind of intercourse between peoples, trading or warfare, carried with it language influences. The Angles and Saxons gained vocabulary from the Scandinavian invaders who swept the country from time to time, but also from the spread of Christianity into the island. The Norman conquest in 1066 changed the official language of England to French, and even though most of the people on the island went on speaking English, much of the influence of the new language persisted. The Renaissance brought an additional flood of words, especially derived from Latin and Greek and often transmitted through French or some other European language. We have continued to borrow—marine terms from Dutch (skipper, yacht), musical terms from Italian (opera, allegro), scientific and technical terms from Latin and Greek (electron, spectroheliograph), philosophical terms from Latin and Greek (epistemology, epicurean). Although Latin and Greek have contributed most heavily, English continues to borrow widely—tomahawk from Algonquian, tomato from Nahuatl through Spanish, naïve and chic from French, assassin and giraffe from Arabic, tea and typhoon from Chinese, and thousands more.

Although most of the words in English have ancestors in Old English or can be traced to borrowed or loan words, many words have developed in the language as combinations or modifications of old words or old words put to new uses. Word forms are created in English in several ways; the following two are the most common:

1. *Compounding.* The process of putting two words together to make a new one has gone on for a long time; when speakers of Old English needed a new name for a flower they relied on their sense of metaphor and put together *daeges*, "day's," and *eage*, "eye," to create *daegeseage*, which became *daisy*. Recently, when we needed a name for a new vehicle, we combined two words to make *spaceship*, and then for the person using it took two Greek roots, *astro*, "star," and *naut*, "sailor," and produced *astronaut*. *Typewriter, mimeograph, television, radiogram,* are all recent compounds. Compounds tend to multiply rapidly by analogy; with *horsepower* and *waterpower* as patterns all sorts of *power* compounds developed, and some have already virtually disappeared: *black power, flower power, gay power.*

2. *Affixes.* An affix is a syllable or group of syllables joined to a word to affect its meaning or indicate its use—in English a prefix at the beginning of a word or a suffix at the end. Usually affixes cannot stand alone and work only when attached to a word or root. Word formation with prefixes and suffixes occurred in Old English and also in languages like Latin and Greek from which English borrows. For example, we have borrowed a number of words that had already been formed with affixes in Latin—*inspect* comes from the Latin *inspicere*, which had been formed in Latin by the prefix *in-* and the verb *specere*, "to see." But the tendency to build new words with affixes has continued in English. Prefixes like *in-, un-, non-, ultra-, super-, anti-*, or *pre-* and suffixes like *-al, -ion, -icle, -or, -ity, -able*, or *-ant* are constantly being attached in new ways to form new words. We have recently coined *superstar* for an outstanding athlete, *deplane* for getting out of an airplane, and *debriefing* for what happens when astronauts report on a mission for which they were "briefed" before they started. Recent fads involving the suffixes *-orium, -orama,* and *-wise* are already luckily fading. *Crematorium* persists as a euphemism, but *lubratorium* and *tiratorium* have not caught on; *fishorama* had only a short life to describe a seafood meal; and it is no longer common for a television announcer to say that he will discuss temperatures "weatherwise."

Building a Vocabulary

Every literate person has at least four vocabularies: a speaking vocabulary, a writing vocabulary, a reading vocabulary, and an acquaintance vocabulary. The first is usually the smallest, the body of words that come readily to the speaker's tongue; even a fairly articulate speaker may use only 2000 or 3000 words. A second vocabulary for every literate person includes the words in his speaking vocabulary plus those he can produce when he has time to think before writing. Some writers are said to have used as many as 50,000 words. A reading vocabulary is still larger, including in addition to words used in speaking and writing words that can be recognized in reading and understood. As a fourth vocabulary, almost everyone adds a body of words that he does not really command but that he has seen or heard before and can understand from context.

We acquire basic vocabularies of these kinds more or less unconsciously, but expanding them usually requires deliberate effort, growing from an interest in words and how they work and using practical procedures like the following:

1. *Learn words in groups.* Since words are related in meaning and through common origins, you can learn a dozen words of a group almost as easily as you can learn one of them.

2. *Work with prefixes and suffixes.* By learning the meanings of a few important affixes you can almost at once add many words to your recognition vocabularies.

3. *Learn a new word thoroughly.* When you look up a new word, check its origin and its various uses. The history of a word is interesting in itself, but it is also an aid to memory.

4. *Use new words.* An obvious way to increase vocabularies is to move words from recognition vocabularies to writing and speaking vocabularies.

19A Following are a list of words and a list of etymologies of these words, but the words and their etymologies are not in the same order. Look up each word in the dictionary and study its etymology. Then find the etymology that fits it in the list, and place the number of the word in the blank after the etymology. For example, the nineteenth word in the list has its etymology listed first; the number 19 therefore belongs in the blank after the example. For words in Old English, Middle English, and Old French you may find different spellings in different dictionaries.

1. alphabet	6. constable	11. jelly	16. tooth
2. ballot	7. dollar	12. kennel	17. undulant
3. Bible	8. fiddle	13. language	18. paper
4. cabbage	9. fowl	14. magazine	19. umpire
5. calendar	10. stranger	15. television	

EXAMPLE: From the French *non*, meaning *not*, plus *per*, meaning *pair,* the third to decide a choice; with a loss of initial *n, a numpire* becoming *an umpire.*   *19*

From Latin *canis*, meaning *dog*, plus a suffix, *-ile*, meaning *suitable for.* _____

From Latin *extraneus*, meaning *on the outside*, through Old French *estraungier.* _____

From Arabic *makhazin*, from *khazana*, meaning *to store up.* _____

From Latin *unda*, meaning *a wave*, plus an ending showing action. _____

From Latin *caput*, meaning *head*, through Old French *caoche*, Middle English *cabache.* _____

From Greek *payros*, name of a water reed. _____

From Latin *Kalends*, the first day of the month, when interest on loans was due. _____

From the first two Greek letters, *alpha* and *beta.* _____

From Old English or Anglo-Saxon *toth*, from an Indo-European base *edont-*, meaning *to eat*; related by Latin to *dental.* _____

From Greek *tele*, meaning *far off*, and Latin *visio*, from Latin *video*, meaning *to see.* _____

From Old English or Anglo-Saxon *fugol*, meaning a bird. _____

From Latin *gelare*, meaning *to freeze*, through Old French *geler.* _____

From Latin *comes stabuli*, meaning *companion of the stables*, that is, *nobleman companion* (of the king) *in charge of transportation.* _____

From Latin *lingua*, meaning the *tongue*, which comes from an Indo-European *dnghwa*, from which English *tongue* also comes. _____

From supposed Latin *disjejunare*, made up of *dis*, meaning *away from*, and *jejunare*, meaning *to be hungry.* _____

From the Phoenician city of *Byblos*, by way of the Greek word for sheets of papyrus, *biblia.* _____

From Italian *ballotta*, meaning *a little ball*, dropped in a box. _____

19B Many English words come from Latin. Sometimes the Latin word has changed little or not at all; for instance, Latin *circus*, a circular place and then a celebration held in a circular place, has become English *circus*. Some Latin words, by slight changes or by combining with other words or affixes, have given us many words. For each of the following Latin words try to find at least ten descendants in English that make some use of the parent word.

1 *dicere (dictus)*

_____   _____   _____   _____   _____

_____   _____   _____   _____   _____

2 *mittere (missus)*

_____   _____   _____   _____   _____

_____   _____   _____   _____   _____

3 *pendere*

_____   _____   _____   _____   _____

_____   _____   _____   _____   _____

4 *currere (cursus)*

_____   _____   _____   _____   _____

_____   _____   _____   _____   _____

5 *stabilis (stabulum, stare)*

_____   _____   _____   _____   _____

_____   _____   _____   _____   _____

6 *facere (factus)*

_____   _____   _____   _____   _____

_____   _____   _____   _____   _____

7 *liber*

_____   _____   _____   _____   _____

_____   _____   _____   _____   _____

8 *vertere* (hint: try this with prefixes, for instance di-, in-, re-)

_____   _____   _____   _____   _____

_____   _____   _____   _____   _____

9 *ducere (ductus)*

_____   _____   _____   _____   _____

_____   _____   _____   _____   _____

19C Familiarity with common prefixes and suffixes in English and a grasp of the manner in which they combine with frequently used root words aid vocabulary development. Following is a list of common prefixes and also a root word with which each prefix can be combined. Using a dictionary, write the meaning of each prefix in the blank following it. Then in the blank at the right write one English word that combines the prefix at the left with the root word in the center column.

EXAMPLE: con- _*with*_   sequi (to follow)   *consequent*

1	de-	_____	clinare (to bend)	_____
2	sub-	_____	scribere (to write)	_____
3	contra-	_____	dicere (to say)	_____
4	inter-	_____	ferire (to strike)	_____
5	in-	_____	dicere (to say)	_____
6	archi-	_____	teacton (work)	_____
7	poly-	_____	pous (foot)	_____
8	pro-	_____	nuntiare (to announce)	_____
9	pro-	_____	mittere (to send)	_____
10	sub-	_____	trahere (to draw)	_____
11	super-	_____	sedere (to sit)	_____
12	trans-	_____	ferre (to carry)	_____
13	bio-	_____	logy (study)	_____
14	bi-	_____	nomos (law)	_____
15	col-	_____	leger (to gather)	_____
16	com-	_____	mutare (to change)	_____
17	counter-	_____	facere (to make)	_____
18	pre-	_____	dicere (to say)	_____

19D The following words were created by compounding either in Old English or in a language from which the compound was borrowed. Look up each word in the dictionary and write the words from which it was formed.

EXAMPLE: freebooter *Dutch vrijbuiter, from vrij (free) + buit (plunder)*

1 delicatessen

2 nostril

3 democracy

4 window

5 garlic

6 barn

7 landscape

8 pajamas

9 hussy

10 municipal

19E In the left column are words created by compounding, in the right the words from which they were formed. In speech the words in the two columns would be distinguished by differences in accent, as marked. In the space at the left write the meanings of the compounds; in the space at the right the meanings of the two words used separately, with the accent as marked. Use the dictionary as you need to.

EXAMPLE: bláckboard   black bóard

1 híghchair   high cháir

2 híghbrow   high brów

3 bláckguard   black gúard

4 géntleman   gentle mán

5 hándout   hand oút

6 loúdspeaker   loud spéaker

7 roúghneck   rough néck

8 chéapskate   cheap skáte

9 bríckyard   brick yárd

10 cópperhead   copper héad

19F Following are pairs of words, similar in meaning, one of each pair originating in Old English and one in French. Remembering that Norman French was the official and court language in England during the period after 1066, although English persisted among the common people, underline the word in each pair that you think is a native English word rather than a borrowing from French. Then check your answers in a dictionary.

1 help, assistance
2 beef, cow
3 begin, commence
4 corpulent, fat
5 judgment, doom

6 deer, venison
7 king, sovereign
8 work, labor
9 wretched, miserable
10 buy, purchase

19G The following words were created through some process other than the two described in the text, compounding and adding affixes. Look up each word and describe its origin in the space following it.

1 kodak

2 bus

3 grovel

4 smog

5 cockroach

6 laser

Objectives: (1) To take advantage of the different sorts of information offered by a dictionary. (2) To use words accurately, economically, and expressively.

Words affect readers and hearers in many ways, mainly by carrying what we call "meaning." But meaning is not simple, and no word has quite the same meaning for any two people. Although a word like *sea* refers to an object, its referent, it does not directly represent that referent but represents a person's thought about the referent.

Referent   **Word**

The word *sea* refers to only one subject or sort of object, but it can call up various things, and thus in a way can "mean" them. To a fisherman it may suggest sea fishing, to a romantic person an island paradise in the South Seas, to anyone who has experienced a storm at sea it may suggest mountainous waves.

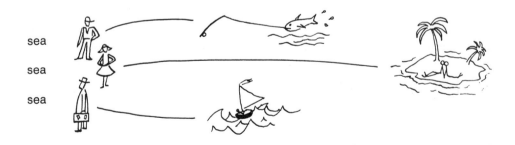

From the time we first hear our parents speak, we live with words; we even think and dream with them. Thus they develop power that we can use with others, power that others can use on us, power for good or evil, for understanding or confusion. The powers of words are many, but speaking roughly they can be included under *denotation* and *connotation*. The denotation of *sea* is its "dictionary" meaning, its communication of the central concept of its referent, a large body of salt water. The connotation of *sea* can be anything that the word suggests, emotional and interpretative parts of the meaning of the word.

We cannot, therefore, think of any word as having a single eternal and absolute meaning. The record of the many meanings and shades of meaning that attach themselves to a word during its history may be extensive and complex—as a glance at the *Oxford English Dictionary* illustrates. *Love* can refer to an emotion, a mythological character, or the wrong end of a tennis score. *Plug* can refer to an electrical fixture, a flattering comment, or a worn-out horse. Even the most extensive dictionary cannot record all the meanings possible for a word. As users of the language, however, we are able to distinguish remarkable variations in meaning because we consider words in their contexts—that is, in association with all the words around them. Notice, for example, that we can distinguish the various meanings of the word *tip* in the following without the aid of a dictionary.

> Take a tip from me, and send her a dozen roses.
> The tip of her nose pointed at her left ear.
> The first batter hit a foul tip.
> The waiter accepted the tip without a smile.
> The old man was chalking the tip of a billiard cue.
> The medium was surprised when I tipped the table.
> Why didn't you tip me off about his plans?

We can understand what the word means by relating it to the company it keeps.

Using a Dictionary

For most purposes, a dictionary supplies the readiest information about a word. Unfortunately, not everybody knows how to use a dictionary, does not know how a dictionary is made and why it is made that way.

Formerly, lexicographers—that is, makers of dictionaries—tried to tell people what was correct or elegant, what was the "best" language. Lexicographers have since learned that trying to police the language is not the most useful thing they can do, and that they could not do it if they wanted to. If there is any such thing as "best" in word choice, then the best is the best for a certain person on a certain occasion. The best words for a scientist discussing his discoveries about skull structure while addressing brain surgeons would not be the best words for the same scientist trying to explain to his little daughter why she should not thump her baby brother on the head with a building block.

That is, language is a tool, and lexicographers now believe they can help users of dictionaries most if they try to describe the tool—only a user of the tool can know what he wants to do with it. Thus a modern dictionary is a compendium of information about words.

The following is an entry from a modern dictionary, the most recently edited at this writing:

gas (gas) *n.* [ModL., word invented by the Belgian chemist, Van Helmont (1577–1644), on basis of *chaos*, air (< Gr. *chaos*, CHAOS), term used by Paracelsus] **1.** the fluid form of a substance in which it can expand indefinitely and completely fill its container; form that is neither liquid nor solid; vapor **2.** any mixture of flammable gases used for lighting, heating, or cooking **3.** any gas, as nitrous oxide, used as an anesthetic **4.** any substance, as phosgene, intentionally dispersed through the atmosphere, as in war, to act as a poison, irritant, or asphyxiant **5.** a gaseous substance formed in the stomach, bowels, etc. ☆**6.** [Colloq.] *a) short for* GASOLINE *b)* the accelerator or throttle in an automobile, etc. ☆**7.** [Slang] *a)* idle or boastful talk *b)* something or someone that is very pleasing, exciting, amusing, etc. **8.** *Mining* a mixture of firedamp with air that explodes if ignited —*vt.* **gassed, gas′sing 1.** to supply with gas **2.** to subject to the action of gas **3.** to injure or kill by gas, as in war ☆**4.** [Slang] to thrill, delight, amuse greatly, etc. —*vi.* **1.** to give off gas ☆**2.** [Slang] to talk in an idle or boastful way —*adj.* of, using, or operated by gas —☆**gas up** [Colloq.] to fill the tank of an automobile, etc. with gasoline —☆**step on the gas** [Slang] **1.** to press on the accelerator of an automobile, etc. **2.** to hurry; move or act faster

The word *gas* in boldface type is the entry word; it identifies the entry and provides the standard spelling. If there were another acceptable spelling it might appear here; the word usually spelled *center* in American English is spelled *centre* in British English. The next part of the entry, (gas) in parentheses and not boldface, is intended to suggest the pronunciation. The symbols *g, a,* and *s* are here not used as letters, but as indications of sounds; the symbols are explained somewhere in the book, in this volume on every right-hand page. When the lexicographer provided only one pronunciation he did not mean to say that all other pronunciations are wrong; he meant to say that this is an acceptable pronunciation, very much more common in good usage in the United States than any other. For words having great diversity of pronunciation the same dictionary gives two or more pronunciations. It lists two pronunciations for *tomato*, but does not clutter up the book with the dozen or more acceptable pronunciations of *orange*. The next letter, an *n* in boldface italics, is an indication of grammatical class, here standing for *noun*. The fourth portion of the entry, enclosed in square brackets, is the etymology.

Following the etymology are the meanings, numbered through 8. Again, the lexicographer is not saying these are the only possible meanings; he knows that there have been meanings now obsolete, that there are technical meanings used by a few scientists, and that there are slang uses—*gas* can mean a fine party in the Harlem dialect—and that there will be more uses tomorrow. What he does mean is that he has studied the word carefully, that the word can be used in the ways he has suggested, and that granted the size of his book and his probable audience, he believes these are likely to be the most useful. He starts with an old and central use, from which a number of others derive, and goes on to a technical use in mining. Number 6 is labeled in two ways; the star indicates that the word is an Americanism, and the abbreviation *colloq.* suggests that in this use the word is colloquial, suitable for conversation but to be used with some caution in writing (on usage varieties, see Chapter 27). For his number 7, the lexicographer uses the label *slang*, meaning that the word may have the charm and vigor of lively speech, but may lack the stability or wide currency of the standard uses he has not so labeled.

A dash after use number 8 warns us of a change, and the letters in boldface, *v.t.*, tell us what this change is. The abbreviation means "verb, transitive," and the whole means that the symbol *gas* can be used as a verb as well as a noun, and the forms *gassed* and *gassing* alert us to a change in spelling. Similarly, we are later notified that the same spelling, *gas*, can be used as an intransitive verb and as an adjective. With the boldfaced entry *gas up*, we come to something still different, what is called in dictionary terminology a *phrase*. The words *gas* and *up*, when used together, can mean something that they do not mean when used alone. That is, *gas up* does not mean that a volatile substance rises toward the heavens; as the dictionary puts it, the phrase means to fill the tank of an automotive vehicle.

20a Word Choice W

*Choose the right word, consulting a good dictionary
if necessary.*

The students who wrote that Chaucer's Knight "had great humidity" and that *The Faery Queene* "was an allergy" were, among other things, confusing *humility* with *humidity* and *allegory* with *allergy*. The Chicago official who asked his audience to join him on a road leading to "higher platitudes of achievement" said more than he intended. No nostrum will prevent slips of this sort, but care and use of the dictionary will help.

20b Abstract and Concrete Words Concrete

*Consider whether a more concrete, specific wording
will not tell the reader more.*

In general, we use *concrete* to describe expressions that refer to things we can see, hear, or feel; *abstract* expressions refer to concepts, attributes, ideas. *Book* is concrete, *literature* abstract. Like *specific* and *general*, however, these terms are relative. *Traffic hazard* is more concrete than *transportation problem; drunk driver* is more concrete than *traffic hazard*. Abstractions are, of course, necessary, but most writers can refine their thinking by using concrete words whenever possible. Especially troublesome are what are sometimes called "blanket" words, which are used almost without meaning, to cover like a blanket everything within the vicinity of the author's idea. Examples currently popular include: *aspect, point, setup, over-all, claim* (verb), *contact* (verb), *situation, picture, deal, factor, put across, put over, condition, circumstances, phase, basic, regard, fundamental, facility, angle, rate* (verb), *worthwhile, unique, outstanding, state* (verb).

Since concreteness is relative, the writer's problem often is to determine the degree of concreteness that is appropriated. A writer may refer to "her red dress." There is nothing wrong with the choice of adjective if *red* is being used only to distinguish the wearer from a girl wearing green. But if the writer is trying to make a reader see the dress, or to tell something about the girl by using the dress as a sign of her character, or to use the word to create an emotion, then he may need to be more precise. He may need to specify that the dress is brick red, Chinese red, blood red, terra cotta, carmine, vermilion, or cerise.

Frequently concrete diction is useful because it helps the writer refer to objects that symbolize a broader concept. Writers can characterize a person by referring to specific objects—a hard hat, a leather jacket, hot pants, horn-rimmed glasses. A man may be defined as a Hitler, a St. Francis, or a Machiavelli. The symbolic use of concrete expressions allows the writer to be both abstract and concrete, general and specific, at the same time. The device has its dangers, since symbols do not have the same significance for all people and readily change. Napoleon is not now a powerful symbol for most Americans, but in France he was a symbol of glorious victory and in some countries a personification of evil.

20c Denotation and Connotation: Slanting   Slant

Reconsider slanted terms, using them only for justified emotional effects.

Because words have connotation, communicate emotionally, they have special power. A poet may use this power to write moving verse; an unscrupulous advertiser or a political demagogue may exploit the same power intentionally to deceive; the unwary student, if he does not consider emotional effects of words, may be betrayed into both misstatement and misunderstanding. Political opponents might refer to the same action as the following.

Mayor Jones, heeding always the wisdom of the common man . . . .
Mayor Jones, pandering to the yawpings of the scum of the community . . . .

The comments have opposite effects largely because they contain words with different connotations, words loaded or slanted to rouse differing emotions.

20d Figurative Language: Metaphor   Fig

Control metaphorical writing to obtain only the desired effects.

Metaphorical writing can be both vigorous and terse. A figure of speech can have both denotative and connotative power, especially when it can work as a symbol. A hard hat, for example, may be a concrete indication of a workingman's occupation, but the term *hardhat* can also suggest the conservatism, belligerence, and resilience of a segment of society. The danger arises in figurative use when figures are incongruously mixed. The legislator who condemned a bill as "a sword of Damocles hanging over a Pandora's box," made himself a laughing stock and probably did not win his cause many votes.

20e Economical Word Choice   **Wordy**

Make style more concise by eliminating needless words.

Good writing requires development, and development requires words, usually many of them, but as long as a writer can say what he wants to, with the appropriate precision and vigor, the fewer words he uses, the better. Often a writer can improve his prose by ruthless use of a blue pencil, cutting every unnecessary word. Wordiness obscures meaning; it does not create a "style." Careless repetition can be especially disconcerting. Often, of course, studied repetition is useful, preferable to the use of clumsy synonyms. *Eye* has no good synonym and must appear often in a discussion of eyes; variation with *optic* or *limpid pool* does not add grace, but neither does careless doubling of a conjunction like *that*. Repetition of the same meaning or idea is called redundancy. Since consensus means "agreement, especially in opinion," *consensus of opinion* is redundant. *Persevere on, refer back*, and *repeat again* say the same thing twice.

20f "Direction" in Meaning   **Dir**

*Revise, substituting more accurate choices for words
used to point in a "false direction."*

Many words can work only in what might be called one "direction," and cannot work the opposite way. A word may be able to work toward a subject but not toward a predicate, toward a modifier but not toward a complement. The student who wrote "Such antics arise interest in the spectators," meant to say something else. Interest may arise, or antics may arouse interest, but as the sentence stands, the direction of *arise* is wrong. Similarly, the direction is confused in "The mixtures of colors up higher on the mountain are accountable to the slides of loose rocks." If the writer's sense of idiom does not clarify the direction of words for him, a good dictionary will help.

20A In the blank after each sentence in the second column, write the number designating the first-column sentence that comes nearest to using the italicized word in the same way. You need not select all the first-column sentences, and you may select one more than once.

1	The individual is more important than the *state*.	**1**	He could not *state* any of the rules. _____
2	He found the mother in a *state* of collapse.	**2**	The President spoke on the *state* of the union. _____
3	Texas is the largest *state*.	**3**	She was in no *state* to be alone. _____
4	Please *state* your objections.	**4**	Speed laws are strict in this *state*. _____
		5	The finances were in a miserable *state*. _____

1	Chemistry was his hardest *study*.	**1**	College work requires more *study* than high school. _____
2	She was born in a brown *study*.	**2**	His paper was a *study* of language changes. _____
3	*Study* is more tiring than manual labor.	**3**	He never worked in his *study*. _____
4	His *study* of Keats is to be published in the spring.	**4**	He decided after careful *study*. _____
5	The sketch was a *study* for his masterpiece.	**5**	The dress was a *study* in scarlet. _____
6	His *study* is paneled in oak.		

1	I thought he was in Mexico, but such was not the *case*.	**1**	In any *case*, you should fill in the forms. _____
2	In this *case* the detectives are baffled.	**2**	The adjective agreed in number and *case*. _____
3	"You have a good *case*," said the lawyer.	**3**	Dr. Johnson had a bad *case* of measles. _____
4	What is the *case* of this pronoun?	**4**	The *case* of the stolen necklace was never solved. _____
		5	He stated his *case* badly. _____

1	Exercise keeps the *body* healthy.	**1**	We went in a *body* to see the new dean. _____
2	The doctor viewed the *body*.	**2**	With flowers they cover the *bodies* of unburied men. _____
3	His legs were short, but he was long in the *body*.	**3**	Gin a *body* meet a *body* Comin' through the rye. _____
4	Put the information in the *body* of the letter.	**4**	I am absent in *body* but present in spirit. _____
5	The Irish landlady was a comfortable old *body*.	**5**	Soul is form, and doth the *body* make. _____
6	A *body* of armed men attacked the City Hall.	**6**	He concentrated attention on the *body* of the argument. _____
7	The doctor found a foreign *body* in his eye.	**7**	Joe sent a left jab to the *body*. _____
8	They spent the evening studying the heavenly *bodies*.	**8**	No*body* knows where he is. _____

20B Anthony Burgess's fantasy, *A Clockwork Orange*, is told in the words of a character who uses a nadsat (teenage) vocabulary of the future. Read independently, most of the words would be nonsense to a reader of English, but many meanings can be guessed from context. A number of the words in the following passage from the opening of the novel have been listed below. Consider each word in its context, and then after it write your best guess at a meaning for the word.

> There was me, that is Alex, and my three droogs, that is Pete, Georgie, and Dim, Dim being really dim, and we sat in the Korova Milkbar making up our rassoodocks what to do with the evening, a flip dark chill winter bastard though dry. The Korova Milkbar was a milk-plus mesto, and you may, O my brothers, have forgotten what these mestos were like, things changing so skorry these days and everybody very quick to forget, newspapers not being read much neither. Well, what they sold there was milk plus something else. They had no licence for selling liquor, but there was no law yet against prodding some of the new veshches which they used to put into the old moloko, so you could peet it with vellocet or synthemesc or drencrom or one or two other veshches which would give you a nice quiet horrorshow fifteen minutes admiring Bog And All His Holy Angels and Saints in your left shoe with lights bursting all over your mozg. Or you could peet milk with knives in it, as we used to say, and this would sharpen you up and make you ready for a bit of dirty twenty-to-one, and that was what we were peeting this evening I'm starting off the story with.

1   droogs

2   rassoodocks

3   mesto

4   skorry

5   veshches

6   moloko

7   peet

8   vellocet

9   horrorshow

10   mozg

20C In the following sentences one word or set of words is italicized. It means approximately what a word in its context should, but there is a more exact word. By thinking, or by using the lists of synonyms in a thesaurus or in your dictionary, write a more exact word in the blank to the right. Change *a* to *an* or *an* to *a* if necessary.

EXAMPLE: Place the check down and *sign* it.   *endorse*

1 She *signed up for* the magazine.   _____

2 After the wreck divers worked for weeks in the sunken ships trying to *save* some of the cargo.   _____

3 Several army officers had been involved in the complicated political *planning* that led to the revolt.   _____

4 The next speaker *turned down* completely all the traditional principles of the party.   _____

5 He promised that he would never *change* from the course he had set when he entered the ministry.   _____

6 Gold, since it can be hammered to the thinnest gold leaf, is obviously a *soft* metal.   _____

7 The new hotel was a *big* structure, dwarfing all the buildings near it.   _____

8 We must now face the *hard* task of clearing the city of the mud and debris left by the flood.   _____

9 They tried to *get* money from the old shopkeeper by threatening to kidnap his grandson.   _____

10 Since nobody else knew how to operate the machinery, the old engineer was *important* to the directors of the project.   _____

11 He determined to *put* his energy to the work of the new group of social reformers.   _____

12 After the long debate all the representatives *were together* in advocating a policy of neutrality.   _____

13 He reported his findings in a learned *talk* before the American Philosophical Society.   _____

14 He has aptitude, but he has never learned the *really effective way* of making a turn.   _____

15 Little Adrian was trying to *get* a bumblebee into his homemade fly trap.   _____

16 A boatswain led the *revolution* against the ship's officers.   _____

17 He was a *critical* sort of person, always finding fault with everything and everybody.   _____

18 Grades are supposedly *proportional* with the student's achievements.   _____

19 I argued, but he would not *receive* the possibility.   _____

20 He only dabbled in philosophy because he had not the perseverance or insight to *deal with* profound problems.   _____

20D The following sentences could be improved by deleting unnecessary, repetitious, or redundant expressions. Cross out the nonessential words in each sentence and write them in the blanks.

EXAMPLE: The gangster went entirely scot-free, in spite of his illegal crimes.

entirely
illegal

1 He was bored by all phases of his line of work and eager for a completely different change.

2 In this modern world of today nobody suggests that we should return back to the horse and buggy.

3 We are now in the process of entering upon a global conflict of worldwide proportions.

4 Many thought that the case of the managing of the divorce was of a very inept nature.

5 In regard to the final result, we were all wondering which candidate would win.

6 Since it was a fourth-down situation, the quarterback decided that what he should do was to kick.

7 When next week rolls around again, we expect to continue further our examination of the plant.

8 He planned to study in the field of philology, although he knew the work would be difficult in character.

9 Although his horse was in an exhausted condition, Roy decided to ride until sundown.

10 He promised that if he won the election that he would concentrate his efforts on the area of economy.

11 The machine is of so complicated a nature that only a trained expert who has been trained in all the many factors involved can repair it.

20E The following might be an abstract from the journal of the first Martian to land in the United States. In the blanks at the right copy sixteen of the italicized words that are most clearly slanted or loaded.

Among the eating habits of these *disgusting* creatures, one revolted us particularly. With the *utmost* concern, apparently, they have assembled *filthy* beasts which have large *sacklike* protuberances between their hind *legs*, with *sloppy, dangling* handles on them. These they massage, though even the *earth-apes* are so *revolted* by the process that they usually do not touch these *snakelike* teats but have them squeezed by *machines*. These *protuberances* emit a *sickly* white *excretion* which the *earth-apes* call *milk*. They treasure and chill it, and then gulp it down with *seeming* relish, giving it even to their *infants*. The *scum* which rises on it, called *cream*, is accounted a delicacy, although it is *slimy* in texture, and readily develops a *jaundiced* appearing crust. This scum of the excretion is allowed to sour, and when it is *agitated* the earth-apes collect from it *greasy* particles called *butter*, without which the *depraved* creatures consider their *staple,* bread, inedible. I tried the *stuff* and found it *nauseating.*

20F Below are three sentences, each with a blank in it and another blank to the right. Consider synonyms of *fool* that you might insert in each sentence; select the best you can find and insert it in the sentence. Insert one that you rejected in the blank to the right. Then, in the space below, explain why you chose the word you did instead of a synonym you rejected. You will find the entry for *fool* in selections from two thesauruses below. You may want to consult the lists.

1 Only a (an) _____ would say that educational opportunities are equal in this society.

_____

2 When I saw what the competition looked like, I felt like a (an) _____.

_____

3 Some _____ had been trying to correct my laboratory notes.

_____

> **fool,** *n.* **1.** [A simple-witted person]—*Syn.* nitwit, simpleton, dunce, oaf, ninny, cretin, nincompoop, bore, dolt, idiot, jackass, ass, buffoon, blockhead, numbskull, booby, boob, clodplate, dunderhead, goose, ignoramus, imbecile, moron, clown, tomfool, wiseacre, witling, donkey, looby, noddy, noodle, innocent, loon, dullard, jolthead, fathead, halfwit, mooncalf, lightweight, dotard, babbler, driveler, Simple Simon, silly; *all* (D): bonehead, mutt, simp, dope, natural, sap, dumb ox, lunkhead, numbskull, dimwit, chump, crackpot.—*Ant.* philosopher*, sage, scholar.
> **2.** [One made to seem foolish]—*Syn.* butt. laughingstock, victim, clown, poor fish, schlemiel, dupe, gull, gudgeon, cully, stooge, fair game; *all* (D): goat, sucker, fall guy, pushover, mess, lug, screwball, crackpot, setup, (easy) mark.
> no (*or* **nobody's**) **fool**—*Syn.* shrewd, calculating, capable; see **able** 1, 2, intelligent 1.
> **play the fool**—*Syn.* be silly, show off, clown; see **joke.**
> **fool,** *v.*—*Syn.* trick, dupe, mislead; see **deceive.**
>
> CHARLTON LAIRD, *Webster's New World Thesaurus*

> **fool,** *n.* idiot, tomfool, witling, dunce, simpleton; clown, buffoon, jester (FOLLY).
> **fool,** *v.* deceive, delude, trick (DECEPTION); pretend, make believe, play-act (PRETENSE); jest, jape, kid (*slang*), spoof (WITTINESS); trifle, play the fool (FOLLY).
> (WITTINESS); trifle, play the fool (FOLLY).
>
> NORMAN LEWIS, ed., *The New Roget's Thesaurus*

20G Italicized expressions in the following sentences have connotations that suggest an attitude toward whatever they refer to. In the blanks write substitutes for the italicized words that would change the attitude of the sentence —often changing approval to disapproval or disapproval to approval. Use substitutes that change connotations but might refer to the same things or acts as the original expressions. Synonym lists in the dictionary or thesaurus may provide suggestions.

EXAMPLE: Miss Ellen *doted on* her pair of *ill-tempered curs.*   *loved*

spirited dogs

1 The Senator *ranted* for an hour *vilifying* the chairman.   _____

_____

2 The *poem* that Alice wrote for her mother was filled with   _____

deep emotion.   _____

3 Big-city *tycoons* were soon *exploiting* the natural resources   _____

of the desert.   _____

4 Jack was so *stubborn* in his business deals because he was   _____

always *pushing* to get ahead.   _____

5 Her *exploits* in high society groups had made her *notorious.*   _____

_____

6 The blue laws were *time-honored* statutes that had effec-   _____

tively *governed* the municipal development.   _____

7 The *courageous* charge of the militia was an *unwise* ges-   _____

ture.   _____

8 After a *reversal* on the banks of the river, the regiment   _____

withdrew into the mountains.   _____

9 The chairman of the committee reported that the uni-   _____

versity was a *hotbed* of *radicalism.*   _____

10 Lucy *became dizzy* from the punch and *went to sleep* on   _____

the sofa.   _____

Objectives: (1) To recognize varying tones in writing and to write consistently in an appropriate tone. (2) To maintain in writing a consistent point of view.

> You don't know about me without you have read a book by the name of *The Adventures of Tom Sawyer*; but that ain't no matter. That book was made by Mr. Mark Twain, and he told the truth, mainly. There was things which he stretched, but mainly he told the truth.

In these opening lines of *Huckleberry Finn* Mark Twain is obviously playing a role. He is pretending to be a young boy, and using the boy's voice. The writing imitates speech, the speech of an uneducated, imaginative young man.

Most writing, especially of nonfiction, does not so obviously assume a character; but within limits a writer is always playing a role. For a laboratory report, a letter to a friend, or an argumentative essay he adopts a voice to suit the occasion—his purposes, his subject, and his audience. The voice, for example, may be that of a thoughtful, reasoning person, of a skeptic asking questions, of an outraged protester, of an amused observer, of a sarcastic critic, or of the writer attempting to be straightforward and sincere. The voice is expressed through the writer's style.

Style is a broad term, difficult to define. In general, it refers to the individuality of writing, to its "character," its distinguishing qualities. Style results from ways in which a writer makes his choices among alternatives, and these choices determine tone and point of view.

21a Tone: Attitude Toward Material and Audience   Tone

Adopt and maintain a tone appropriate to the subject matter and to the audience.

"Good morning!" can be said in a dozen different ways—casually, reluctantly, ominously, cheerfully, or too cheerfully. It can indicate that the speaker slept badly or slept well. It can please one listener and annoy another who has a headache. The effect depends on the speaker's tone of voice and also on the appropriateness of that tone for the mood of the listener. *Tone*, as it is used in discussing writing, grows from the notion of tone of voice in speaking; it refers to the writer's attitude toward his subject and toward his audience. The writer tries to select and maintain a tone that will get the results he wants. There are no rules, but some hints may help:

1. *Suitability to subject, medium, audience.* Although "writing down" to an audience seldom helps, a highly technical scientific article is not likely

to communicate much to the readers of a popular children's magazine. On the other hand, attempts at a joking tone usually only harm a report that describes a serious experiment.

2. *Maturity and taste.* A student who writes a boasting account of his triumphs in a high school track meet, as though the meet were a world-shaking event, is likely to be humorous when he does not mean to be. The tone fails because the writer seems to lack maturity and good sense in judging what he did.

3. *Sincerity and simplicity.* Although serious imitation of a good style has helped writers improve their own, borrowing tricks or seemingly clever devices seldom succeeds. Relying on worn-out metaphors—"the old pigskin" for a football—does not make sports writing clever or racy, and attempts at "literary" style may sound like old melodramas: "Little did I know what heartbreak the day was destined to bring." Usually a student does well to write naturally, sincerely, honestly, directly.

4. *Objectivity and emotion.* Exaggerations and protests do not usually portray strong emotion. One common failure of tone is sentimentality, an over-assertion of emotion, the attempt to claim more emotional impact than the facts warrant.

5. *Humor.* Forced humor usually ruins tone. Humor is most likely to succeed when it is presented with a straight face.

21b Point of View   PV

Maintain a consistent point of view—in time, space and person.

To keep faith with his audience, the writer should speak with the same voice—through the same person—and keep the reader aware of that person's position in space and time. Difficulties with person are not likely to occur when the writer has assumed a character, as Twain assumed the role of Huckleberry Finn, but they may arise in objective reports when the writer shifts about among *I, one, he,* and *you.* Shifts in space may occur in descriptive writing if the writer locates his narrator somewhere and then allows him to see what he cannot possibly see from his position. Some shifts in time are needed in writing that involves both present and past facts. Notice the verb forms in the following:

> The first chapters of *David Copperfield appeared* when Dickens *had* already *published* more than half a dozen novels. *David Copperfield is* auto-biographical in many of its details. Dickens *wrote* that of all his books he liked this novel best. It *has* always *been* a favorite of Dickens enthusiasts. The novel *introduces* a number of interesting minor characters.

The first sentence establishes a position in which the writer is in the present looking back; verbs in the other sentences vary to show how facts and events are related to this position in time. But shifts in tense are to be avoided, and they are warranted only when they reveal actual differences in time.

21A   Following are brief passages from works of fiction in which the writer is using the voice of a first person narrator. For each passage (a) write a sentence telling what sort of person you think the narrator is, and (b) list two or three characteristics of the passage that influence your guess about the character.

1   The frost was working out of the ground, and out of the air, too, and it was getting closer and closer onto barefoot time every day; and next it would be marble-time, and next mumblety-peg, and next tops and hoops, and next kites, and then right away it would be summer and going in a-swimming. It most makes a boy homesick to look ahead like that and see how far off summer is.

a

b

2   This is our first separation since we have been engaged, nearly 17 days. It will be 17 days tomorrow. And the hotel orchestra at dinner this evening played that old thing "Oh how I miss you tonight" and it seemed as if they must be playing it for my benefit though of course the person in that song is talking about how they miss their mother though of course I miss mother too, but a person gets used to missing their mother and it isn't like Walter or the person you are engaged to.

a

b

3   Monday. Breakfast tray about eleven; didn't want it. The champagne at the Amory's last night was *too* revolting, but what *can* you do? You can't stay until five o'clock on just *nothing*. They had those *divine* Hungarian musicians in the green coats, and Stewie Hunter took off one of his shoes and led them with it, and it couldn't have been funnier. . . .

a

b

4   Harry, you been jacking me up about how I been neglecting Rotary here lately, so I'm just going to break down and tell you something. Now I don't want you to take this personal, Harry, because it's not meant personal at all. No siree! Not *a*-tall! But, just between you and I, Harry, I'm not going to be coming out to Rotary lunches any more. I mean I'm quitting Rotary!

a

b

21B Following are brief excerpts from two famous pieces of writing and a "translation" of each into a widely different style. On separate paper write a brief comment on the kinds of changes the parodist has made. Indicate which of each pair seems more dated to you and why. Then try to continue each of the parodies for a few lines—five or six lines of the speech from *Julius Caesar* in the style of the *Mad* burlesque and two, three, or four sentences of the *Declaration* in the style of Mencken's version.

1

Friends, Romans, Countrymen,
    lend me your ears!
I come to bury Caesar, not to
    praise him.
The evil that men do lives after
    them,
The good is oft interred with
    their bones;
So let it be with Caesar. The
    noble Brutus
Hath told you Caesar was ambitious.
If it were so, it was a grievous
    fault,
And grievously hath Caesar
    answer'd it.

        WILLIAM SHAKESPEARE, *Julius
        Caesar*, III, ii, 79–85.

Friends, Romans, hipsters,
    Let me clue you in;
I come to put down Caesar, not
    to groove him.
The square kicks some cats are on
    stay with them;
The hip bits, like, to down
    under;
So let it lay with Caesar. The
    cool Brutus
Gave you the message that Caesar
    had big eyes;
If that's the sound, someone's
    copping a plea,
And, like, old Caesar really set
    them straight.

        Mad, January, 1958.

2

When, in the course of human events, it becomes necessary for one people to dissolve the political bonds which have connected them with another, and to assume among the powers of the earth the separate and equal station to which the laws of nature and of nature's God entitle them, a decent respect to the opinions of mankind requires that they should declare the causes which impel them to the separation.

We hold these truths to be self-evident: that all men are created equal; that they are endowed by their creator with certain inalienable rights; that among these are life, liberty, and the pursuit of happiness. . . .

        THOMAS JEFFERSON, *The
        Unanimous Declaration of the
        Thirteen United States of America*

When things get so balled up that the people of a country got to cut loose from some other country, and go it on their own hook, without asking no permission from nobody, excepting maybe God Almighty, then they ought to let everybody know why they done it, so that everybody can see they are on the level, and not trying to put nothing over on nobody.

All we got to say on this proposition is this: first, me and you is as good as anybody else, and maybe a damn sight better; second, nobody ain't got no right to take away none of our rights; third, every man has got a right to live, to come and go as he pleases, and to have a good time whichever way he likes, so long as he don't interfere with nobody else.

        H. L. MENCKEN, *The Declaration
        of Independence in American*

21C Following are four accounts of dramatic incidents written by different authors in different styles. On separate paper write four different accounts of an incident, imitating each of the four styles of the passages.

As material for your imitation, assume that Adrian Burkham has received notice that he is failing chemistry. He is afraid that if he fails chemistry he will not be taken into the fraternity to which he is pledged. He believes also that if that happens he will be ruined for life; his family will be shamed, old friends will desert him, his girl will refuse to go with him. He would have to consider quitting school and getting a job, if he could find one. Accordingly, he goes to see Professor Mark Manley, who is said to be a good scientist, but rather gullible, likely to accept convincing excuses and plausible fibs.

1 "Hold," cried Ludlow, motioning to the valet to withdraw. "Mr. Venerout, an uncle should be tender of the errors of one so dear as this cruel, unreflecting girl. You cannot think of abandoning her to so frightful a fortune?"

"I am not addicted to abandoning anything, sir, to which my title is just and legal. But you speak in enigmas. If you were acquainted with the place where my niece is secreted, avow it frankly, and permit me to take those measures which the case requires."

". . . Cruisers and manors! What in the name of mysteries is thy meaning? The girl is not here; you declare she is not on board the Coquette, and there remains only—"

"The brigantine!" groaned the young sailor. . . .

JAMES FENIMORE COOPER, *The Water Witch*

2 I wish with all my heart, my readers could see the valiant Von Poffenburgh, as he presided at the head of the banquet; it was a sight worth beholding—there he sat, in his greatest glory, surrounded by his soldiers, like that famous wine bibber Alexander, whose thirsty virtue he did most ably imitate—telling astounding stories of his hairbreadth adventures and heroic exploits, at which, though all his auditors knew them to be most incontinent and outrageous gasconades, yet did they cast up their eyes in admiration and utter many interjections of astonishment. . . . Thus all was rout and revelry within Fort Casimir, and so lustily did the great Von Poffenburgh ply the bottle, that in less than four short hours he made himself, and his whole garrison, who all sedulously emulated the deeds of their chieftan, dead drunk, in singing songs, quaffing bumpers, and drinking Fourth of July toasts, not one of which, but was as long as a Welsh pedigree or a plea in chancery.

No sooner did things come unto this pass, than the crafty Risingh and his Swedes, who had cunningly kept themselves sober, rose on their entertainers, tied them neck and heels, and took formal possession of the fort. . . .

WASHINGTON IRVING, *History of New York*

3 "What happened between you and Neva Norrell that night?"

Joe ran his tongue nervously over his dry lips. "She told me her husband was a writer, a citizen of Holland. He was out . . . and . . ."

"And," he asked gently.

"Well—she made a sort of play for me."

Shomar was serious. "Marble will want to know whether you slept with her that night."

"No, I didn't. I left before the boiling point."

The Israeli laughed lightly. "Don't get upset. A man has been murdered. In the apartment of a kept woman, to use an archaic expression. And who is killed? A lover. So the captain will want to know whether she had a fling with you, for kicks, maybe. So maybe you become a suspect, eh? Another jealous lover."

HENRY KLINGER, Wanton for Murder

21D Revise each of the following passages, correcting any shifts in point of view. Write in the blanks only the passages that require revision.

1 Any person who wants to succeed has to learn the techniques of their trade. You cannot hope to be a good writer unless you know how to handle words, any more than one can be a good plumber if you don't know how to use a pipe wrench.

2 In the beginning of the novel Mr. Bennett made some sarcastic comments about the way his wife was always trying to get his five daughters married. As the novel progressed, however, it is apparent that Mr. Bennett is genuinely interested in the welfare of his family.

3 No matter how often a person has rehearsed their lines, opening night may find you suffering from intense stage fright.

4 After the volunteer workers finished trimming the trees and shrubs and took all the branches and dead leaves to the dump, the campus began to look presentable again.

5 What happened in our high school was what they have called the drug culture. Other students say there were pushers on the school grounds, but personally I cannot honestly say that I had ever seen any.

Objectives: *(1) To apply writing principles discussed*
in earlier chapters to writing in impromptu situations.
(2) To analyze an examination question and write a
unified and economical answer.

A student going home for his first vacation is likely to report his experiences
in certain ways to his father or mother and quite differently to his former
schoolmates. He is so accustomed to adapting what he says to his old friends
and acquaintances that he does not need to study or practice what we might
call the rhetoric of familiar conversation.

Some kinds of writing frequently needed in college composition, however, may not come so naturally. In this and the following two chapters we
shall consider three different sorts of composition likely to be important in
college work and specialized enough to warrant particular attention. The first
we might call the impromptu reply, and we can include within it class discussion, impromptu themes, and various sorts of examinations.

Oral Discussion

Good discussion requires knowing how to talk, when to talk, and when
to keep quiet and listen. Most people listen too little, and badly. Many people
talk too much, and badly. The following, however, is good discussion. It reports a conversation in a newspaper office after a young black, Dowdell, had
been killed by a police officer during troubles at the University of Kansas.

> [The] executive editor wanted to put a picture of Dowdell and the
> policeman on the front page but [the editor] said he wasn't sure that was a
> good idea. "The boy is dead," he said. "His picture belongs on the front
> page. The officer's on the second."
> The executive editor: "The headline will read, 'Negro Youth Dies in
> Gun Battle.'"
> The editor: "It wasn't a gun battle."
> Executive editor: "The officer fired a warning shot—the Negro fired
> back—then the officer fired back."
> The editor: "I guess it was a gun battle. O.K."

These speakers are professional journalists; they are trained in dealing
with evidence and with words. They speak only when they have something to
say, and then they speak to the point, probably because they have already
made up their minds what to say—no hemming and hawing. They give the
other person a chance to speak. They listen. They even change their minds
when somebody else makes a good point.

In a class, discussion may be more or less than this. If the instructor asks, "What kind of charge will you find in an electron?" the answer, "Negative," is enough. But many questions or instructions are drafted so that a one-word answer is not enough. If the instructor had said, "What use do electrical charges in the human brain have in speech?" an adequate answer would require at least several sentences. And these sentences will be the better for being built into a paragraph.

That is, a good answer is a brief, oral composition. The speaker will do well to decide carefully what he wants to say, construct a good topic sentence, organize his material in accordance with some plan, include plenty of evidence—evidence that is both specific and relevant—and draw a conclusion if one is warranted.

Impromptu Themes and Examinations

An impromptu theme is very much like the answer to a question, except that the writer is given more time to prepare it. It can be both longer and more carefully worked out. If a trial lawyer says to a witness, "Now tell the jury what happened on the evening of March 16, 1973," he is in effect asking for an impromptu narrative. The witness need do no more than recount events in chronological order as he recalls them. An impromptu theme requires something more, but not more than a student should expect to do when he prepares his first draft; he should plan his essay, outline it briefly, draft his topic sentence with care, and proceed as he would expect to when writing a formally prepared paper—except that he has to hand in his first draft, and may never have a chance to revise it.

Contrary to some student opinion, examinations are not subtle devices for mental torture best prepared for by sleepless nights, black coffee, benzedrine, or crib notes. They are, rather, opportunities for the student to demonstrate his ability and knowledge; they give him a chance to show in an orderly way what he knows about a subject. Furthermore, ability to handle examinations in an adult way has many nonacademic uses—for example, in gaining the rights to practice law, medicine, or architecture, or in qualifying for professional advancement, civil service, or special training. As composition, they can be thought of as a series of questions and answers, like questions in class, except that they are usually written. The answers may be so brief that a single word will suffice, or even a symbol like T or F in a blank space. If longer answers are required, the examination becomes, in effect, a series of impromptu themes with the topics proposed by the instructor. The following are suggestions for preparing for examinations and writing them:

1. *Prepare the subject.* No substitute for consistent work throughout a course has yet been discovered; without prolonged preparation the student probably cannot hope for much, except to resolve to use good sense the next time. Last-minute efforts to memorize chapter headings or to skim a roommate's notes are not likely to help greatly.

2. *Think about the course.* Most teachers want students, not parrots. Good teachers look for students who show evidence of independent work, of

lively and critical minds. The student should try to see relationships among parts of the course, and among the course and other subjects.

3. *Survey the course.*   Make a list of the most important principles involved and be sure you know concrete evidence to support each. A good device is to ask yourself what *you* would ask if you were the teacher and what you would look for in the answer.

4. *Review.*   Start your review early, and concentrate on the material. Trying to outguess the teacher may help, but usually the same amount of attention given to the subject helps more. Often outlines of important subjects in a course help organize a review.

5. *Keep your head and use it.*   Do not become panicky about what you do not know; make the best of what you do know. Survey the whole examination, budget your time, and decide what you expect to do. Read the questions with great care, and be sure you know exactly what they require. Most examinations are planned; notice the purpose of the examination.

6. *Use the examination.*   Examinations are of many types, but three are perhaps most common. One type, popular in mathematics and science, is composed mostly of problems; the instructor is interested in the student's ability to solve the problems accurately and to understand the principles behind them. "True-false," "multiple-choice," and other "short-answer" examinations are common in many subjects; they require exact knowledge and very careful reading of the questions. The essay question should be handled like any other composition.

7. *Read the question with care.*   A good answer sticks to the point of the question. Barring ignorance or stupidity, more unsatisfactory answers stem from hastily read questions than from any other fault. When an instructor drafts a question he is likely to be checking for a specific thing. A good answer to a different question is not, for him, a good answer. If the student skims through a question, picks up a few words that mean something to him, and makes a wild guess on the basis of them, he is likely to produce an unsatisfactory reply. The instructor is likely to conclude either that the student cannot read or that he is trying to bluff.

Essay or discussion questions usually deal with large subjects, subjects so large that a student could not cover them completely in the limited time of a test period. But the questions also usually specify limits—suggest that the student discuss a limited part of the large subject or discuss it from a limited point of view. Consider, for example, the following:

> Discuss Wordsworth's attitude toward nature and mention two instances in which other Romantic poets express views about nature similar to his.

The student who hastily notices "Wordsworth" and "Romantic poets" in the question and starts out to put down at random anything he can recall from his notes or his reading related to these broad subjects is almost certain to produce a bad answer. Such topics as Wordsworth's biography or the political backgrounds of the Romantic period are likely to be irrelevant. The question sets specific limits, of which the student should take advantage; his answer would probably be organized about different aspects of Wordsworth's views of nature, illustrated with specific examples from his writing, with mention finally of two examples from other poets. Following are further examples of common types of essay questions.

a. *Did the introduction of blacks from Africa have any permanent effect on American English?*   Taken literally, the question might be answered *yes* or *no*. A good answer, however, will require analysis of the question, generalized conclusions, and specific evidence. For example, the student might notice that the presence of a large number of black dialectal speakers must have altered pronunciation in the South, that such speakers hastened the decline of inflected verb forms, and that Africans brought with them some words, like *goober*, that entered into the common word stock.

b. *How did the Federal Reserve Act of December, 1913, alleviate some of the defects of the old national-bank system?*   The student need not waste time proving that the new act brought improvements; this is assumed in the question. But the answer must show enough of the details of both the old system and the new act to answer the question *how*.

c. *Discuss the school busing agitation as evidence of the difficulty of enforcing an unpopular law or court decision.*   An answer will require more than a survey of attempts to boycott buses, to substitute private for public education, and the like. The student must consider what are the powers of governments other than federal to thwart federal intentions, and what, in a democracy, are the powers of the citizens, organized and unorganized, to oppose governmental action, either passively or by militant means.

d. *Compare and contrast the concept of imperialism as it is allegedly practiced today by United States industry in Latin America with imperialism as it was practiced by Great Britain in India and France in Indo-China during the nineteenth century.*   An adequate answer would require showing that there is some similarity between what is called industrial "imperialism" today and the political imperialism as practiced by some European nations during the preceding century, but that there are also great differences. The answer would also require specific evidences of each.

8. *Write your answer like a well-constructed paragraph or short theme.* Recall what you should have learned by this time in this course. Think about your subject; you are likely to find that analysis, with some definition, is your best approach. But whatever your method of development, have one. Prepare some preliminary notes; if these take the form of an outline, so much the better. Draft your topic or theme sentence to say just what you want it to, no more and no less. Remember what you have learned about sentence structure and word choice.

9. *Reread and correct your paper.*   No matter how rushed you are, plan for time to reread your paper and check it, both for fact and for composition. There is no surer way to convince your instructor that you are incompetent than to turn in a paper full of misspellings and other evidences of carelessness. You may even discover on rereading that you have written *a million* when you meant *a billion*, or that you have left out a word like *not* and changed the whole direction of your discussion.

22A The following is a paragraph from *The New York Times Encyclopedic Almanac*, 1971.

> Many users of drugs are unaware of the capacity of these chemicals to do harm, or blithely ignore the dangers, while experts on narcotic and hallucinogenic drugs find increasing cause for alarm in their untoward effects. Even marijuana, long considered safe, is losing its benign reputation. Although it seems clear that most U.S. smokers of "pot" are not significantly harmed by occasional exposure to marijuana, recent clinical reports and laboratory research have reminded the scientific community that Cannabis plants contain alkaloids that can, taken in sufficient quantities, produce profound perceptual distortions and hallucinations in almost anyone. Fortunately the tetrahydrocannabinol content of American marijuana is fairly low in contrast to that of some samples from Mexico and the Far East. If hashish, the popular and more potent Eastern product of Cannabis, becomes popular in the United States, the likelihood of "bad trips" and antisocial or self-destructive behavior will increase. Even with currently available "pot," a few individuals use it to such excess that they suffer psychologic derangements or spend most of their time experiencing the drug's effects to the exclusion of other interests and activities.

1 Write two questions that an instructor might ask that could be answered by expanding materials in this statement.

EXAMPLE: What seems to have been the state of our understanding about the effects of marijuana by about 1970?

2 Write two questions that an instructor might ask that would require relating this material to some other material.

EXAMPLE: How is our ignorance of the effect of drugs reflected in the major campaign platforms for 1972?

22B Study each of the following examination questions; then in the spaces describe in detail the kinds of information that a good answer would require. You are not, of course, expected to know the subject matter, but you can describe requirements as in the discussions of questions above.

EXAMPLE: Distinguish between a synthetic and an analytic grammar.

Answer: The answer would require definitions of each type of grammar and a contrast of the differences between them. Examples of each might help to clarify the definitions.

1 Discuss the population explosion in relation to the problems of pure water.

2 How did British regulation of American trade help provoke the American Revolution?

3 Discuss volcanism and its possible role in the formation of the earth as we know it.

4 Why and when did the problem of the modern American ghetto arise?

5 Analyze the major difficulties in American foreign policy in eastern Asia.

6 Do racial differences affect intelligence?

7 Can the principles of Mendel's Law be applied to heredity in human beings?

22C

OBJECTIVE: To formulate principles for writing a good answer to an essay question.

INSTRUCTIONS: The evidence below includes an essay question and numbered answers by various students. In the blank after each answer, write notes about what is good, bad, or inadequate in it.

EVIDENCE: Discuss the relationships between crime and life in the American ghetto.

1 There is lots of relationships between crime and life in the gettoes. This relationship can be seen in many ways. Some of the ways it can be see is in the relation ship between them. Which is one of the ressons Sociolgists are intrusted in the Gettos. Much can be done about this, if any body is intrusted enough too do it.

2 The ghettos breed crime, and crime makes life in the ghettoes worse. In Harlem, the Hough area of Cleveland, and in Watts, a suburb of Los Angeles, all kinds of crimes, from murder and rape to larceny, are several times as common as in neighboring, more affluent communities. In the ghettos schools are poor, there are few sanitary and health facilities, and most of the people have low incomes or none at all. In such conditions crime flourishes. At the same time, crime makes life worse in the ghettos. People who have little legal or police protection become easy victims of gambling rackets, heroin pushers, and both organized and unorganized crime. Raising the standard of living in ghettos would not stop crime, but apparently it would help.

3 Helping the people in the ghettos is a very interesting problem, and I am interested in it. Our textbook said, and a woman who talked to us said the same thing. That there is a lot of relationship between crime in the ghettos and the number of schools, how old they are, and things like that. One thing that impressed me is something the woman said. Almost everybody that gets raped gets raped by somebody she knows. And in the ghettoes everybody know's everybody else. Another thing that interested me is something else the woman said. She said the word ghetto comes from a Italian word that means foundling.

4 That is what I have always said, and there is a lot of evidence for it, although of course the evidence has to be circumstantial. You cannot really prove it, because there isn't any control. You have to have a control if you are to prove anything, And here there isn't any control, because how can you get one? Thats one reason it is hard to get any action, because you cant prove it. But as I have always said, it is a nacional disgrac, and something should be done. Every one has a rite to as good an education as everybody else.

CONCLUSIONS: (Sketch back through your observations in the spaces above. Then, in the space below, write out what seem to be the four most important principles to be observed in writing a good essay answer.)

1

2

3

4

*Objectives: (1) To select topics for writing about
literature that can be developed from analysis of the
work itself or from relating the work to background
material. (2) To write about literature by making
generalizations from study of a work and supporting
the generalizations with specific illustrations.*

Some students object to being asked to write about literature, and they may
have a point. If they are immediately practical they may say that knowing
about Homer and Shakespeare is not likely to get a person a job, or to help
him keep the job he has already. Some students object for quite different
reasons; they say that trying to understand literature takes too much work,
that nobody knows what should be said about literature anyhow since one
man's opinion is as good as another's, and that literature as it is taught in
most colleges is not relevant to modern life. It is about people the students
never heard of, and about things they are not interested in.

But most questions have more than one side, and the instructor who
assigns a theme on literature may have a point, too. Many students have
trouble writing because they cannot think of anything to say; literature is a
sure-fire subject. Any student who reads a novel or a play or a poem will
almost certainly have something to say, even if it is only that he does not
like what he has read. Meanwhile, the student will have gained practice reading, and most students need to read more, and more acutely, than they do.
Lastly, reading and writing about literature may show a student something
about art, and what art means for civilization—and of course it means more
than many people realize. Then, of course, there are those students who
like to write about literature because they love literature. Whatever the pros
and cons, many instructors do assign themes on literature. This chapter is
intended to suggest to the student how he can write such themes, whether
he wants to or finds he has to, and write them better and with less pain
than he might otherwise. First, however, here are some things *not* to do.

Any writer, especially any student trying to grow into a cultured man
or woman, should be honest with himself and everyone else. Honesty is appropriate in any writing, but plagiarizing about literature is uncommonly
tempting because it seems to be so easy. The writings of well-known authors
are summarized in reference books like encyclopedias and collections of plot
summaries, and more recent books may carry on the jacket or elsewhere a
sketch of the plot and comments by reviewers. If a writer needs any of this
material, he should copy it accurately and give due credit, using quotation
marks for quoted material (see Chapter 3 and **25i**). Doing one's own thinking
and one's own writing is not only the right thing to do; it is more fun.

Most people who publish comments about literature know a great deal about it. They have read thousands of books, and have worked for years to understand and evaluate literature. When such a critic writes, "Angela is Smith's most engaging woman character," he is offering an opinion that is based on extensive background. He has read every word that Smith has published, much of it several times—and perhaps a lot that Smith did not publish, but left in letters and the like. He has read what other critics have written, and he may have spent years maturing his estimate of Smith. He has every right to speak as one whose opinions must be respected, but a beginning student should not try to imitate him. A student's own experience with literature can be a very good thing, interesting to him and to others, but he should present it for what it is. He should not pretend to a competence that, as yet, he could not be expected to have.

Here, then, are some sorts of writing about literature that a relatively inexperienced critic can appropriately attempt:

1. *A summary, condensation, or digest.*   A student can condense a piece of writing or "tell the story" of a novel, play, or short story. This is probably the easiest thing to do, but the instructor may demand more than a summary because he wants to encourage the student to think, weigh, and evaluate. He has good reasons for this attitude, but even a good summary can be more difficult than it seems. Being entirely objective, maintaining the balance in the original, and choosing concrete details is not easy. At a minimum, preparing a summary requires reading the book from beginning to end, every word, no skipping or skimming. After all, the author wrote every word, and nobody can do him justice without complete reading. Close examination will require another reading, but at least the critic should check back through the book to confirm his first impressions. A good summary usually requires some quotations; they should be identified with quotation marks.

2. *The subject, meaning, or purpose.*   What is the book about? What does the author seem to be trying to say? Every book has an idea, usually a main idea and several subsidiary ideas. Serious writers have something to say and try to say it. Of course, most books are not written by serious literary artists, and may be about very little. But one can say something about even books with relatively trivial themes—pointing out, if it is true, how the ideas are conventional or the author's purpose only to amuse or entertain. More serious books are harder to write and harder to discuss, partly because serious books are concentrated, and they may be varied and subtle. What did Shakespeare mean to say in *Macbeth*? Apparently one thing he meant was that crime corrupts the criminal. But is this all he meant to say? Macbeth and Lady Macbeth commit the same crime, but the effects on them are quite different. Trying to decide just what an author meant may be rewarding.

3. *The conflict or tension within the book.*   Conflict is almost inevitable in literature—if everybody knew the subject and agreed about it, why write the book? In a novel or play, the conflict is often expressed in the plot, in what happens. Or it may appear in characters who clash, because they hold opposing beliefs or because they are personally incompatible. In a book about ideas and conduct, the clash may be between beliefs, attitudes, and the like.

4. *Psychological and social problems.*   Does the book faithfully reflect human psychology, showing what kinds of creatures men and women are? Does it probe into modern social problems? Some years back there was a flood of novels about the problems of farmers in the Middle West and Far West, the difficulties of people who needed money against those in the East who had money. More recently we have had novels about the difficulties of growing up a black, especially in the ghettos.

5. *The writer's means of getting his effects.*   Various writers, treating essentially the same subject, will write quite differently. Two nineteenth-century historians described the French Revolution. One tried to help us discover cause, to trace movements, to analyze results. Another tried to help us see the drama of a chaotic time, to experience the enthusiasm of mobs and sense the tragedy of death. The American novelist, Frank Norris, often used an interesting combination of massed detail with highly symbolic objects. In his novel *McTeague* he describes in great detail the courtship of his principal character, a big, stupid fellow, telling us just what he and his selfish girl friend said, did, and ate. At the same time he keeps calling our attention to a huge gold tooth that hung outside McTeague's office—he was a quack dentist. The tooth signified at once avarice and pompous incompetence.

6. *The general effect of the book?*   The background of a book may build up until it becomes the dominant effect. A historical novel, which may have a rather silly or conventional plot, may be so convincing in detail that we feel we have had the experience of living in another time and place. Even a novel like John Barth's *The Sotweed Factor*, which many critics have admired for its wit and irony, may give the reader such a vivid picture of life in early Maryland that he will want to describe what it was like to live along the Chesapeake Bay in the eighteenth century.

7. *Characters and characterization.*   Not all literature is about people and what they are like, but character study provides one of the most enduring charms of fiction, biography, and other writing that centers in human beings. A character study becomes more intriguing if we can believe that a fictional character, in addition to seeming real, is typical of something. Yossarian in Joseph Heller's *Catch-22* is not only a highly engaging young man; he also comes to typify modern protest against the insanity of war.

8. *Relationships to other books.*   Comparing books can be revealing, although doing so may take more background than many students have. Likely prospects for comparison are two books by the same author, two treatments of the same subject, or two books in the same literary tradition.

9. *The relationship of a book to its time, place, or tradition.*   A topic like this one, also, may require some background, but young people who are not professional critics may have special background that will help. For example, a veteran who has served in the air force might consider *Catch-22* as a picture of air warfare. A student with some reading background might compare it with other novels of the Second World War. Or he might consider it as an example of what is sometimes called "black humor."

10. *Form and genre.*   There are ways of writing, and these ways become formalized into what are sometimes called *genres*. The novel is a *genre,*

and classes of novels may be thought of as constituting lesser *genres*—the historical novel, the novel of black protest, and the like. A book may be discussed as a representative of its *genre*. Perhaps most distinctive are the various sorts of poetry, but prosodic study can become specialized.

11. *Language.* All literature is written in language, and many revealing studies have been made of the language authors have used, its effectiveness, and why the author chose the language he did. This sort of thing can be attempted better if the critic has studied modern linguistics. Or he may have special background that will help him approach such an aspect of language as dialect. A Jewish student in the New York area might check the Yiddish idiom of a modern writer, or a student living along the middle or lower Mississippi River might check the dialect spoken there now with the dialects that Mark Twain recorded in *Huckleberry Fin.*

12. *The reputation of the book.* What have other people thought of the book? The reputation of some writers varies greatly; Herman Melville is now one of the most admired American novelists, but during his lifetime few people read him and most of the reviews of his books were unfavorable. Reading a review is no substitute for the book, but it can supplement a reading, and a student writer can well compare and contrast reviews of books. Many magazines carry reviews, and some, like the *Saturday Review, TLS* (the London Times *Literary Supplement*), *The New York Times Book Review*, and the *New York Review of Books*, print many reviews.

Prewriting for a Theme on Literature

The first thing to do, of course, is to read the book, all the way through, all of every page. The prospective critic may skim it first if he wants to; for many books a preliminary skimming may help, but it should not be used to replace the actual reading. Sooner or later the critic should ask himself, "Do I like the book?" The most likely answer is that he likes it somewhat, or some parts of it, or in some ways. Whatever the answer, it should lead to other questions: Why did I like or dislike it? What did I like or dislike about it? He should then check his answers against the book itself. If he has told himself that he did not like the principal character because she did not seem to be a human being, he had better do some rereading, partly to confirm or discredit his first impression, partly to get concrete evidence to use in his paper. Is the trouble that the writer had not done his job very well, or is the real fault that the reader had not read very carefully?

Collateral reading may help. Knowing something about a writer's life may illuminate what he wrote and why. Well-known writers, especially the older ones, will have been the subject of biographies, and they appear in encyclopedias, and the like. Writers are likely to have been the subject of articles in magazines. But the critic will do well to read the author's work first, and make up his own mind before he reads what others have said.

23A

OBJECTIVE: To understand, appreciate, and describe a poem.

INSTRUCTIONS: Read the poem below several times, thinking about it. Then, in the space provided, make notes in response to the numbered questions.

EVIDENCE:

> I'm nobody! Who are you?
> Are you nobody, too?
> Then there's a pair of us—don't tell!
> They'd banish us, you know.
> How dreary to be somebody!
> How public, like a frog
> To tell your name the livelong day
> To an admiring bog!
>
>   EMILY DICKINSON

1   Who seems to be speaking in the poem?

2   To whom does the poem seem to be speaking?

3   What is the poem about?

4   Having answered **3**, above, are you sure this is the only possible answer? Try listing two or three more things that the poem may be about?

5   Did you like anything in the poem, or anything about it?

6   What do the words "how public" tell about the poet or the poem? Advertisers pay a lot of money to be public.

7 What is the impact of the last two words in the poem?

8 Having answered questions **5–7**, do you now have any further or different ideas concerning what the poem is about?

CONCLUSION: Check back through your notes. Making use of them, write a paragraph on a separate sheet of paper in which you bring together the most important things you have to say about the poem.

23B You probably know *West Side Story* in one of its various versions. Recall that Tony has formerly been a leader of the Jets, but now has a job, that the girl to whom he becomes engaged is Maria, whose brother Bernardo objects to her having anything to do with a person that he calls an "American."

1 In a broad way, what is the conflict in the story?

2 Is there anything that you might call inner conflict? For example, how does Maria's inner turmoil reflect the conflict in the whole story?

3 Is there anything ironical in the fact that Tony is one of those who are killed?

4 Does *West Side Story* give a convincing picture of some kind of life? If so, select some significant details.

5 Does *West Side Story* deal with any modern problems? If so, select an incident in the story that dramatizes this problem.

6 Look back through your notes, and then write a short paper saying what *West Side Story* is about? You may conclude that it is about several things, some more prominent than others. (If you have not read or seen a version of *West Side Story*, or have but do not recall it sharply enough to discuss it, select the best film you know, and ask yourself questions about it like those above.)

OBJECTIVE WRITING: 24
THE INVESTIGATIVE PAPER

*Objectives: (1) To write objectively, using and
evaluating evidence from printed sources. (2) To document
research writing according to a standard form.*

In the early part of this book writing from personal experience was recommended, partly because it is the easiest to start with. Everybody has something to say; he has background he can call up, and he has beliefs and opinions he can express. But for many purposes personal writing is not adequate.

Modern society, especially a specialized and socialized technological society like that in the United States, requires great bodies of objective fact. Consequently, it needs objective writing. Of course nothing can be entirely objective. Even an electronic measuring device will vary, and no statement based on supposed fact can be without fault; but writing can be objective enough for most practical purposes, and every student needs to read and write objective prose.

An Objective Approach to Writing

Factual writing requires at once an objective attitude and facts with which to write. A writer needs to be objective and to develop techniques for doing so. Anyone is likely to say, "The play begins at eight." An experienced journalist, however, is more likely to write, "The high school production of *She Stoops to Conquer* is scheduled to begin at eight p.m." The reporter knows that amateur productions are often late, and that the unqualified statement that the play will begin at eight is factual only in a limited sense.

The journalist finds a way to report the expected production by using verifiable facts and restricting his statement to these facts. That the play is scheduled at 8 p.m. is a fact. The school's calendar of events lists the play at 8:00 p.m.; the playbill gives the time as 8:00 p.m., and so does a bulletin from the principal's office. That is, that the play has been scheduled at a given hour is an event, a recorded event, something that at the time of writing is over and done with. It can be reported as a fact; accordingly, the reporter says that and nothing more.

In statements growing from more complicated bodies of fact, a scientist or a scholar uses essentially the same approach as does the journalist, relying on verifiable fact as far as possible. When he finds he must go beyond his facts, he is careful to make his opinions conservative and to label them clearly. For example, the United States Center for Disease Control made an announcement clearly intended to warn the public that the threat from rabies in the United States is increasing and that something should be done. Being a scientific body, however, the Center made its statement objective insofar as possible, announcing that in the continental United States the reported cases of rabid animals rose from 3,276 in 1970 to 4,392 in 1971. Thus far the Center could speak with confidence; presumably the staff has records for each one of these 4,392 cases. But obviously this is not the whole story, although it is the basic objectively documentable evidence. Accordingly, the Center warned that the increase "may actually have been much greater than these figures indicate because only a small proportion of cases of rabid animals is ever reported at all." The staff was objective so far as objective evidence was available, and where adequate evidence was not available it labeled the guess with the phrase "may actually have been."

This last distinction raises a problem, one too complex to be more than mentioned here. What does the writer do, if he is trying to be objective, but the evidence is not plentiful enough or reliable enough to permit him to be sure? Writers face such uncertainties all the time. Strictly speaking, we know nothing. We do not even know that the sun will come up tomorrow, although the chances are so good that we even predict the time of its rising to the second. Most events are much less certain, but even so we must discuss them, and we usually do best if we discuss them as objectively as possible. Such discussions require careful weighing of evidence, the writer trying to be honest with himself and with his reader about how sure he is when he draws a conclusion. Instead of saying, "I think thus and so," he is likely to say, "the evidence suggests that," or "insofar as this evidence can be trusted, we can assume that," or something of the sort. That is, writing objectively requires the development of considerable skill in making clear the degree of one's certainty or uncertainty.

Materials for Objective Writing

A good library contains hundreds of thousands, perhaps millions, of volumes, and each of these volumes contains various sorts of information. Obviously, looking for a useful needle in this haystack of material is hopeless without help. In emergencies a librarian can help, but the student should appeal to library attendants only after he has made an honest effort to find what he wants himself. The library staff has arranged the library to work mainly as self-service; asking staff members in addition to do the student's work is an imposition. Besides, the writer is the only person who knows what he wants. The best help in finding materials, therefore, is a knowledge of how a library is organized and of available reference tools.

The most regularly useful materials in a library are of two types; individual items like books and pamphlets and serial publications, periodicals. Books and pamphlets are arranged on shelves according to a regular system, and in American libraries cards are prepared for each item: (1) a card for each author or editor, (2) a card for the title, and (3) one or more cards for the subjects treated in the book. These cards are filed alphabetically in drawers, the whole constituting an index known as the card catalog of the library. Materials published serially—articles in newspapers and magazines or in professional, scholarly, or scientific journals—cannot be conveniently shelved as individual items. Usually the library binds a number of copies of a periodical into a volume, lists the general titles of the series it holds in the card catalog or a separate list, and provides periodical indexes through which the student can locate individual articles. The most common of these indexes are mentioned below. Publications of one other sort, documents, are sometimes useful to specialists, are often shelved in special collections, and can be located through the *United States Document Catalogue.*

Library Reference Tools

Most American libraries use one or both of two systems in cataloging books, the Dewey Decimal System or the Library of Congress System, but the borrower need not understand either system to use it. He need only copy the call number accurately. Actually, a library card carries a considerable amount of useful material, so that a student who learns to interpret such a card can learn much about the book. A Library of Congress card looks like the following:

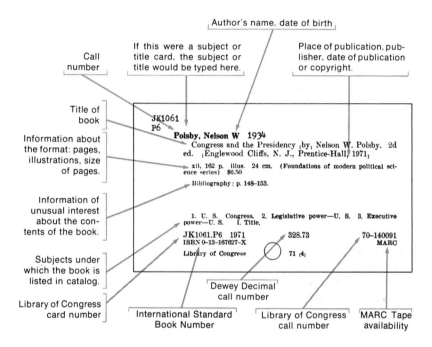

As we have seen, articles and other pieces in periodicals do not usually appear in the card catalog, but must be sought in an index. For most purposes the handiest is *Reader's Guide to Periodical Literature, 1900– .* It indexes many popular and semipopular magazines, listed in the front of each volume. It is *cumulated*; that is, little volumes come out every month, but these are re-edited and re-edited, so that eventually all the articles published in the indexed magazines for a five-year period are brought together into one volume. The user should check the dates to be sure he has the index volume or volumes for the period he wants to cover. To save space, all indexes are more or less skeletonized (see page 203).

The *Reader's Guide*, useful as it is, does not index all periodicals, and the student may need to consult the *International Index* or one of the indexes of materials in individual subjects. The readiest place to locate specialized

197

indexes is Constance M. Winchell, *Guide to Reference Books*, 8th ed. (Chicago: American Library Association, 1966).

In addition, all libraries have a collection of works for ready reference —encyclopedias, dictionaries, bibliographies, handbooks, and the like. These are much more numerous than most students can imagine, and more useful. Most beginning writers do not refer to them enough. Volumes like the *New York Times Almanac*, the *World Almanac*, the *Dictionary of National Biography*, and the *Century Dictionary and Cyclopedia* can be used both to enrich a writer's composition and save him time. But like all tools, they can be misused. They are good places to start an investigation, but they are at best cursory and are sometimes compiled by people who are not experts and are sometimes out of date. Even a work like the *Encyclopaedia Britannica*, which purports to be under constant revision, lags far behind modern scholarship, and should not be trusted as any kind of up-to-date, informed authority.

Preparing a Bibliography

For any but the simplest sort of objective study, the writer should start by preparing a bibliography. If he is to write with any competence he will need to know what has been published and he will do well to start with what is called a trial bibliography. He tries to locate all available printed materials on his subject. At a minimum he should consult encyclopedias and other general reference works that may be pertinent, look up the subject in the card catalog, check other books by the same authors he finds there, and check periodical indexes, the *Reader's Guide*, and any more specialized indexes that treat his subject.

As he locates books and articles he will later want to consult, he should keep an orderly record of his findings. One system is so clearly the best that it is used by practically all scholars and professional people concerned with research. The writer supplies himself with bibliography cards—3″ × 5″ are standard—or slips of paper cut to uniform size. Whenever he finds a book or article that he thinks may be useful, he makes out a card for it, checking his note for accuracy. If he prepares the card carefully and files it, he will never need to look up that item again. The system should be followed rigidly. Beginners sometimes resent doing this; it takes a little time. They may be tempted "to just jot this one down," on the back of an envelope or in a notebook. The result is that their bibliography is a jumble and they cannot find what they want when they want it; experienced research workers have learned that this sort of misdirected effort only wastes time. For the form of recording bibliographical data, see page 203.

24a Restricting Research Subjects   **R Subj**

Choose an appropriate subject for objective writing, one that can be treated objectively and adequately restricted.

Not every subject is suited to objective approaches, and objective investigation must always precede objective writing. "Why I Am a Republican" and "Life with Father and the Television Set" are not suitable. The first is likely to be mostly opinion and the second mostly reminiscence. Neither would "Our Military Adventures in Asia" be a fit subject; it could be objectively studied, but the subject, as phrased here, is far too large. Hundreds of books have been written on it, and hundreds more will be. "The Green Berets in Laos" would be much better, although it would require some further restricting. "Conflicting Opinions on the Tonkin Gulf Affair" would have possibilities, for although the writer would here be dealing with opinions, he could deal with them objectively. "Save Our Eco-systems!" is not a fit subject for a brief, objective essay, but "The Rising Pollution Level at the Skagway Duck Marsh" is more promising.

Restricting an objective subject is like restricting any other subject, but the problem may become acute because most young writers have little idea how much material is available, and cannot be expected to until they are well along in their research. By that time they will have spent considerable time investigating aspects of the subject that they are never likely to develop. Analysis usually provides the best means of restricting a topic; see 1a.

24b Footnote Form   Fn

Document objective writing adequately, employing
modern techniques insofar as they are appropriate for
the writing at hand.

Truth is always uncertain, and even the objective writer can approach no closer to it than the evidence he relies on. Accordingly, the reader has every right, not only to know what this evidence is, but where it came from, so that its validity can be tested. The writer is obligated to supply that information.

Documentation can be more or less formal. Notice the following:

> Many times in the course of our name giving, the Indian name was translated into its English equivalent. As the survey of place names in South Dakota puts it, 'When a creek is called White Thunder, Blue Dog, or American Horse, the Indian influence is obvious, since these adjectives are not those which a white man would use with these nouns. Four Horns, Greasy Horn, and Dog Ear are other examples.' The survey neglected to mention Stinking Water and Stinking Bear creeks, both of which are further convincing and delightful illustrations of this same process.
>
> ALBERT H. MARCKWARDT, *American English*

This might be called light documentation. The book is semipopular, and very sensibly, the author thought that this much documentation was sufficient; he indicates that he is quoting from a reliable source. In other words and for other purposes, Marckwardt, who is a careful scholar, would have provided less limited information. Contrast the paragraph above with the following:

Although the study of morphemes can never perhaps be put on a strictly scientific basis,[1] there still remains much to be done in identifying, analyzing, and understanding this characteristic of language structure. The purpose of this paper is to prevent an extensive list of one type—the final root-forming[2] or terminal[3] morpheme—and to make certain tentative suggestions concerning the phenomenon in English.

MORTON W. BLOOMFIELD, "Final Root-forming Morphemes."

The following footnotes appear at the bottom of the page:

[1]See Dwight L. Bolinger's important article, "Rime, Assonance and Morpheme Analysis," *Word*, VI(1950), 117–136. Cf. also his earlier "Word Affinities," *American Speech*, XV(1940), 62–73.

[2]So called by Leonard Bloomfield, *Language* (New York, 1933), pp. 245–246.

[3]Bolinger's term in "Rime," p. 120.

This might be called close documentation. It interrupts the flow of text more than most readers of popular books and articles prefer, but it does permit close study. We can learn what Bloomfield is relying on, and if one is working in a good library, which would have the bound volumes of a periodical like *Word* and Leonard Bloomfield's book, he can identify these quotations very quickly if he wishes to.

Obviously, this system rests on footnotes, and these footnotes require notes taken as part of the prewriting. For such a system the best practice is to take notes on cards or uniform slips of paper. Following are two sample cards that might be taken from the matter quoted above:

> Place Names—Indian
>
> Marckwardt quotes "The survey of place names in South Dakota" for obvious fact that names like American Horse, Blue Dog, and Stinking Bear Creek are translations of Indian names.
>
> Marckwardt, *Am. Engl.*, p. 155.

> Vocabulary—Morphemes
>
> Morton Bloomfield endeavors to list characteristics of one type of morpheme, which had been called "terminal" by Leonard Bloomfield and "final root-forming" by Bolinger.
>
> M. Bloomfield, "Final," p. 159.

Such a card contains three essential parts: (1) an indication of the contents so that it can be filed with other cards on the same subject; (2) the note, and (3) identification of the source of the note, usually composed of the last name of the author, a shortened form of the title, and the page reference or other identification. Some style sheets recommend numbering bibliographical items; if that system is used, the number of the bibliographical entry would appear here. By consulting his bibliography card (for form, see **24c**), the writer could prepare the following footnotes for these:

[1]Albert H. Marckwardt, *American English* (New York: Oxford University Press, 1958), p. 155.

[2]Morton W. Bloomfield, "Final Root-forming Morphemes," *American Speech,* 38(1953), 158.

The style in these footnotes is based on that recommended in the *MLA Style Sheet*, 2nd ed., which is standard for many sorts of scholarly publications. As will be apparent from the previous examples, basic items in footnotes for the two main kinds of publications are as follows:

Books—name of author, exactly as it appears on title page; comma; name of book, exactly as printed on title page, underlined; parenthesis; place of publication; colon; name of publisher; comma; date in Arabic numerals; close parenthesis; abbreviation for page or pages; page number or numbers in Arabic numerals; period.

Article—name of author as it appears in connection with article; comma; name of article, within quotation marks, including comma before close quotation mark; name of periodical, underlined; comma; volume number in Arabic numerals; year of publication, within parentheses; comma; page number or numbers in Arabic numerals; period.

Special circumstances call for some variations on these standard entries. Here are the most common for books. If a book has more than one author, as many as three are mentioned; for a book with more authors, only the first is mentioned followed by the words "and others." If a book is published in more than one volume, the abbreviation for *page* or *pages* is not used, but the volume number is given in Roman numerals, followed by a comma, followed by the page or pages, as above.

[3]René Wellek, *A History of Modern Criticism: 1750–1950* (New Haven: Yale University Press, 1955–   ), IV, 259–61.

If the book being cited is not the first edition, the edition should be given. If the book has an editor, he should be mentioned. The following is an acceptable form providing for both these conditions:

[4]Geoffrey Chaucer, *The Works of Geoffrey Chaucer*, ed. F. N. Robinson, 2nd ed. (Boston: Houghton Mifflin, 1957), p. 86.

Anonymous books are usually cited only by the title. For standard reference works only the title is sufficient, although the edition should be mentioned if any but the first edition is being cited, and if the book is arranged alphabetically, the entry rather than the page is given, as in the following:

[5]*Webster's New World Dictionary*, 2nd ed., under *style*.

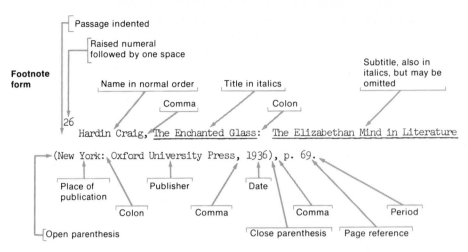

Footnote form

Passage indented

Raised numeral followed by one space

Name in normal order

Comma

Title in italics

Colon

Subtitle, also in italics, but may be omitted

26 Hardin Craig, The Enchanted Glass: The Elizabethan Mind in Literature

(New York: Oxford University Press, 1936), p. 69.

Place of publication

Colon

Publisher

Comma

Date

Comma

Close parenthesis

Page reference

Period

Open parenthesis

Note: For inclusive pages, reference is pp. 69–72. For work of more than one volume, style is I, 82.

The forms above serve for the first reference to a work. Thereafter an abbreviated form can be used—as Bloomfield does, in the quotation above. Usually for the second reference the last name, a shortened form of title, and the page reference is sufficient, as below:

[6]Marckwardt, *American*, p. 10.

Footnotes are numbered consecutively; they are usually accumulated at the bottom of the page, at the end of the article, or immediately after the citation mark. In this case they are ruled above and below. Unless, as in the Bloomfield quotation above, the citation is to a word or phrase, the citation numeral occurs at the end of the sentence, or at the end of the paragraph, whichever is more fitting.

Following are special cases that arise in connection with articles. For an article published in a book the following is an acceptable form:

[7]Garland H. Cannon, "Sir William Jones's Persian Linguistics," in *Portraits of Linguists* (Bloomington, Ind.: Indiana University Press, 1966), I, 36–57.

Some periodicals are not paged as volumes; for such works the individual number must be cited, for which the following may serve as a model:

[8]Rodney Fox, "Attacked by a Killer Shark!" *The Reader's Digest*, 87, No. 520 (1965), 51–52.

Citations to newspapers can become complicated; for many, the name, volume, date, and page will suffice, except that the date should be specific, (Feb. 15, 1972), but the important requirement is that the reader be able to find the citation. If details like the section are necessary, they can be added before the page number.

24c Bibliography Form   **Biblio**

Make bibliographical entries conform to accepted style.

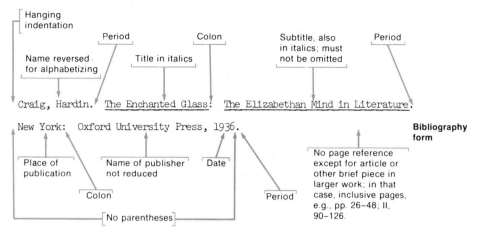

Hanging indentation

Period   Colon   Subtitle, also in italics; must not be omitted   Period

Name reversed for alphabetizing   Title in italics

Craig, Hardin. *The Enchanted Glass: The Elizabethan Mind in Literature.*

New York: Oxford University Press, 1936.   **Bibliography form**

Place of publication   Name of publisher not reduced   Date

No page reference except for article or other brief piece in larger work; in that case, inclusive pages, e.g., pp. 26–48; II, 90–126.

Colon   Period

No parentheses

Note: In both forms mention of an editor not treated as author follows the title; for a book of more than one volume, mention of the number of volumes appears before the data on publication.

All publications conform to some style sheet. The style described below is based on that in the *MLA Style Sheet*, 2nd ed., which is standard for many publishers and scholarly journals. Others vary slightly. It differs somewhat from the recommendations for footnotes. The diagrams at the top of these pages will make the difference clear.

A bibliography is a list of works found useful for a paper, particularly those that are cited. The following entries will illustrate some of the special problems for an anonymous work, for an article published in a collection, and the like:

Baugh, Albert C. *A History of the English Language.* 2nd ed. New York: Appleton, 1957.

Chaucer, Geoffrey. *The Works of Geoffrey Chaucer.* Ed. F[red] N[orris] Robinson. 2nd ed. Boston: Houghton Mifflin, 1957.

Fox, Rodney. "Attacked by a Killer Shark!" *The Reader's Digest,* 87, No. 520 (1965), 47–54.

The Home Mechanic's Handbook: An Encyclopedia of Tools, Materials, Methods, and Directions. New York: Van Nostrand, 1945.

Lewis, C[live] S. *The Allegory of Love: A Study in Medieval Tradition.* 1936; rpt. New York: Galaxy–Oxford Univ. Press, 1958.

Sapir, Edward. "Language." *Encyclopaedia of the Social Sciences.* New York: Macmillan, 1933.

Wolfe, Tom. "A Sunday Kind of Love." *The Kandy-Kolored Tangerine-Flake Streamline Baby.* New York: Farrar Straus, 1964.

To make up a bibliography entry, or to supply the information for a footnote, the research worker should record the following information on his bibliography card: (1) the author, exactly as the name appears in the publication; (2) the title, the name underlined for a book, the title in quotation marks for an article, followed by the name of the periodical, underlined;

(3) the bibliographical information, place, publisher, and date of publication for a book, number of volumes if more than one; volume, year, and pages for a periodical article. The research worker can add any convenient information, the library call number, the library in which the book is available, a quick guess about the usefulness of the publication, and the like.

In some bibliographies and in most periodical indexes, the material is somewhat skeletonized. The research worker will need to expand abbreviations, recognize that titles and the names of authors may be reduced, and information skeletonized. Practices vary, but all publications will give some indication of how details are abbreviated. Following is a selection from the *Reader's Guide* with a card that might result from one entry:

```
GRAND CANYON
   Grand  Canyon  by  helicopter.  B.  Thomas.
      il Travel 133:46-50 Je '70
   Heck  of  a  hole  in  the  ground.  il  Newsweek
      75:23 Je 22 '70
   Trees  on  the  rim;  photographs.  P.  D.  Dun-
      can. Am For 76:12-15 Jl '70
GRAND  CANYON  NATIONAL  PARK
   Moods  of  the  North  Rim:  Grand  Canyon  Na-
      tional  Park.  J.  Fain.  il  Nat  Parks  &  Con
      Mag 44:4-7 My '70
```

A bibliography card for the first entry would look like the following:

```
THOMAS, B.

   "Grand Canyon by Helicopter,"

Travel,  133 (1970), 46-50.

                  (Illustrations;

                  apparently no

                  bibliog.)
```

24A Utilizing the blank spaces below, record the information requested in the following:

1 Using the card catalog of a library, find the author, publisher, date, and place of publication of a book called *In the Shadow of Man.*

2 Using the same source, find out how many pages there are in a copy of James A. Michener's *Hawaii.*

3 Using the same source, look up a history of modern criticism by René Wellek. It is in several volumes; try to find out from the card if he has finished it yet.

4 Using the same source, find the title and the details of publication for the latest volume the library has written by Vladimir Nabakov.

5 Using *Reader's Guide*, locate an article printed in 1972, by Stanley Kripner and Richard Davidson, about what the Russians were doing with parapsychology and record the information necessary to find the article itself.

6 Using *International Index*, locate an article in a British publication concerning a recently discovered manuscript and write the citation into the following blank. Again, you will need to expand abbreviations.

7 Using a standard encyclopedia, locate a brief biography of Jan Gaston Darbous and write the citation appropriately in the following blank.

8 Using the card catalog, make an appropriate entry for a book by William Langland as it was published in an edition of 1886 (the date will be in Roman numerals, MDCCCLXXXVI).

9 Using the card catalog, make an appropriate entry for a recent book about the Civil War. (Hint: you may have to start with *United States, History of.*)

24B The following is a bibliography of Samuel Taylor Coleridge, scrambled and full of errors. Rearrange it in alphabetical order by the authors' last names, and by using the style on page 203 and the card catalog in your library, correct and complete the items.

Doug Bush. Mythology and Rom. Trad. in Eng. Poems. 1938. 453 pp.

Trail, H. D. *Social England*, ten volumes London 1896, 1897 (Trail is ed.)

C. H. Hereford, Age of William Wordsworth, the (London, the Mac-Millan Co.)

Beers, H. Anthony. "A history of English romanticism in the 19th cent." Ox. U. P. 1901, page 167.

Ernest Bernbaum: Guide through the rom. move. Scribner's and Sons, 1949.

Colridge, *Works, Complete*, Shedd, ed., 7 v., 1884, Lon., etc..

Lowes, Livingstone (enlarged, 1930) The road to zanadu (New York, N. Y., in 1927.

E. Schneider. Colridge's opium and Khubla, Kan., (1953, New York)

Chambers, E. "Samuel Taylor Coleridge," 1938, London, 398 pages

Cam. Hist. of Engl. Lit. volume 11

Alardice Nicoll, Hist of early 19th C. drama, 1800–50, two volumes, nineteen hundred thirty, New York, McMillan & Co.

24C Before attempting this exercise you will do well to review Chapter 4 for suggestions on ways of making your notes detailed and usable. It is particularly important that you distinguish exactly between quoted matter and your summaries. Now read the following passage carefully:

> In Richland, the brand-new spotlessly clean town of thirty thousand inhabitants, built at the close of the war for the employees of the atomic factory twelve to twenty-five miles away, fear of contagion through the invisible radioactive particles and rays amounts to an obsession.
>
> In public and continually repeated courses everyone who comes to live in Richland learns the atomic age's alphabet of fear:
>
> *Alpha rays.* Positive charged helium nucleuses emanating out of the atom. Cannot penetrate the skin but can do great damage if they enter the body through small open places.
>
> *Beta rays.* Electrons. Slight power of penetration. Penetrate about a third of an inch through the skin. Great danger of burns.
>
> *Gamma rays.* Can penetrate from the outside into the body. Weaker in the mass than other forms of rays but the most difficult to ward off by protective measures because of their strong penetrative power.
>
> *Neutrons.* Danger! Harmful in the highest degree. According to speed they penetrate different depths into the tissue. In the case of strong radiation internal organs are paralyzed.
>
> The force of the threat is matched by the strength of the defense against it. Dr. Compton, head of the scientific armaments development in the Second World War, stated before the Special Committee of the Senate: "The atomic energy program involves by far the most dangerous production process ever undertaken by man." In 1942 some of the American atomic experts still believed it would be practically impossible to protect the workers in the atomic industry, then existing only on paper, against the rays produced by nuclear fission. Until then there had been altogether about three pounds of radium in human possession. Now in the nuclear burners literally millions of pounds of radioactive material of widely different varieties were generated by the influence of the atom demolisher. The scientists saw clearly that enormous quantities of life-menacing rays were being generated as byproducts of nuclear fission. Safety measures of such scope and severity had to be taken as had never before been remotely necessary in the protection of industrial health.
>
> ROBERT JUNGK, *Tomorrow Is Already Here* (New York, 1954), pp. 108–109.

Now make out five cards with the key words, Radioactivity—danger of, having the following content: (1) details of Richland and quotation concerning the inhabitants' fear of contagion; (2) summary of four sources of danger, with quotation on neutrons; (3) quotation from Compton; (4) summary of change after 1942 with significant quotations from Jungk; and (5) contrast of characteristics of beta and gamma rays.

24D The following paragraph is very general. Read it and then by using reference tools provide more specific information that could be useful in rewriting the paragraph. Write the title of the reference work or works you used and the information you found in spaces below each numbered suggestion. Also correct in the margins any errors in the paragraph that you catch through reference volumes.

As almost everyone knows, there has been a revolution in the study and teaching of language. Perhaps it all goes back to people like Sir William Jones (1746–1794), Jacob Grimm, and Wilhelm von Humboldt, but in America, one of the pioneers was E. Sapir. His ideas were taken up by Carl Carpenter Fries, who had the advantage of being able to write books that would shock teachers. All this led to a monumental little volume by Gnome Chomsky, called *Syntactic Structure*. By this time, *linguistics* was a fad, although nobody could agree as to what linguistics is.

1 Who were Jones, Grimm, and Humboldt?

2 Who was Sapir; what books did he publish during his lifetime?

3 Who was Fries? How did he shock teachers?

4 When is "by this time"?

5 Is it true that "nobody can agree as to what linguistics is"?

24E The following is a paragraph concerning a poem written by Henry Adams.

A copy of the "Prayer of the Virgin of Chartres," reprinted in the Appendix of the present volume, was found in its author's wallet after his death early in 1918, but the poem had been composed many years before. "By way of relief from boredom," wrote Adams, February 25, 1901, to Elizabeth Cameron, "I have returned to verse, and have written a long prayer to the Virgin of Chartres, which I will send you presently, to put in your fire. It is not poetry, and it is not very like verse, and it will not amuse you to read; but it occupies me to write; which is something—at sixty-three. . . ." About seven years later he sent a copy also to Margaret Chanler. "It is sad stuff," he told her, "but felt, as you see."

ROBERT A. HUME, *Runaway Star: An Appreciation of
Henry Adams* (Ithaca, N. Y., 1951), pp. 166–67.

The following note cards are based upon the passage and intended for an article on Adams:

1. wrote poem late in life — sent them other people — in appendix present volume — Adams

2. Poems – Prayer to Virgin
Written by Feb. 25, 1901; copy promised Elizabeth Cameron in letter of that date, in which Adams says it "Is not poetry...is not very like verse, and it will not amuse you...."
cited in Hume, *Star*, 166-67

3. Adams — virgin
I have returned to verse and have written a long prayer to the Virgin which I will send you pretty soon to kindle your fire. It is sad stuff, but felt as you see. Copy to Chandler.
Hume

4. "Prayer to the Virgin of Chartres" found in Adams's wallet after death, early 1918. Referred to in letter to Elizabeth Cameron, Feb. 25, 1901. Presumably sent her copy. Some seven years later another copy to Margaret Chandler.
Hume, *Star*

5. Hume does not like Prayer to Chartres. It is sad stuff and it will not amuse you to read though it may be all right by way of relief from boredom. Robert A. Hume, *Runaway Star*, Cornell University Press, copyright 1951, and Geoffrey Cumberlege

6. Character — modesty
Adams modesty and humor evident in his comments on his Prayer to the Virgin of Chartres, which he called "sad stuff," and offered copy to woman friend, Elizabeth Cameron, saying it would serve "to put in your fire."

Make out a score sheet for the six cards, noticing the following: (a) Are there appropriate key words at the top of the card? (b) Is the material in the card detailed enough to be useful? (c) Is it accurately taken? (d) Is quoted matter properly handled? (e) Did the writer seem to understand the passage and take notes that fairly represented it? (f) Granted that the writer has made out an adequate bibliography card, does the note have appropriate identification of the source? Obviously note card 1 has no key words at the top and note card 2 has what seem to be good key words. Therefore, you would make no check under (a) for 1, but you would make a check for 2 under (a). Now complete the score.

*Objective: To develop ready use of standard
punctuation practices.*

A language develops as speech; writing follows as an attempt to record the language, to transfer the effects of speech into a more enduring medium. In a broad way the result is a writing system, a body of conventions that taken together permit rapid and relatively exact reproduction of language that might otherwise be spoken. Inevitably, the system is mainly arbitrary, the result of codified tradition, although logic lies back of at least parts of it.

For English, the most obvious part of the system is an alphabet of letters, which suggest the sounds of speech and can be built into words. The words can be built into sentences; in writing and reading sentences, marks of punctuation are useful, since they show in part how parts of sentences are related and how sentences are related to one another. The commonest uses of punctuation marks are the subject of this chapter.

Since punctuation clarifies meaning and since meaning is so varied, a few rules for using punctuation—or even a few hundred rules—can never suffice to prescribe how punctuation marks shall be used in all circumstances. In Modern English punctuation works on four broad principles: (1) it marks off a sentence and shows how clauses and phrases within it are joined or separated; (2) it distinguishes the normal sequence of verb, subject, and complement; (3) it separates elements not sufficiently isolated by function words and sets off elements that interrupt the sequence of ideas within a sentence; (4) it serves conventional uses in series, statistics, abbreviations, and the like. Styles in punctuation vary somewhat; accordingly, no strict rules work infallibly, but practices follow general standards. Persons trained in the use of language—writers, editors, teachers of English—seldom disagree materially about what punctuation is appropriate for any given sentence. The student will do well to follow directions as exactly as possible; attempts to punctuate "by feel" are likely to work only for the most experienced writers.

---

25 Follow Standard Punctuation Practices   **P**

*The punctuation is inadequate or non-standard; revise
to clarify meaning or to provide emphasis.*

Notice the following:

An organic fiend, she would cook only home-grown vegetables and small children, and dogs that wandered into her garden were chased out with a broom.

So punctuated, the sentence seems to refer to an insane person, a fiend indeed. If the sentence is repunctuated, the "fiend" becomes a harmless eccentric:

> An organic fiend, she would cook only home-grown vegetables, and small children and dogs that wandered into her garden were chased out with a broom.

That is, punctuation can strengthen, reveal, or even change meaning. For ready reference the main uses of punctuation marks may be surveyed as follows:

. The *period* marks the end of many sentences and has some conventional uses (see **25a**).

? The *question mark* (also called interrogation point) follows a direct question (see **25a**).

! The *exclamation mark* (point) may follow an expression of strong emotion or feeling (see **25a**).

: The *colon* may separate independent clauses (see **25b**); it also has conventional uses (see **25j**).

; The *semicolon* separates independent clauses (see **25b**), and can separate items in a series (see **25d**).

, The *comma*, the most common punctuation mark in English, has a wide variety of uses (see **25c–h**).

— The *dash* may mark a sharp break in a sentence or may set off parenthetical material (see **25k**). It is made with two hyphens on the typewriter.

' The *apostrophe*, used to mark omissions, is primarily a spelling device (see **26g**).

" " *Quotation marks* enclose sentences or parts of sentences reproduced as spoken or written (see **25i**). Single quotation marks (the *apostrophe*) are used to set off a quotation within a quotation.

( ) *Parentheses* may be used to set parenthetical material apart from the sentence; it also has conventional uses (see **25l**).

[ ] *Square brackets* enclose material inserted within a quoted passage and for some conventional uses (see **25l**).

. . . The ellipsis marks an omission from something quoted (see **25a**).

25a End Punctuation; Period Fault   **P1**

Use a period or other form of end punctuation.

Sentence structures vary widely, but most end with a period. Exceptions are those that ask a direct question or convey a sense of great excitement. Use of a period to mark an expression not a sentence is called a *period fault,* and usually reflects a flaw in sentence structure (see **12a**). Failure to use a period where needed produces the *run-together* or *fused* sentence. It usually suggests confused sentence structure (see **25b**).

The following uses of end punctuation are also common in Modern English:

The *exclamation mark* is used in direct quotation involving interjections like "Ouch!" or "Help!" and may be used after quotations expressing great excitement or emotion, as in "He's a hijacker! Stop him before he can get on the plane!" but modern practice discourages the use of marks of exclamation except for very special effects.

Direct question. A question mark follows a direct question—that is, a question phrased in the exact words of the speaker.

I asked her, "Do you really mean that?"

The question mark is not used if the sentence takes the form of an indirect question, that is, a question that is attributed to someone, not quoted from him, as in the following:

I asked her if she really meant that.

Question within sentence. The mark is required after an interposed question:

Anybody who wants to breathe clean air—and who does not?—should support the anti-pollution laws.

The question mark is also used conventionally, sometimes within parentheses, to indicate that a fact, especially a date, is questionable:

Canterbury Tales is the work of Geoffrey Chaucer, 1345(?)–1400.

The use of the question mark for humorous purposes (*She then offered one of her intelligent? remarks*) is not usually in good taste.

Question as request. A request, or a command politely put as a question, may end either with a question mark or a period.

Will you kindly sign and return the enclosed form?

Ellipsis. Three periods (. . .) constitute the punctuation mark called the ellipsis, and signify omission of part of a quotation. If the words left out make up an entire sentence or several sentences, the period marking the end of the quoted sentence preceding the ellipsis is retained. In such cases, four periods appear in sequence, one being a true period and three the ellipsis. Notice the following quotation from C. G. Lichtenberg in *Reflections*:

Sometimes men come by the name of genius in the same way certain insects come by the name of centipede—not because they have a hundred feet, but because most people can't count above fourteen.

The passage could be somewhat shortened by ellipsis:

Somtimes men come by the name of genius in the same way certain insects come by the name of centipede . . . because most people can't count above fourteen.

Abbreviation. Although American usage is changing and periods are often dispensed with in such abbreviations as USA, PhD, MD, HUD, CIO-

AFL, ICBM, ESP, WASP, in American usage one finds them in A.D., Mr., Mrs., Ms., a.m., p.m., etc. A good dictionary will include abbreviations.

25b Punctuating Independent Clauses   P2, RT, CS

*Repunctuate so that you mark off an independent clause,
or consider redrafting the sentence.*

Independent clauses, so called because they have the structure of a complete sentence, are usually punctuated in one of three ways:

1. They are treated as separate sentences (see **25a**).
2. They are separated within the sentence by a semicolon.

> A woman may have trouble being recognized for her genius; she may have even more trouble being forgiven for it.

3. Within a sentence, they are joined by a coordinating conjunction (*and, but, for, yet, so*) with a comma preceding the conjunction (see **25c**). A semicolon, however, not a comma, is used when the second independent clause is introduced by words known as "conjunctive adverbs"—like *hence, then, therefore, however, nevertheless, in fact, moreover.*

> When God made woman he brought an end to boredom; however, he also brought an end to several other things.

For the position of the conjunctive adverb, see **16d**.

Besides these three methods of punctuating independent clauses within the same sentence, two others are standard, but less often used. Short similar clauses in a series are sometimes separated by only a comma, as in the old proverb:

> Man is the head, woman is the neck, but the neck turns the head.

Occasionally a colon separates independent clauses when the second clause specifies or exemplifies the idea of the first (see **25j**).

A sentence in which independent clauses are joined without punctuation is called a *fused* or *run-together* sentence. Use of a comma between clauses when a semicolon or period is needed is called a *comma fault* or *comma splice*. The error usually involves a failure of language to express thought. Correction may demand rewriting, perhaps by making part of the sentence subordinate.

ORIGINAL: Alice checked the locks on the windows and bolted the door, then she grabbed a blanket and curled up on the sofa.

REVISION: Alice checked the locks on the windows and bolted the door; then she grabbed a blanket and curled up on the sofa.

REVISION: After she had checked the locks on the windows and bolted the door, Alice grabbed a blanket and curled up on the red sofa.

REVISION: Alice checked the locks on the windows, bolted the door, grabbed a blanket, and curled up on the red sofa.

A semicolon solves the problem, but reducing one clause, as in the last two revisions, strengthens the sentence.

Use adequate punctuation between clauses joined by
coordinating conjunctions.

Coordinating conjunctions (*and, but, for, or, nor, yet, so*) may link independent clauses, but normally the conjunction should be preceded by a comma. Notice the following:

> Our committee got involved in women's lib on the campus and the problem of getting rid of nuclear wastes from the power plant was forgotten.

Without a comma before the conjunction *and*, the sentence is likely to be misread until the end. One might notice, however, that if the *and* joins two lesser parts of a sentence, words or phrases as against clauses, the meaning is clear without the comma.

> Our committee got involved in women's lib on the campus and in the problem of getting rid of nuclear wastes.

25d **Punctuation in a Series**   P4

Except in special circumstances, use commas to
separate items in series.

Commas serve to separate elements in series, whether the sequence is made up of words, phrases, dependent clauses, or independent clauses (see **25b**).

> The policeman signaled through traffic to go, right-turn traffic to go, left-turn to hold, while his out-stretched, white-gloved, authoritative hands effectively warned all cross traffic to wait its turn.

Some styles, notably in newspapers, permit omission of the comma before *and* in a series, but the comma should never be omitted before the conjunction if it is *but* or *or*.

Not all units that make up a sequence are conceived to be "in series." Words like nouns and adverbs are usually in series, but modifiers are in series only if each modifies separately. Compare the following:

> He swore the conventional, legal oath.
> He swore a good round oath.
> He swore an unbelievably naïve oath.
> The oath was naïve and insulting and useless.

The first sentence requires a comma, because *conventional* and *legal* modify *oath* separately. The same oath was both of these. The second sentence does not require the comma because *good* and *round* make up a single modifier, and the third does not require a comma because *unbelievably* modifies *naïve*, not *oath*. The series in the last sentence does not require commas because all modifiers in it are joined with *and*. Such constructions should be reserved for very special effects; for most uses, commas plus the final *and* are standard. Two ready tests may help identify modifiers in a series; if the modifiers can be reversed, or if *and* can be inserted between them, the modifiers are usually in series. Unfortunately, the test does not always work. A sequence composed of numerals and adjectives of size, number, color, and age seldom require commas as punctuation: two big black crows; twenty-three little brown men; a crabbed old man; a pale young woman.

When items in a series are complicated, or themselves contain punctuation, semicolons may substitute for commas.

ORIGINAL: The board was made up of Chancellor Calvin East, administration, Prof. Leland Howard, faculty Avery McLane, Liberal Arts 3, student body, and Elizabeth Wharton grounds and buildings.

REVISION: The board was made up of Chancellor Calvin East, administration; Prof. Leland Howard, faculty; Avery McLane, Liberal Arts 3, student body; and Elizabeth Wharton, grounds and buildings.

Commas alone confuse in this sentence; semicolons are needed to make clear the division into categories.

25e Punctuation of Nonrestrictive or Parenthetical Modifiers   P5

Set off restrictive modifiers and parenthetical matter, but not nonrestrictive modifiers.

Modifiers needed to identify subject or complement—those called *restrictive*—are not set off by punctuation. Modifiers not essential to the subject-verb-complement combination but which supply nonessential information—the *nonrestrictive modifiers*—are set off from the element they modify. Compare:

All the skiers who had trained for cross-country racing finished the course.
All the skiers, who had trained for cross-country racing, finished the course.

In the situation described in the first sentence, presumably some skiers had not trained; the clause identifies the finishers as only those who had trained and presumably concerns the value of the training. The second sentence reports that all skiers finished; the clause tells something about these skiers, but does not identify any of them as distinguished from some others. As a rough test to identify restrictive modifiers, the writer can try dropping the modifier. If the sentence is essentially changed, as in the first sentence of the pair above, the modifier is restrictive. If the subject-verb-complement core is not changed, as in the second sentence, the modifier is nonrestrictive.

Usually, restrictive and nonrestrictive modifiers can be distinguished by pauses in the flow of the sentence and by changes in the pitch and stress if the passage is read. In the sentences above, the reader would say, *All the skiers who trained* with little pause or change in either stress or pitch. The same reader, saying the second sentence, would pause after *skiers* and would pronounce *skiers* with falling pitch. He would then start the clause, pronouncing *who* with greater stress and at a higher pitch.

Various sorts of qualifiers following the word to which they refer are usually nonrestrictive and require commas: Technically known as *appositive modifiers, verbal modifiers, general modifiers*, and *parenthetical expressions,* their need to be set off by commas is shown by the voice-pitch test. Examples are:

APPOSITIVE: John, *the piper's son*, was a rascal.
VERBAL: The fullback, *having muffed the punt*, was benched.
GENERAL: You, *of course*, will understand. (*In general, accordingly, that is, for example, for instance*, are a few of many general modifiers set off by commas. When general modifiers are essential to the sense of the sentence they are not set off, as in: *Of course you understand*.)
PARENTHETICAL: Examples, *as will be seen*, are easy to come by. (When the interpolated parenthetical material interrupts the sentence sharply or dramatically, dashes or parentheses rather than commas may be warranted; see **25k, 25l**).

Final qualifying clauses, especially those beginning with *although*, are often set off by commas. The voice pitch test helps here also. In the two sentences below, the comma contributes to a subtle difference.

I signed up for the Army after I was drafted.
I signed up for the Army, after I was drafted.

25f Punctuation after Introductory Modifiers   P6
Punctuate for clarity after introductory modifiers.

Introductory modifying clauses and other long or complicated modifiers are set off from the rest of the sentence by commas. The punctuation is especially necessary, even with a short modifier, if the reader might otherwise have difficulty identifying the point at which the modifier stops. Compare:

In the morning we knew we had been sleeping among a horde of hungry chiggers.
In the morning, light streamed through the windows.
Being exhausted from thirty miles of mountain climbing and inexperienced in the ways of the chigger, we lay down expecting a good night's sleep.

25g Punctuation with Geographical, Temporal, and Metrical Material   P7
Use punctuation to separate or to combine statistical material.

A number of conventional uses of the comma convey information about places, times, and measurements.

1. *Dates*: Commas are generally used between elements of a date. The year is so set off; the month and date are not separated. With inclusion of times of day and abbreviations, the need for commas grows.

At 9:05 A.M., Monday, May 8, 1972, the plane took off.

Some styles permit omission of commas in brief indications of date: "In March 1972 she began. . . ." In one style now gaining acceptance the day precedes the month and year with no commas: "20 March 1903." Whatever the style employed for dates, the writer who wishes to spare his readers' confusion aims to be consistent.

2. *Addresses*: In the address of a letter separate lines are accorded to the name of the addressee, the house number and street name (or number), and the city, state, and zip code area. Until recently city and state were placed on separate lines, and this may still be done, with the zip code either on the same line with the state or separate. Now, with machine reading, city, state, and zip number frequently are put on the same line.

> Miss Jane Smith
> 432 Albany Avenue N.E.
> Seattle, Wash. 98506

In written, or spoken, communication: "Jane gave as her address, 432 Albany Avenue Northeast, Seattle, Washington, 98506."

3. *Other statistics*: Commas commonly separate measurements, divisions of a whole, and other statistical details. The last element in a series of divisions, such as those of a book, is usually separated from what follows by a final comma, but the last of a series of parts of a measure is not.

> The bridge was exactly 127 feet, 4 inches long.
> The quotation appears on page 47, lines 2–20, of his last novel.

25h Commas to Clarify Constructions   P8
Insert a comma to clarify the construction.

Commas are sometimes needed to separate words that may be mistakenly run together (*Whatever is, is right*) or to emphasize or clarify a structure when a function word is not used (*No money, no supper. He knew that he was wrong, that he had spoken hastily*).

25i Punctuation with Quotations   P9, Quot
Provide punctuation appropriate to the quotation in its context.

An exact reproduction, word for word, of material spoken or written by another, is enclosed within quotation marks. Conventions governing punctuation of quoted material include the following:

1. *Direct quotations.* Words recorded as spoken or written are enclosed in double quotation marks.

> "On your marks," he called.
> Wherever he saw a tree and grass, Peter remarked that "this would be a good place for a picnic."

A series of words as short as one word or two or three taken directly from a source should be enclosed in quotation marks.

> Two thousand years after Virgil, farmers still share with him concern for weather that will "make the crops rejoice."

2. *Special usages.* Quotation marks are sometimes used to call attention to a way of talking or writing peculiar to a particular country, region, social class, or person.

> The New England farmer calls a field from which hay is harvested a "mowing."

Quotation marks are no longer used to distinguish slang or colloquial expressions that bear the taint of slang. If the use is appropriate, no apology in the form of quotation marks is required.

3. *Indirect quotations.* Indirect quotations do not require quotation marks, but words quoted directly within an indirect quotation must be marked.

> DIRECT: Full of confidence, John said, "I can do that easily."
> INDIRECT: Full of confidence, John said he could "do that easily."

4. *Words out of context.* Use of a word as a word may be indicated by use of quotation marks. However, italics are increasingly coming to serve the purpose of identifying a word—or letter or other symbol—so used.

> The proper noun *John* is the subject, *or* The proper noun "John" is the subject.

5. *Titles.* Although italics are commonly used for titles, quotation marks may be employed when (1) italic type is not available and (2) when a short work is to be distinguished from the larger work that contains it (see **26h**).

> Riley's "When the Frost Is on the Punkin" appeared in *Riley Farm-Rhymes.*

6. *Quotations within quotations.* American practice requires that single quotation marks be used when a quotation is quoted.

> "I am not going to give her any candy," said Orrin, "until she says 'pretty please.' "

7. *Introductions to quotations.* When the person quoted is identified by use of an expression like "John said," it is separated from the quotation by a comma, or commas, or a colon (see **25j**).

> Joan said, "I have a sweet tooth."
> "I have a sweet tooth," Joan said.

8. *Position of quotation marks.* The beginning and end of every quotation is marked by quotation marks. If a quotation consists of two or more paragraphs, the open-quote mark is used to begin each paragraph, but the close-quote mark is used only at the end of the final paragraph. In printed text, long quotations may appear without marks if a substitute typographical device (smaller type, maybe indentation) serves the purpose. In typewritten

material, closer spacing of lines and wider margins may serve to identify long quotations.

9. *Quotation marks and other marks.* Usually, the close-quote mark occurs after end punctuation (see **25a**), and close-quote marks always occur after a period or comma. If the close-quote mark occurs after part of a sentence, however, it comes before any mark of punctuation except the period or comma. Notice the following:

Would you say he had lost his "cool"?
"Would you say his 'cool' was all he lost?"

25j The Colon   **P10, :**

Use the colon for specialized purposes, not as the
equivalent of a semicolon.

The colon is now mainly used to introduce something, often a series, or for formal purposes. Common uses are the following:

1. *Series.* It is used, as in the sentence immediately preceding this one, before a series that has been introduced by a completed statement.

2. *Independent clauses.* When the second part of a sentence composed of two independent clauses has been introduced by the first and the second clause clearly repeats or clarifies the first, a colon may be used to introduce it.

John drove on sustained by two convictions: his gas supply was enough to see him to the other side of the pass, and the road was bound to be better there.

3. *Conventional uses.* The common conventional uses of the colon are in literary citations, in the formal salutation in a letter, in statements of time. Notice the following:

Exodus 6: 1–6   Dear Miss Hadley: 4:20 p.m.

25k The Dash   **P11, Dash**

Use the dash to mark a sharp
break or to fit conventions.

In typewritten material, the dash is composed of two hyphens with no space between or on either side. In handwritten material, the dash should be unbroken and fill the space between two words. It marks a break in the flow of the sentence where the writer wishes to bring the reader up short. It is commonly limited to the following uses:

1. *Emphasis.* The dash emphasizes a sharp break in thought.

Horace said, "I like girls—*all* girls and all *girls.*"

2. *Interruption.* The dash may mark a dramatic or striking interruption, may set off a modifier more distinctly than a comma does.

> The inner city is the home of the landless poor—blacks squeezed out of southern agriculture side by side with Puerto Ricans, familiar neither with English nor with the life style of white Americans.

3. *Summation.* Occasionally a long series, of subjects or of modifiers, calls for a dash and usually a pronoun summarizing the list.

> Daybreak at 4 a.m., the sun still low at noon, a cool, sunlit twilight lasting past 10 p.m. bedtime—these were Olive's memories of a summer in Nome.

4. *Introduction.* A dash may introduce a list less formally than a colon; occasionally it may be used to introduce a clause anticipated by the one preceding.

> He saw the gate open and heard himself cry—"I'm going to ride him! I'm going to win!"
> He was asked to give examples of proper use of half a dozen prepositions—
> *at, by, in, of, off, via, per.*

5. *Convention.* A conventional use of the dash occurs in literary citations.

> "All wastefulness is offensive to . . . taste."
>   THORSTEIN VEBLEN, *The Theory of the Leisure Class*

The dash may be used in informal arrangements, as of categories, etc.

> The field sciences—geology, ornithology, botany, archeology.
> The laboratory sciences—physics, chemistry, physiology.

25l Parentheses and Brackets   P12

Make appropriate use of parentheses or brackets.

Parentheses are used to enclose additional material not part of the sentence structure. Dashes are similarly used (see **25k**).

> My scapegrace uncle (he was the one who was a gigolo for a time in Madrid) made an improper proposal to me when I was too young to know what he meant.

Brackets are used to enclose matter inserted into a direct quotation, or into material already enclosed within parentheses.

25m Inappropriate or Excessive Punctuation   P13, No P

Remove excessive or misleading punctuation.

Punctuation is intended to help readers comprehend. Unwisely used, it distracts or obscures. The notion that any pause warrants a comma—or even a dash—is responsible for some inappropriate punctuation and excessive punctuation. Three kinds of redundant punctuation, with samples, follow:

1. *Separation of main sentence parts.*

ORIGINAL: Every man on the team, had been out with an injury.

REVISION: Every man on the team had been out with an injury.

The comma in the original is unnecessary. Worse, it separates the subject and verb. A comma separating and isolating a restrictive modifying clause would have the same effect.

ORIGINAL: Mario saw through the attempt, to separate him from his money.

REVISION: Mario saw through the attempt to separate him from his money.

For most purposes, the second clause is restrictive and essential and should not be set off by a comma; see **25e**.

2. *Unnecessary comma with* and. A comma is called for before *and* in completion of a series and before a conjunction joining independent clauses (see **25d, 25**), but not in most other uses.

ORIGINAL: We walked all around the square, and back to the house.

REVISION: We walked all around the square and back to the house.

3. *Unnecessary comma before final clause.* The final clause that serves as complement, or one that is restrictive, requires no comma to set it off from the rest of the sentence.

ORIGINAL: Doris fully expected, that Mack would not kick the goal.

REVISION: Doris fully expected that Mack would not kick the goal.

25A

OBJECTIVE: To test the use and value of punctuation.

INSTRUCTIONS: Below are series of words that as they stand have little or uncertain meaning. In the spaces provided try to repunctuate them in one or more ways so that meaning becomes clearer.

EXAMPLE: okay okay okay those invoices then let's get out of here
                Okay? Okay! Okay those invoices. Then let's get out of here.
                Okay, okay. Okay those invoices then. Let's get out of here.

EVIDENCE:

  1   John she said you should not go

  2   I want you to take off the storm windows tomorrow you can go to the beach if you want to

  3   four and four are eight but the square of four is sixteen the square of sixteen is but who can do that in his head anyhow is it four and four are eight or is it is eight I never can remember

  4   you you say that that you can come down that hill and not break your neck why you you wouldn't know a giant slalom from next week would you now

CONCLUSIONS: What are some of the ways in which punctuation alters sentences?

SUGGESTION: Make up a sentence that will have several meanings, depending on the punctuation.

25B

OBJECTIVE: To discover how two or more independent clauses should be punctuated.

INSTRUCTIONS: Fill in the blanks at the right. If you believe a sentence is punctuated in accordance with standard practice, write C; if not, improve the punctuation and copy the new punctuation into the column, along with the preceding word. Check earlier portions of this chapter if necessary.

EXAMPLE: I took seven double martinis from the tray and when nobody was looking poured each drink out the window, everybody stood around waiting for me to collapse.

window;

EVIDENCE:

1 The game was played on a wet field and neither team could rely on its passing attack. _____

2 We were driving the chickens into the yard through the gate, at the same time my little brother was letting them out again through a hole in the fence. _____

3 The new light was only half an inch long but was more powerful than conventional lights ten times its size. _____

4 The salesman at the perfume counter was very co-operative and brought out samples of expensive perfumes. _____

5 I have a fine alarm clock with a two-tone bell but I still manage to be late for my eight-o'clock class. _____

6 Under the new plan retired employees could stay at the company home but could not receive pensions. _____

7 There was little skating that winter, the pond would freeze at night and thaw and crack during the day. _____

8 Nobody in the stands could tell which horse had won, in fact, the officials could not tell from photographs. _____

9 My piano lessons were not very profitable, I was always too tired to practice. _____

10 The field trip took us far into uninhabited country and gave us a look at unusual geological formations. _____

11 Ice was forming on the wings and the strong wind was blowing us off course. _____

12 We knew that the play would be dull and that we would have to stand in line to get seats. _____

13 The machine has brought many changes to our way of life but man has not always benefited from them. _____

14 Much of Sir Walter Ralegh's poetry has been lost and only about thirty short pieces survive. _____

CONCLUSIONS: Study the entries you have made in the right-hand column. Summarize your results in the space below. Do your conclusions differ in any way from those in **25**, **25a**, and **25b**?

25C

OBJECTIVE: To discover what punctuation changes are appropriate when part of a sentence is reduced to a dependent clause.

INSTRUCTIONS: Examine the sentences below. If a sentence is well constructed and appropriately punctuated, write C in the blank to the right. If not, or you can improve it by reducing an independent clause to a dependent clause, do so and write the first three words of the dependent clause in the blank to the right. You may change the remaining independent clause in any way sense requires. If in doubt, consult the earlier portions of this chapter.

EXAMPLE: Required courses are part of every curriculum in our college and I do not like mine very well.   *Although required courses*

EVIDENCE:

   1 The old man sat in the park feeding pigeons, at the same time his house burned down.   _____

   2 Just as Mike and Louise were turning the corner they were stopped by a car, this car was loaded with men carrying rifles.   _____

   3 The new freezer would hold over 450 pounds of food, this freezer had a capacity of sixteen cubic feet.   _____

   4 Soap operas have an appeal for a large number of people, so it should certainly be encouraged as radio entertainment.   _____

   5 The president of our student body is always true to a number of democratic principles and these principles I admire very much.   _____

   6 Modern furniture is functional; nevertheless I prefer eighteenth-century furniture with its graceful, stylized lines.   _____

   7 Mary came out of the salty water and when she did she discovered she was covered with a white alkaline film.   _____

   8 First Chuck would dig the holes and then I would drop the cedar posts in and tamp the earth hard around them.   _____

CONCLUSIONS: Examine your evidence in the column to the right. In the previous exercise you described punctuation for independent clauses. How does the punctuation differ for dependent clauses? Use the following space to describe the difference:

Do your conclusions differ from those in **25b, 25e,** and **25f?**

25D

OBJECTIVE: To determine how independent statements should or should not be combined, and how such changes are reflected in punctuation.

INSTRUCTIONS: Below are several examples of independent but related statements. In the spaces provided, try various ways of combining them or keeping them separate.

EXAMPLE: she said she was glad to die nobody eats in heaven there would be no dishes to wash

She said she was glad to die. Since nobody eats in heaven there would be no dishes to wash.

She said she was glad to die because, since nobody eats in heaven, there would be no dishes to wash.

She said she was glad to die; nobody eats in heaven, and accordingly there would be no dishes to wash.

EVIDENCE:

1 complex organisms have in them the germs of death one-celled creatures seem to be immortal.

2 you cannot get blood out of a turnip you cannot shoe a running horse by asking the impossible you may get the best possible

3 various people drink for various reasons some say they are thirsty some say they are afraid they will become thirsty some can think of nothing better to do

CONCLUSIONS: Some writers say there are three major ways of combining independent clauses or keeping them separate. Do you find this to be true?

Can you draw any conclusions about which sorts of clauses should be kept separate, which combined, and which made subordinate?

25E

OBJECTIVE: To find out how inserted material should be handled.

INSTRUCTIONS: Insert any commas you find to be needed. For later checking, write in the blanks to the right each word that precedes a comma you have added. Naturally, not all blanks will be filled.

EXAMPLE: The boy who had dropped the spider down my neck _____
was looking vaguely at the ceiling. _____
(no further punctuation is necessary)

EVIDENCE:

1 I found myself facing an elderly gentleman who appeared _____
so benign and important that I was sure he must be the president. _____

2 The street car which was the first one, that had come for _____
ten minutes was so full it left me standing in the pouring rain. _____

3 Lincoln who was known at that time only as a gangling _____
clerk of a general store threw the man down and rubbed his _____
face in the mud. _____

4 Anyone who wants to stay out of the dean's office will do _____
well to keep his "crib" notes in his pocket. _____

5 The Department of Grounds and Buildings employs a few _____
aging morons who go about with hoes poking ineffectually at _____
weeds. _____

6 I decided to try the new chemistry instructor who looked _____
to me as though he might not be careful about checking labo- _____
ratory reports. _____

7 I decided to talk with Nick who had worked the summer _____
before as a trucker for an oil-drilling rig. _____

8 The desk which was army surplus and looked like it had _____
a flattened rivet which was always letting the typewriter down _____
on my knees. _____

9 I studied the police lineup which, by the way, had been _____
gathered for my benefit, but I could not distinguish the man who _____
had hit me. _____

10 Golf long my father's favorite pastime, bored me until I _____
learned that it could be used for social purposes acquiring dates _____
for instance. _____

11 My Uncle Tony to the public Professor Anthony Bellini _____
taught in a small, impoverished college Hopkington Institute, and _____
Aunt Martha had her private term for anything empty "a pro- _____
fessor's pocket." _____

12 Of course the linoleum carpet, which was cracked and broken around the edges had been put down only, as Mother said until Father got around to fixing the floor.

13 Nothing not even the prospect of an F in economics would keep Jane from playing after dinner.

14 Some chocolate-covered peanuts, apparently had been smashed on the green sofa the only really expensive piece of furniture we had.

15 Unfortunately the Siamese kitten, called Meow Tse Tsung because he was always yowling and obviously wanted to be a dictator was clawing at Father's hat an expensive new gray fedora.

16 I cut the only blossoms we had some bug-chewed yellow iris, and stuffed them in an old cracked vase in a jumble known for politeness as a flower arrangement.

17 Rolling along over western Wyoming the state that was to become my home, I first smelled what seems to me now the finest odor I know the tangy, pungent, exotic fragrance of wet sagebrush.

18 The African lobster tails although they had been quick-frozen had less flavor than our native Maine lobsters.

19 Thank God for the Mississippi river; without it, nobody could tell where Minneapolis ends and St. Paul begins.

20 Aster Wilson who was in charge of makeup and who had learned what she knew from an old professional that had retired to run a newsstand in Birmingham showed me how to gray the upper eyelid and brush the eyebrows with pencil so that you can counteract the effect of the lights without looking like something that more properly belongs in a museum cage among the beetles.

21 The young hoodlums driving a car that they had stolen from the high school parking lot were stopped for a routine check by officers who wondered why youngsters of their ages were out at 4:30 a.m.

22 I was playing Petruchio in *Kiss Me Kate* an adaptation of *The Taming of the Shrew*. In the final scene in which Kate is supposed to take off her bonnet she came in with nothing on her head not even the mob cap that she had worn in an earlier scene.

CONCLUSIONS: When should elements not part of the SVC pattern be set off by commas?

You may wish to check to see how your conclusions accord with those in **25e, 25f, 25k,** and **25d**.

25F

OBJECTIVE: To check control of the use of punctuation for conventional purposes.

INSTRUCTIONS: Insert necessary punctuation in the passage below, and copy into the blanks at the right the punctuation and the words that immediately precede the added punctuation.

EXAMPLE: George Washington, the first president of the United States, slept here.   *States,*

EVIDENCE:

The wit who tried to distinguish between ancient and modern men by saying that the moderns are the men who earn their living whereas the ancients were those who urned their dead was omitting, among others the Egyptians who preserved their dead by mummification a practice made necessary by Egyptian religious beliefs. Mummification for which they developed elaborate techniques, was intended to preserve the body so that it could be recognized by the god of immortality, Osiris and by the Egyptian's soul. Each baby that was born to an Egyptian mother presumably had with it two companions ka and ba. Ka, which might be called a soul a sort of guardian angel stayed with the Egyptians if possible but if ka became lost, for whatever reason his charge became dead. That is death was being without a ka. Ka, being immortal, did not die and anybody who got to the other world might hope to find his soul, his ka there before him. Ba the other companion of each Egyptian, a soul but a soul of a different sort was supposed to reside in the viscera especially in the stomach or heart. Ba did not forsake the body entirely not even at death but it was likely to fly around except at night when it returned to the tomb for fear of evil spirits of whom there seem to have been a good many in the Nile Valley, all the way from Cairo to Khartum. If ba, returning from one of his flights was unable to find the body which he had left he would necessarily wander off. The Egyptian, as a result would die a second time.

The Egyptians, accordingly who were nothing if not ingenious developed means of preserving the body in shape to be recognized by the god of immortality, Osiris, by the body's twin ka, and by its inhabitant ba; that is, the Egyptian learned techniques of embalming or more properly, mummification. The body which was to be mummified was brought to an embalmer's shop usually a tent set up behind the home of the deceased. By using various instruments mainly probes and ingeniously designed hooks the embalmer drew the brains out through the nose, and then

through an incision in the groin removed the viscera except the   _____
heart which was allowed to remain in place and preserved them   _____
in small vessels from the ancient delta city of Canopus the   _____
Canopic jars which can be seen in many museums. The body was   _____
then submerged in brine except for the head which remained   _____
above water. After a considerable period, usually about fifty days   _____
the body was removed dried, and treated with chemicals a mix-   _____
ture of sodium carbonate sodium bicarbonate and sometimes   _____
other sodium derivatives. Incisions were made at several less   _____
visible points of the body especially between the toes and fingers   _____
at the knees and under the elbows in order to drain off the fluids   _____
of decomposition which might otherwise rot the body. The skin   _____
was anointed with oils and unguents, and sometimes with the   _____
Biblical balm of Gilead, and wrapped in linen in bandages about   _____
two three or four inches wide and as much as twenty feet long.   _____
Each layer of linen was sealed with hot liquid resin and with   _____
whatever may have fallen into the resin provided the embalmer   _____
was a bit careless. One mummy for instance contained the   _____
corpses of two mice which seem to have fallen into the hot resin   _____
and remained unnoticed by the embalmer. One wonders if the   _____
mice also attained the other world accompanied by their mouse-   _____
ba's. The art of embalming apparently reached its height in Cairo   _____
Egypt during what is called the New Kingdom sometimes dated   _____
from Amenhotep 1590 B.C. to Ramses III who may have died   _____
March 16 1199 B.C.   _____

CONCLUSIONS: For which arbitrary, conventional uses of punctuation were you uncertain? Describe these as exactly as you can.

Check these uncertainties against the earlier sections of this chapter. Copy here the numbers of sections that you need to review in order to use punctuation in a standard way to reveal conventional relationship within the sentence.

*Objective: To develop facility in handling
conventional devices essential to the writing system.*

As we have seen in Chapter 25, writing works through a system, inevitably an arbitrary system. For English, as for most languages that can be used in written form, the system relies extensively on symbols and codified practices that all literate users of the language know, and the more literate know so well that they can use them unconsciously. In Chapter 25 we considered one extensive body of these symbols, those known as punctuation. In this chapter we shall bring together the more useful remaining symbols and practices.

26a   Manuscript Form   M

*Check requirements for standard manuscript form and
revise your manuscript accordingly.*

Material formally submitted, whether for a class requirement or for publication, follows conventions, some of which are arbitrary, some of which promote exactitude and ease of handling. Editors and teachers prefer type-written copy, double-spaced, on good white paper, 8½ x 11 inches. The type should be clean and the ribbon sufficiently inked for clarity. Most teachers accept handwritten papers, but are likely to require that the writer use black or blue-black ink, on full-ruled paper (not narrow-ruled notebook paper), and that the writer be careful to distinguish between capital and lower-case letters and between similar letters like *a* and *o*. All manuscript should have generous margins, at least an inch and a half at the top and left, an inch at the right and bottom. On the typewriter, paragraphs should be indented about five spaces; a space should follow internal punctuation, and two spaces should follow a sentence. In handwritten copy, these differences should be approximated. For classes, brief papers are often folded lengthwise and longer papers are left flat. All papers should carry identification on the outside, as though on the front of a book or magazine. This identification should usually include: (1) the student's name, (2) the class and section for which the paper is submitted, (3) the theme number, (4) the date, (5) the name of the instructor. Papers submitted for publication carry the name and address of the author and an estimate of the number of words in the manuscript.

Diagnosis of Spelling Problems

English spelling presents problems, and for some students it becomes a major problem. In a few languages—such as Finnish, for which writing de-

veloped rather late—writing records sounds with considerable accuracy: the
Finnish schoolboy does not have to work hard on spelling. For most languages, however, written transcription is only a rough approximation of
sound, often—as with some words in English—a very rough one. The spoken
language changes more rapidly than the more stable written language; spelling cannot keep up with the changes. *Colonel* was spelled as it was pronounced when it was introduced into English; its pronunciation was compressed, but its spelling remained stable. Furthermore, speech in English
produces subtle variations in sound that only a cumbersomely long alphabet
could reproduce completely. As a result, English spelling has to be learned.

But learning spelling—even for the adult who has not bothered to learn
it in elementary school or who has convinced himself that he has a "psychological block"—is not so difficult as it is often considered. Usually the poor
speller has never tried to learn systematically and over a long enough time to
let new habits become set. This section suggests a way of approaching spelling systematically—by analyzing individual problems and then correcting
specific weaknesses. In other words, by using diagnostic tests the student can
discover the nature of his individual weaknesses in spelling. He can then
simplify his work by concentrating on the trouble spots. The first step is to
take each of the following tests, recording the results on the table on this page
for easy reference. Each test consists of a series of selected words that are
to be written from dictation, without previous study. Your instructor may
dictate the words to you, or you may ask someone else to dictate them. From
the results you can plan study. For instance, if you make a low score on test 1,
you regularly misspell a few common words. You may thus appear to be a
"bad speller," but if this is your only low score the cure is relatively easy.
You have only to isolate the words you habitually misspell—perhaps using
the list on page 237 under the head *Additional Spelling Demons* and memorize their spellings.

Diagnostic Test Scores

Test	Subject	Number Correct	Score
1	Common Spelling Demons	_____	_____
2	Spelling by Sound	_____	_____
3	Words No Longer Spelled Phonetically	_____	_____
4	Plurals, Possessives, Omissions	_____	_____
5	Compounds, Hyphenation	_____	_____
6	Doubling of Consonants	_____	_____
7	Final Silent *e*	_____	_____
8	Spelling with *y* Plus Suffix	_____	_____
9	Combinations of *e* and *i*	_____	_____
10	Words Having Similar Spellings	_____	_____
11	Words Having Similar Prefixes and Suffixes	_____	_____

1. *The Common Spelling Demons*

receive	to	affect	rhythm
separate	friend	principal	pronunciation
their	familiar	similar	appearance
too	grammar	occurred	arguing
athletic	quiet	disappointed	professor
its	tragedy	sentence	principle
definite	acquaintance	weather	it's
until	losing	Britain	interest
all right	business	environment	chose
privilege	whether	coming	referring
writer	humorous	studying	existence
loose	benefited	embarrass	immediately

Double the number correct, add two points, and record the number right and the score in the table above. Since these words are all common, though often misspelled, even a moderately low score—80 for instance—indicates trouble. The words occur so often that difficulties with only a few make a paper look illiterate. You should be able to spell every word in the list. Look up any word you misspelled in a dictionary, learn everything you can about it, and recall the correct spelling every day for two weeks. Think up any device you can to remember unusual words; for instance, *alright* is not all right but *all right* is.

2. *Spelling by Sound*

sobriety	animosity	monstrosity	mesmerism
peculiarity	impecuniousness	supererogation	prestidigitator
prerequisite	diphthong	strenuous	moiety
impracticable	operational	oleander	oleaginous
indubitable	recuperate	aborigines	hedonism
ridiculousness	manumit	caveat	stoically
criticism	impetuous	cosmography	perspicacity
individual	predestination	eleemosynary	emoluments

Triple the number correct, add four points, and enter the scores in the table above. These words may not be familiar, but they are spelled much as they sound. A low score here indicates difficulty in "sounding out" words.

3. *Words No Longer Spelled Phonetically*

government	restaurant	interest	library
joists	attention	against	clothes
literature	villain	recognize	different
laboratory	glacier	really	dictionary
statue	often	cellar	ocean
naturally	knife	parliament	gradually

Multiply the number correct by four, entering your scores in the table above. These words are not spelled phonetically now because the sound of the word has changed. If you made a low score here, you might notice that many of these words are related to others that have changed but little. *Govern* is still pronounced about as it is spelled, although *government* often is not. Some other spellings you can remember by comparisons. The *t* in *nature* used to be pronounced like the *t* in *mature*, but it has changed to the sound usually written *ch*. This change is not uncommon in English; it appears in *righteous* as against *right*, for instance.

4. *Plurals, Possessives, and Omissions*

(Note: to be entirely successful, this examination must be dictated by the instructor or by someone who can use the forms correctly in sentences.)

oriole's	people's	students'	of my father's
doesn't	students	the mothers'	boys'
forty days	yours	boy's	day's time
Henry's	they're	one's	there's
it's	Henrys	theirs	radios
hour's work	solos	Negroes	James' (James's)
heroes	two dollars' worth	wives	Mothers Day
student's	life's	lives	hers

Triple the number correct, add four points, and enter your scores in the table above. Even a moderately low score here indicates that you do not understand something about plurals or the use of the apostrophe. By examining which words you misspelled, you can diagnose your trouble. Confusion arises here because *students, student's,* and *students'* sound alike but have different meanings. The difficulty is that you do not understand the spelling of plurals (see **26e**), or the use of the hyphen (see **26g**), or both. You would do well to look up these sections and master the rules.

5. *Compounds, Hyphenation*

(Note: to be entirely successful, this examination should be dictated by the instructor or by someone who can use the forms correctly in sentences.)

post-mortem	courthouse	court plaster	courtroom
court-martial	homemade	homework	home rule
home economics	home-brew	home plate	homestretch
rapidly eaten	half-eaten	half eaten	down-at-heel
down-and-out	down and out	slowly moving	slow-moving
high-powered	high power	two-by-four	badly needed
ten- and twelve-foot	day labor	daylight	day by day
day-by-day	daydream	day coach	day nursery

Triple the number correct, add four points, and record your scores in the table above. A low percentage indicates that you do not understand compounding and hyphenation (see **26e**).

6. *Doubling of Consonants*

Write the following words from dictation:

stopping	dinner	preferred	netted
hide	full	necessary	recommend
embarrassed	bus	pastime	cunning
benefited	misspell	buss	coming
committed	professor	spitting	committing
occurred	coming	spiteful	commitment
dine	marry	helpful	finer
hidden	ridden	excellent	written

Triple the number correct, add four points, and record your scores in the table above. A low percentage here indicates that you do not understand the doubling of consonants or have not learned the exceptions. In general, a doubled consonant indicates a preceding short vowel in an accented or single syllable (*control, controlled*). Some exceptions are conventional (*come, coming*) although they may follow a pattern (*full, helpful, careful*), but a few follow a rule: A consonant is not doubled after a short unaccented vowel (*benefited*).

7. *Final Silent* e

rid	judging	curable	writing
ride	astride	siding	noticeable
rating	striding	relieving	wholly
typing	lovely	slide	truly
courageous	boredom	slid	argument

Multiply the number correct by five and enter your scores in the table above. A low percentage here indicates that you do not understand that in general a final silent *e* indicates a preceding long vowel (*rid, ride*). It is usually dropped before an ending beginning with a vowel (*riding*) or to avoid an awkward sequence (*wholly*). It may be retained to indicate that a preceding *c* or *g* is "soft" (*noticeable, courageous*).

8. *Spellings with* y *Plus a Suffix*

try	studies	entries	spies
trying	flies	shanties	lied
tried	valleys	O'Mally's	lies
busy	histories	stays	lyes
business	rays	turkeys	paying
studying	alleys	spying	paid

Multiply the number correct by four and record your scores in the table above. A low percentage indicates that you do not understand the rule for *y* plus a suffix. In general, when a suffix beginning with a vowel is added to a word ending in *y*, the *y* is changed to *i* (*try, tried*). It is not changed if the suffix begins with *i* (*trying*), if *e* precedes the *y* (*monkeys*), or if the word is a proper name (*the Alfred Frys*).

9. *Combinations of* e *and* i

receive	weird	shield	seizure
retrieve	neighbor	either	seine
reprieve	seize	relieve	seignor
height	believe	brief	siege
leisure	sovereign	deign	sieve

Multiply the number correct by five and record your scores in the table above. A low percentage indicates that you do not know or are not applying the rule for *e* and *i*. The old rhyme describes most usages: Write *i* before *e*/ Except after *c*/ Or when spoken as *a*/ In *neighbor* and *weigh*. There are some exceptions, of which the following are the commonest: *height, foreign, sovereign, weir, weird, leisure, either, neither, seize*.

10. *Words Having Similar Spellings*

assent	lye	advise	affect
ascent	sight	advice	effect
decent	cite	tents	stationary
descent	site	tense	stationery
sense	there	lead	roll
scents	they're	led	role
cents	your	Britain	principle
lie	you're	Martian	principal

Triple the number correct, add four points, and record your scores in the table above. A low percentage means that you are not distinguishing between similar words. Look words of this sort up in the dictionary, learn everything you can about them, and treat them as in **27a**. For instance, *stationary* concerns *place*, but *stationery* is used for *letters*.

11. *Words Having Similar Prefixes and Suffixes*

superintendent	dabble	purpose	experience
permissible	attendance	intolerant	inheritance
feasible	sacraments	amenable	intense
attendants	immense	incidents	intents
sufficient	innocents	incidence	correspondence
unable	innocence	unsure	correspondents
perquisite	monuments	insecure	extravagance
prerequisite	indestructible	pervade	entanglements
sentence	sociable	prevision	invisible
impassible	instruments	eatable	irreverent
intelligible	proposable	edible	irreverence
label	hindrance	dominant	perform
			preform

Double the number correct and record your scores in the table above. A low percentage here indicates ignorance of prefixes and suffixes. Careful use of the dictionary will help here, since some affixes can be distinguished by sound and meaning, *pre-, pro-, per-,* and sometimes *de-, di-*. As suffixes,

-ants and *-ents* indicate plurals and *-ance* and *-ence* indicate an abstraction (*residents, residence*). *Un-* and *-able* come from Anglo-Saxon, and there is some tendency to use them with words of native origin (*uneatable, unsure*), whereas *in-* and *-ible* appear more frequently with Latin derivatives (*inedible, insecure*). The use of *-ance, -ence, -ants, -ents* is erratic, but can sometimes be inferred from careful pronunciation (*sacraments*) and more frequently from the pronunciation of related words in which the stress has not shifted from the vowel in the suffix (*variants, variation; sacraments, sacramental*).

Additional Spelling Demons

To the words in 29a that you should know without fail, add the following. Your instructor may assign them for special study.

they're	choose	equipped	led
there	choice	affect	lonely
occurring	performance	tries	preferred
occurrence	similar	tried	surprise
definitely	profession	forty	explanation
define	unnecessary	fourth	fascinate
believe	began	criticism	immediate
belief	beginner	criticize	interpretation
occasion	beginning	apparent	thorough
writing	controlled	sense	useful
description	controlling	conscious	noticeable
precede	argument	studying	noticing
referring	arguing	varies	probably
success	proceed	category	imaginary
succeed	procedure	embarrass	marriage
original	achieve	excellent	prejudice
conscientious	achievement	repetition	disastrous
accommodate	controversial	consistency	passed
comparative	possess	prevalent	past
decision	heroine	intelligence	acquire
experience	heroes	mere	busy
prominent	opportunity	opinion	Negroes
pursue	paid	possible	among
shining	villain	ridiculous	height
practical	accept	summary	character
woman	acceptable	attendant	hypocrisy
acquaintance	predominant	attendance	operate
exaggerate	independent	difference	planned
incidentally	particular	recommend	athletic
disappoint	technique	appearance	challenge
desirability	transferred	convenience	fundamentally
knowledge	discipline	you're	quantity
ninety	basically	familiar	accidentally
personal	conceive	suppress	liveliest
personnel	considerably	where	philosophy
than	psychology	whose	speech
then	psychoanalysis	realize	synonymous
principal	analyze	really	conceivably

*Correct the misspelling and consider whether a principle
of English spelling or the violation of a specific
rule is involved.*

Writing can and should be free of misspellings. Spelling is easy for some people, but very hard for others, including many good students. In fact, some of the most intelligent people have trouble learning to spell. But spelling can be learned, especially if the writer will take the trouble to understand the spelling system, will diagnose his own spelling problems (see the diagnostic tests, above), and will work at the job systematically. Some faulty spelling results from temperament, but even habits can be changed. Carelessness probably accounts for more misspellings than anything else, but people can learn to be careful, and quite easily. Some spelling can readily be corrected by rule; for the most useful rules see **26c–26g** and the tests above. The way *not* to learn to spell is to go on looking up the same words again and again, and forgetting them at once. Misspellings have reasons behind them; one of the best ways to learn to spell is to identify the reasons and eliminate them.

26c Capitals   **Cap, lc**

Capitalize according to accepted conventions.

In English, most capitalization follows a clear rule, which is simple although exacting: *Capitalize any word that is a proper name.* If little Mary says to her father, "Give me some ice cream, Daddy," *Daddy* is capitalized because it is his name, at least so far as Mary is concerned. If Mary's mother says, "Ask your daddy to give you some ice cream," *daddy* is not capitalized because *daddy* is not now Mr. John Jones' name. Mrs. Jones is merely recognizing Mary's parent and that fathers are common phenomena. Similarly, in *Jackson Union High School*, the words *high* and *school* are capitalized because they are parts of a proper name, but the same words would not be capitalized in "I attended high school," because they are not now part of a name, even though the writer is thinking of only one high school. In "I lived in the South," *South* is capitalized, but the same word is not capitalized in "I went south."

Some words are capitalized by convention; words designating a country or race are capitalized (*Yugoslavia, Britain*). The following are capitalized: the pronoun *I*, the first word of a sentence or of a line of poetry, and the first letters of the principal words in a title (see **26j**). References to the deity are usually capitalized, and initials and abbreviations may be capitalized (see **26i**). Words that have been proper names, but have come into common use, are not capitalized (*The word* quisling *is derived from a Norwegian, Vidkung Quisling*). If in doubt, consult a good dictionary.

*Hyphenate, join, or leave as separate words in accordance
with modern practice, consulting a good dictionary if
necessary.*

Compounding causes trouble because it is partly logical, partly arbitrary, and is constantly changing. Consider the airplane. It was invented as a device to fly on air with one or more planes and was accordingly described as an *air plane*. When it acquired a sort of identity of its own it became an *air-plane* and now, using parabolas, not planes, for wings and relying so much on jet propulsion that it has less and less use for air, it is an *airplane*. This process has been completed in thousands of words (*midnight*), and is in process in others (*mid-gut*). Logic influences usage, but current practice is often arbitrary (*post office, courthouse*), and if in doubt, the writer must consult a dictionary. In general, hyphenation is avoided in nouns except for (1) newly made nouns as above, and (2) combinations that would otherwise be confusing (*He figured the come-and-go of the metal.*).

Many words not hyphenated in the dictionary are hyphenated or left separate by standard practice as follows:

1. Verbs and adjectives are hyphenated when they are newly formed from two or more words (*Air-season the lumber*). We write *airline* hostess because airline has become a word, but *air-line railroad* because a straight road can be said to follow an *air-line*.

2. Modifiers in series are not hyphenated if the former can be thought of as modifying the latter (the *slowly turning roast*, but a *slow-turned roast*).

3. When alternative words enter into a compound, the hyphen follows each alternative (*four- and six-point* bucks).

Compounds with *self* are usually hyphenated (*self-conscious, self-help*), although not if the word *self* has a suffix (*selfless*). Prefixes that are not also words are usually not hyphenated (*midsummer, nongovernmental*) except before capitalized words (non-*Communist*).

---

*Use the standard plural form, distinguishing between
plurals and possessives, consulting a good dictionary
if necessary.*

Plurals: commonly the plural is formed by adding *-s* (*days*). If the sound of the plural adds a syllable, and the word does not end in *e*, *-es* is added (*masses*). A few archaic plurals survive (*deer, oxen*) for which a dictionary can be consulted. Words recently borrowed and ending in *o* follow the rule (*radios*), but older words add *-es* (*potatoes*). In a few words ending in *f* or *fe*, the *f* changes to *v*, sometimes with an added *e* (*hoof, hooves*). Symbols and words out of context form the plural by adding *'s* (*two p's*). For most words ending in *y*, the *y* is changed to *i* before the plural is added; for examples and exceptions, see table 8 above.

Plurals from languages other than English cause trouble partly because in the original language plurals are made differently than in English, and the form used in English may be unusual or changing. For example, *agenda* comes from Latin; it is plural, meaning things to be done. But it looks like an English singular, and hence a new plural is developing, *agendas*. In Latin, the singular is *agendum*, and accordingly a third English plural has developed, *agendums*. Something similar is happening with *data*, plural of the Latin *datum*, and many more, such as *alumnus, alumni; alumna, alumnae; cactus, cacti; jinn, jinni*. All this is so complicated and even so shifting that most of us can only rely on a good dictionary.

26f Numbers   **Num**

*Follow standard form for numbers, spelling them
out if necessary.*

Numbers that can be written in two words are spelled out in standard English; accordingly, all numbers one hundred and below are written. Two sorts of exceptions warrant notice: (1) If several numbers are used in a passage and at least one is large, all are written in figures, and (2) figures are used in certain standard contexts, in dates, addresses, bibliographical material, and in complicated decimals and percentages. Numerals are not used to open a sentence, and numbers are not written both as figures and words except in legal documents.

26g Apostrophes, Possessives, Contractions   Apos; Poss; Cont

*Revise, using apostrophes accurately to mark possessives
or omissions, and using contractions consistently.*

The apostrophe marks an omission in a standard contraction (*doesn't the war of '76*) or in dialect (*goin', prob'ly*), but since the possessive form was mistakenly supposed to involve an omission, the apostrophe has become the usual mark of the possessive, the apostrophe preceding the *s* in the singular (*the cat's meow*) and following it in the plural (*the cats' meows*). Nouns of specification follow the rule for possessives (*a year's sentence, ten cents' worth*). In compounds, the last element takes the sign of possession (*my brother-in-law's car*), and in phrases indicating joint possession, only the last requires the apostrophe (*Jim and Mary's date*). The following possessive forms do not require the apostrophe: *his, hers, its, ours, yours, theirs*. (NOTE: thus *its* is possessive, *it's* the contraction of *it is*.)

26h Italics

Underline to indicate italic type in accordance with modern practice.

Italic type, indicated in manuscript by underlining, is the accepted indication of most titles (see **26j**), the commonest method of indicating foreign words not yet anglicized (*laissez faire*), and a device for marking words used out of context (*so* is to be avoided as a conjunction). For other examples, see **26g**. For many of these uses, quotation marks were formerly standard (see **25i**), but italics are increasing in popularity, except in newspapers, which are mostly set by machines that have no provision for italic type. Italics may also be used for contrast, especially in headings, as in the passage above beginning *Underline to*, and elsewhere in this book—for example, in the explanation of punctuation marks in **25**.

26i Abbreviations

Limit the use of abbreviations in standard writing.

Abbreviations are usually avoided in writing except in lists and in footnotes, bibliographies, addresses, and the like. The exceptions are few: common forms of address used with proper names (*Mr., Mrs., Dr., Jr., Ph.D., S. J.*, and similar designations, but not *Rev., Sen., Gov., Prof.*, or *Pres.* in formal writing); *Before Christ* and *Anno Domini* when used with a date (*B.C., A.D.*); standard abbreviations when used in informal, technical, or business writing (*cf., e.g., no. etc.*); some government agencies and groups commonly known by their initials (*NATO, CIO, NLRB*). Except in footnotes, bibliographies, and the like, the following are spelled out: states and countries (*New York, United States*), details of publication (*volume, page*), addresses (*avenue, street*), months and days (*March, Tuesday*), business terms and others not specifically excepted (*company, mountain, saint*). Contractions (*I'm, doesn't*, and symbols for *and*) are inappropriate in formal writing (see **26**).

26j Titles

Use the standard form for a title.

The title of any brief piece of writing, including a theme, is written toward the top of the first page, centered, and separated from the body of the composition by a blank line if handwritten, by at least four spaces if typed. Titles of longer works are centered on a title page. Principal words, usually all except articles and prepositions, are capitalized, but a title at the head of a composition is not underlined or enclosed within quotation marks. When titles are quoted, the older practice was to treat them as quotations, but in the best modern practice, titles are printed in italics, indicated in manuscript by underlining. There is one exception—a brief work that is part of a collection. For example, a poem cited in a sentence with the name of the collection from which it is taken or an article in a magazine is enclosed within quotation marks and the inclusive work printed in italics. For examples of titles, see **24b**.

26k Word Division   **Div**

Divide words in accordance with standard practice,
consulting a dictionary in doubtful cases.

Except in print, which is rigid, division of words is to be avoided. The rules are complicated enough so that, if words are to be divided, most writers must consult a dictionary, but a few rules will handle most words. The hyphen is always on the first line, not the second. Words are divided by syllables. No word should be divided so that fewer than two letters appear on either line. Double consonants are usually separated by the hyphen unless the two letters represent one sound (hy-phen). Consonants usually attach to following vowels (di-vine), but prefixes and suffixes are generally kept intact (dis-arm).

26A   Revise the following passages using appropriate devices for manuscript form and copy the corrected passages into the space after each paragraph in the order in which they occur.

1   Apparently, tallness is worth money, according to an insurance co. in philadelphia, Pa, in a survey covering two hundred and seventy thousand men, thought they found correlation between the size of the insurance policies and the size of the men. Those who averaged 6 ft. 4 in. in height carried insurance which averaged 8180 dollars each; whereas the 5-footers averaged four thousand nine hundred seventy-nine dollars ($4,979) or approximately $200 an in. In another study salesmanagers averaged 5 ft. ten in.; whereas salesmen averaged only five foot nine inch. Bishops averaged 5′ 10½, but rural preachers averaged only 5′ 8¾″.

2   According to a column in the new York times called national pastime, a sort of baseball has been played for 100's perhaps 1000's of years. A monument in canterbury cathedral shows a youth, presumably a norman, holding a bat and seemingly about to throw a ball. The statue dates from about a. d. twelve-fifty, and some authorities trace baseball to approximately three thousand b. c. The longest game in major-league history was played in the national league, may one, nineteen twenty, when the dodgers then still in Brooklyn but not yet known as the bums, battled the Boston braves to a 1 to 1 tie in 26 innings. In the shortest Big League game the New York and Philadelphia national league teams played at the polo grounds Sep. 28 1919. The time was fifty-one minutes; the score New York six; Philadelphia, one. The *Times* records the first game played for commercial purposes as follows: the first admission charges to a baseball game were inaugurated at Fashion race Course on Long Island in 1859; Brooklyn played New York and 1500 spectators paid fifty cents each to see the game.

3   Geoffrey Chaucer, 1345?–1400, made his monk praise hunters, saying he would not give what he called a pulled hen for the text which, as the middle english has it, says thei ben nat holy menn; but not all writers have been admirers of hunters. Bernard Shaw, the british playwright, who delighted his audiences with plays like saint joan and the devil's disciple, insisted that the man who uses a camera or an artist's canvas to preserve wild beasts in their native liberty is, as the playwright put it, a thousand times a better sportsman than the malignant idiot who shoots them and gets photographed sitting on the corpse. Similarly, dr. Samuel Johnson, author of rasselas, lives of the poets, and the famous work he called The Dictionary seems to have had no admiration for hunters. "it is very strange and very melancholy," he said, "that the paucity of human pleasures should persuade us ever to call hunting one of them." On the other hand, homer, supposedly the author of two ancient greek works, the iliad and the odyssey, wrote, "It is wiser to go killing wild deer on the mountains than to do battle against your betters."

4   He quoted the following passage from the new York Times magazine: the rev. henry v. sattler of mission church, roxbury, mass., discussing the kinsey report on women, said, "you can't put love and spirituality on an ibm card." I told him I had never heard of rev. sattler, and that i did not trust these machines mfg. by big cos.

5   No doubt horace greeleys advice Go west, young man," was pertinent in it's Day, when the USA was mainly an Agricultural Country, and the west was full of un-tamed land. Our's, however, is the Agr of the *knowledge explosion*, the Era of the computer, so that the movement is now away from the Land, back to the Citys. It was also the day before the space age blight hit Seattle, Wa., and before LA and san Francisco, Cal., became the Centers of great smog producing Communities. Now the advice might better be, go South, or wherever they still have "fresh air and clean water."

26B In each of the following sentences underline the one word misspelled and write it spelled correctly in the blank to the right, first looking it up in the dictionary.

1 The principal said that it was alright for the laboratory to be used for studying grammar.

2 Too many athletic events were accidently scheduled for the week.

3 The woman tryed to commit suicide after listening to the criticism of her chief.

4 The professor seemed to loose his sense of humor after forty appearances of similar familiar themes.

5 It occurred to many citizens that the government had had to little experience in foreign affairs.

6 In the beginning we benefited from the recommendations.

7 The prejudices of the heroes embarassed their friends.

8 Every arguement in the parliament that day was presented in a fascinating speech.

9 As soon as the hall was quite, I began to look for an opportunity to escape.

10 The character of a villian cannot always be described successfully.

11 My acquaintance with business did not affect my dicision to marry.

12 I did not believe that the professor had lead a very happy existence in such an environment.

13 Many restaurants possess separate dining rooms which are convenent for small parties.

14 I did not know untill too late that her mother had been lonely during her visit.

15 I was willing to reccommend him to the hotel, but I could not get accommodations for him immediately.

16 To many of the cooks their were no adequate principles concerning the preparation of excellent broth.

17 The writer had not received sufficient compensation for the tragedy he had writen.

18 I was conscious of no definite rule that preformances should begin at eight o'clock.

19 Certain criticisms exagerated the differences which finally developed among the players.

20 The experience of truely working together was pleasant for everyone.

21 I said, "Your arguing about nonsense because your ideas are similar."

22 The new military personal were allowed few privileges.

23 I do not carry loose change in my pocket for fear of loosing it.

26C   The following sentences contain errors in spelling, particularly in compounding, plurals, and use of the apostrophe. Underline all misspelled words and write them correctly in the blanks to the right. If you are uncertain, be sure you understand the principles involved, restudying the appropriate sections above. (Your instructor may require that you write after each revised word the number of the section that treats the principle.)

EXAMPLE: Mother *didnt* put me in the *go cart*.   *didn't / gocart*

1   "After all, " I said, "its its kitten."

2   The author of hamlet was born in no hamlet.

3   I cant understand why he say's cant-hook is cant.

4   Being already an hour late, the slowly-moving moving van irritated the mover's.

5   Glancing down Skid Row, I observed that the perrenial down-and-outers were still down and out.

6   I would have had the days only home run if I hadn't been out run to home plate just when the game seemed to be ours.

7   I dug the doctor's half moldly onions, which had been half frozen in the seasons early frost.

8   I learned to make home made bread in home-economics classes'.

9   I have worked for more than an hour, and I haven't yet found all of the two authors' mistakes.

10   Ones troubles may be taken lightly by his older sisters' friends'; Mary's and Jane's school chums referred to James's sacroiliac pains as Jims jim jams.

11   Its not yet obvious to our boys gang that the back-to-school movement dooms its less-work-and-more-ice-cream-program.

12   Today coach Day decided to take a day coach for a two day trip.

13   The so called two by six is so called because it is two by six inches.

14   The assistant superintendent insisted that his Yaqui Indian government wards could do three, five and seven strand plaiting and did so in their day-to-day routine as recorded in the Fort-Yaqui record-charts.

15   The air-line officials, speaking for the air line, insisted on air hardened steel but rejected air seasoned lumber.

16   The diatetics-expert rolled the baby beef liver in wheat-germ.

17   The boy wonder driver made a left turn at a no left turn intersection and stopped beside a no parking sign in Twenty Second Street twenty blocks from his destination, the school-house.

26D By using manuscript devices such as capitalization and italics, along with punctuation, write each of the following sentences in two different ways so as to produce two different meanings.

EXAMPLE: hear it pop

a *Here it pop.*

b *Here it, Pop?*

1 see it go pop pop

a _____

b _____

2 pop pop see it go pop

a _____

b _____

3 does pop go pop

a _____

b _____

4 tom crashed into the house mother

a _____

b _____

5 mum mum is the word

a _____

b _____

6 the word mum is short

a _____

b _____

7 did you get the milk bill

a _____

b _____

8 how can you miss smith

a _____

b _____

9 what would you like to eat ladies

a _____

b _____

10 okay bill me for the steak

a _____

b _____

26E Write in the blanks after each of the following sentences any words that should be in italics. Not all blanks will be filled.

1 He said that now was an important word in the sentence and he would not eliminate it. _____ _____

2 She decided that what was savoir faire to a Frenchman might be just plain horse sense to her. _____ _____

3 The teacher said that that that that that boy used should have been omitted. _____ _____

4 He could remember how to spell difficult words like innuendo and supersede because he knew their origins. _____ _____

5 The teacher wrote good at the end of the paper even though much of the work was poor. _____ _____

26F Each of the following contains two errors in capitalization. Write the words you think should be changed correctly in the blanks after each sentence.

1 When he was learning to play the spanish guitar, his mother and father often wished he had taken up russian roulette instead. _____ _____

2 My mother entered College when I did and started a major in Psychology along with regular courses in science, languages, and social studies. _____ _____

3 The Student Council was the only instrument of Government in which all Classes from freshman to senior were represented. _____ _____

4 The New York Mets Baseball Team was again expected to win the championship of the Eastern Division. _____ _____

5 When Father first settled on the farm in Lassen County, my Mother talked only of the east and the chance of returning to it. _____ _____

Objectives: (1) To develop a sense for varieties of
language in modern English usage. (2) to learn to
apply this understanding in particular locutions.

Many people think of "English" as correcting blunders or learning not to
make them. Any user of this book should soon discover, if he did not know
it already, that using the native language well involves much more than
learning to say "smarter than I" rather than "smarter than me." But being
able to use language that will not sound crude, or ignorant, or unintentionally
funny can help. This is called *usage*, the use of language so that it will be
inconspicuously acceptable at the time and place, and will work for the
audience that reads or hears it.

Dialects and Usage

Dialects are healthy in language, and the student has only to cultivate
useful ones. A dialect is a way of speaking that is natural to considerable
bodies of people, and everybody speaks one or more dialects. He has to; it is
part of being human, but many people do not understand this. They think
that a dialect is the way foreigners speak—and the word can be used that
way—but essentially a dialect is a way of speaking, and we all have our ways
of speaking. Within limits, one can change his dialects, but when he does, he
does not stop speaking a dialect. He just learns another dialect or exchanges
an old dialect for a new one.

Mainly, there are two sorts of dialects: (1) geographical dialects, influenced by the place where a person grows up, and (2) social dialects, influenced
by one's personal relationships, by education, by one's family, and the like,
Anything that separates people from one another will be reflected in dialect,
and the main ways people are kept apart are by space or by social barriers.
Englishmen and Americans speak differently for many reasons, but primarily
because there is an ocean between them and has been for a long time. College
professors usually speak differently than do truck drivers. Some college
professors can drive trucks and some truck drivers become college professors,
but on the whole the groups speak differently because they have different
cultural backgrounds and live different sorts of lives.

Most of us need not worry much about our geographical dialects. They
take care of themselves. A student born in Baltimore may be the victim of
a little humor if he goes to school in Chicago, and vice versa, but nobody is
likely to be much penalized because he speaks a dialect of another place. To
many people strange geographical dialect is quite attractive. During the
1960's the United States had three presidents, one who spoke a Massachu-

setts dialect, another who spoke a Texas dialect, and a third who spoke a dialect of Southern California. If dialect hurt any of them, it did not hurt him enough to keep him from being elected.

Social dialects are different. They can hurt a student, or help him. Suppose the student is a Puerto Rican living in a poor section of New York, a Chicano living in a Mexican quarter of the Southwest, an Indian who has grown up on a reservation, a black whose parents moved from a backward part of the South and lives in a northern ghetto. The chances are that his parents could not speak very good English. He will learn their dialect and the dialects of other children, who probably also did not have very good models on which to base their speech.

Such a dialect is likely to be good language, in the sense that it is useful to people. No one need be ashamed of having learned the language of a Cleveland ghetto or of migrant agricultural workers. But people who know only such a dialect will be penalized if they try to get and hold certain jobs or move among educated people.

This evident prejudice is of course unfortunate. People should not be penalized because of the language they learned as children, but they will be. That is the fact, and while one may want to work to change things, to encourage people to be more considerate of their fellow men, the first job of any student who has not learned standard English naturally is to learn it as best he can. Anyone who expects to have a responsible place in the modern world needs to be able to use a standard dialect, even if he has to learn a second way of speaking in addition to the one he learned naturally.

That some people are penalized for their dialects may be unjust, but it is human enough. There are fashions in language as there are in clothes and hair. Sixty years ago all girls wore their hair long, and they were not decent unless they did. Then they bobbed their hair and curled it, and any girl with long hair was considered funny. At this writing, long, stringy hair is in fashion again, but human nature being what it is, one of these days girls will be cutting off their hair once more. Language goes through such fashions, too.

But there are special reasons why some speech is not fashionable and can damage a student who has ambitions. Unpopular ways of speaking are often associated with ignorance, crudity, and even with stupidity. Accordingly, anybody who talks like ignorant persons is likely to be thought ignorant, or not bright enough to learn. Such prejudices may be unfounded; intelligent people learn unpopular dialects, but they are likely to be penalized in their social life and in their pay checks unless they learn standard English.

Of course the generally approved dialect may not be "correct" in any real sense, or the unpopular dialect "incorrect." Consider the past tense of the verb *to eat*. The standard form is *ate*, but some dialects use a term that might be spelled *ett*. If one considers the history of the language, *ett* would be a more logical form than *ate*, but *ate* has become standard and *ett* is now commonly considered "bad grammar." Accordingly, one had better learn to say *ate* not *ett*, if he did not learn it naturally as a child. Similarly, although *ain't* is historically and logically a good word, it is now out of fashion in most parts of the United States. The smart young person will learn not to use it.

This is the problem of usage, how to learn to use the language so that it will serve well as a medium of expression and exchange. No rigid rules are possible; society and language are both too varied and flexible for that. Most speakers and writers who use English well develop a sense for usage and adapt what they say and write almost unconsciously to their varied audiences. But a broad recognition of functional variations and usage levels will help. The following are useful generalizations about usage:

Formal.   Formal English is used for official papers like laws and legal documents, reports of scientific and scholarly research, and the like. All literate persons should be able to read such composition, but not many have to learn to speak or write it.

Informal.   Informal English is the serious means of communication of cultured people. It is the kind of writing likely to appear in the better books and magazines and in the serious discussions of educated people. If a good college student cannot handle this language, he should try to learn to.

Colloquial.   This is the language of everyday talk—the word *colloquial* is related to words like *vocal* and *voice*. In this use it can be thought of as meaning "suited to talking." It is, of course, very useful language, but may not be precise, controlled, permanent, or current enough for writing.

Vulgate or *nonstandard.*   Roughly speaking, this is what is often called "bad grammar," or "slang," words and ways of saying things that are either out of fashion or have never become accepted as good informal or colloquial English. Actually, such words and constructions are not very numerous compared with what is called "good grammar," but at first glance they seem numerous, and some students will have to learn one by one to avoid them. The more common have been brought together in the Glossary that follows. The student can expect the instructor to refer him to one of these usages simply by writing *Glos* in the margin.

Glossary

a, an   Alternative forms of the indefinite article, with the choice determined by sound. *A* is used before words beginning with a consonant sound (*a liberation movement*), even though the first letter is a vowel (*a university*). *An* is used before words beginning with a vowel sound (*an orbit*). *An* was formerly used before *history* and *historian*, but *a* is now usual. Etymologically, *a* and *an* stem from an old form of *one* and retain some of the meaning of *one*.

above   To be avoided for all but very formal uses like "the above remark."

accept, except   *To accept* means to receive. (*I* accept *your conditions.*) *To except* means to exclude. (*If you travel, the company repays you for business expenditures, but* excepts *personal expenses.*) As a function word, *except* indicates an exception. (*They all came* except *Marilyn.*)

Accusative case See *Objective case.*

Active voice See *Voice.*

actually A broad intensifier, frequently overworked.

A.D. Abbreviation of *Anno Domini*, "in the year of (our) lord," used for dates after the birth of Christ but appropriate only when A.D. and B.C. could be confused. It comes before the number as in *A.D. 50.*

ad Informal shortening for advertisement, inappropriate in formal English.

adapt, adept, adopt *To adapt* is to improve by altering. (*He* adapted *the old brake to fit the new motorcycle.*) *To adopt* is to accept or take as one's own. (*The class* adopted *my plan.*) *Adept* means skillful. (*Soren is so* adept *as a mimic that she can imitate most birds.*)

Adjective Adjectives modify nouns and some noun-like words (*a* hot *afternoon*); see **16b.**

Adverb Various sorts of modifiers have been called adverbs. Some modify a whole sentence or a large part of it. (*Certainly, he is wrong.*) Some modify verbs. (*He spelled* badly.) Some, now often called intensifiers, modify other modifiers (*a* very *bad beginning.*) Many answer such questions as *why, when, where,* and *how.* Many end with *-ly,* but some do not. (*She should come* soon. *He can run* far.) For distinctions between adverbs and adjectives, see **16b.**

advise, advice The first is a verb, the second a noun.

> We *advise* all students to seek good *advice.*

adviser, advisor Both spellings are acceptable; the *-er* ending is more common.

affect, effect The first is a verb, the second either verb or noun.

> The weather does not *affect* the schedule. The *effect* of the schedule is to promote uniformity. We can *effect* a change in the schedule but not in the weather.

agenda A list of matters to be considered or things to be done. It is the Latin plural of *agendum* but is often used as a singular in English with its own added *s* forming the plural, *agendas.*

aggravate In formal English the word means "intensify" or "make worse." Informally, it is used to mean "annoy" or "provoke."

> INFORMAL: The noise *aggravated* her.
> FORMAL: The noise *annoyed* her.
> FORMAL: The old remedy only *aggravated* her disease.

agree Idiomatically we agree *with* others, *to* a suggestion, *on* a program.

alibi Used formally only in the legal sense, evidence that the defendant could not have been present when a crime was committed. Informally it is synonymous with "excuse."

all (of) When followed by a noun, this construction can be improved by deleting the *of.* Retain it when followed by a pronoun.

> He could not win over *all of* them with *all* the charm he could command.

all right, alright Although its use is increasing, *alright* is generally accounted a misspelling of *all right*.

all ready, already The *all* modifies *ready*. *Already* means prior to some specified or understood time.

> The players were *already* on the field, *all ready* for the kickoff.

all the farther (further) Colloquial excess for "as far as."

alumna, alumnus An *alumna* is a female graduate, an *alumnus* is a male. *Alumni* is the plural of *alumnus* and is used for groups including both sexes; *alumnae* is the plural of *alumna*. The Anglicized plurals, *alumnuses* and *alumnas*, are nonstandard.

among, between The formal, and mathematically sound, distinction calls for *between* two and *among* more than two.

> The marbles were divided *between* Jim and Bob. All the marbles were distributed *among* the first-grade boys.

amount, number *Amount* refers to a sum or mass or bulk. *Number* refers to a group made up of separate, countable units. *Number* is a collective noun, singular when applied to a unit, plural when designating individuals.

> A *number* of children were in the room. The *number* of his good deeds is beyond belief. The *amount* of snow that fell was slight.

and which, and who Awkward and unacceptable except when the following clause is coordinate with a previous clause introduced by *which* or *who*.

> NONSTANDARD: The rose was his finest, *and which* he expected to enter in the show.
>
> STANDARD: The rose, which was his finest *and which* he expected to enter in the show. . . .

angle Popular but trite, see **20b,** in expressions like, He's got the right *angle* on money. What's your *angle?*

Antecedent The word or construction that identifies a pronoun or pronominal modifier is called its antecedent (see **17e**).

anxious The restricted, standard meaning is "apprehensive," or "worried," but the word is now often used in the near-contrary sense of "eager."

> FORMAL: He was eager [not *anxious*] to attend the flower show. The patient was *anxious*, anticipating surgery.

anybody, any body; anyone, any one Combined these words make the pronoun form; separate, the first portion becomes a modifier.

> *Anybody* may watch. Was *any body* found?
> *Anyone* can see that. Can *any one* see that?

any more Standard only in the negative use.

> STANDARD: School rules are not strict *any more*.
> NONSTANDARD: Teachers are more permissive *any more*.

anyways Anyway or anyhow is preferred.

anywheres Nonstandard. The *s* should be omitted.

apt See *liable*.

area Loosely, even redundantly, used to refer to a subject of study, a scientific discipline, or a field of activity.

> He was a student of [not in *the area of*] biochemistry.

around Informal when used for *about*.

> There were about [not *around*] twenty of us there.

Articles *a, an*, and *the* are used as determiners to point out nouns (see *a, an*, and *the*). Numerous nouns and noun expressions, including terms for common phenomena, require no article. Plural nouns including all members of a class usually require no article.

> When *autumn* came the hills were ablaze with color. *Birds, bees*, and *flowers* abide by their own rules.

Abstract and general nouns usually need no article.

> *Poetry* and *philosophy* teach the art of *literature*.

as Not standard as a substitute for *that* to introduce a noun clause.

> *It seems to me that* I am mistaken; *not It seems to me as I*. . . . As is nonstandard when used as a subordinating conjunction to suggest cause and effect. "As we were on the fifty-yard line, we had a good view of the play" can be made more precise by substituting for *as* another word—*because* or *since*. *As* is nonstandard also when used as a preposition instead of *like*. See *like*.

as if, as though These conjunctions should ordinarily be followed by a past conditional form, not by a present or past indicative. (*He looks as if he had been through a ringer*.)

as (so) long as Both are acceptable except in expressions involving time or space (see *not . . . as*).

> The lawn is *as* (not *so*) *wide as* the street. He was not gone *so long as* he might have been.

as to Standard at the start of a sentence to point out.

> *As to* your credits, they seem to be in order.

> *As to* seldom suffices as a substitute for *about* or *of*.

> He spoke to Mary *about* [not *as to*] her classwork.

aspect An abused word. See *Jargon*.

at Redundant with *where* (see *where at*).

athletics Plural in form but may be singular.

auto *Car* is the more common short form of *automobile*.

awful, awfully Vague, and overworked, intensives. The formal sense of *awful*, awe-inspiring, is worn thin as *awfully* good or bad.

bad Likely to be confused with the adverb, *badly* (see **16b**).

B.C. Abbreviation of *before Christ*, used with dates that might be confused with those of the Christian era, as in *60 B.C.*

be The verb *be* or *to be* is irregular. The commoner forms are *to be*, infinitive; *being*, present participle; *been*, past participle; *am*, first-person present singular; *are*, second-person present singular and all present plurals; *is*, third-person singular; *was*, first- and third-person past singular; *were*, second-person past singular and all past plurals. *Were* is also used in the subjunctive and conditional moods; see *Mood*. In formal use, *be* is preferred for the imperative and subjunctive.

because   Standard to introduce a modifier, but not a noun clause (see 13c).

> I say "Eh?" because I do not hear well. The reason I say "Eh?" is *that* (not *because*) I don't hear well.

being as, beings as   Nonstandard for *since* or *because*.

beside, besides   *Beside*, a preposition, means "by the side of." Besides may be a preposition or an adverb, meaning "in addition to" or "except."

> He sat beside his mother. The lecture was dull, and besides I needed the sleep.

between   See *among*.

blame   As a verb: *He blames me for the weather.* As a noun: *I accepted full blame.*

blond, blonde   Originally a French word, the feminine *e* is often employed to specify a woman; but *blond* is acceptable as an adjective or a noun without regard to sex.

broke   Informally used to mean out of money, it is not used formally except as a verb.

bunch   Overused, imprecise synonym for group.

burst, bust   In every tense, the verb is *burst; bust* or *busted*, with connotations of insolvency is nonstandard. The meanings of *bust* as a noun are not related to accountancy.

but   In older practice, *but*, when used as a preposition, is followed only by the objective case (*all but him*) but it is now commonly followed by a pronoun in the nominative case, especially when it is part of the subject—"whence all but he had fled."

but, hardly, only, scarcely   In standard English, negative words are avoided with another negative (see *Double negative*).

but that, but what   Both are nonstandard, perhaps because redundant, when used for *that*. But they appear in respectable journals, as in, *There is little doubt but that he will be nominated.*

can, may   In formal speech or writing, *may* refers to permission and *can* to ability. (*May* I go downstairs? I *can* run upstairs.) Informally, *can* is often used in both senses; it may even be essential to distinguish permission from possibility. (*I can do as I like about this but you may have to get permission.*)

can't help but, can't hardly   Double negatives, avoided in standard English.

case   Except in specific uses (*a case at law, a case of ammunition*) a weak term best avoided; see Jargon.

censor, censure, censer   To censor is to scrutinize written material such as wartime news stories, and to remove objectionable content. To censure is to reprimand. A censer is a container for incense.

certain   Often used redundantly—"this certain person" or "that certain development." It can readily be confused with *certain*, meaning sure or exact. *Particular* is preferable.

circumstances   Misused and overused in jargonic writing. Compare:

> He was in *comfortable financial circumstances*. He *had enough money*.

cite, sight, site   One *cites* a reference and *sights* a sail. A *sight* (noun) is seen. One locates a building *site*.

claim   Worn thin. See *Jargon*.

clause   In the most common use, the term *clause* means any part of a sentence that, standing alone, could be a sentence. That is, a clause may be what in this book is called an SVC. See Chapter 12.

cliches   See *Trite expressions*.

Collective noun   A collective noun in singular form indicates an assemblage (a *body* of men, a *swarm* of bees). See **17g**.

Colloquial   From the Latin, *colloquial* describes language appropriate in conversation but not in formal writing.

Comparison of modifiers   See page 27.

complected   Dialectal or colloquial for *complexioned*.

Complete sentence   A sentence is complete if it has a subject, a verb, and a complement if needed. "If needed" are the critical words, and they apply to each element in the SVC; see **12a**.

Conjunctions   Conjunctions reinforce coordination and subordination. *Coordinating conjunctions* join like elements to form complete patterns or parts of patterns (see **17a**). *Subordinating conjunctions* join a dependent clause to something else (see **17c**). For the use of pronouns as conjunctions, see *Pronoun*.

Conjunctive adverb   Conjunctive adverbs connect parallel clauses and, at the same time, modify within a clause (see **17b**).

conscience, conscious   *Conscience* is that faculty which makes one aware of his own morality; *conscious* is an adjective meaning aware.

contact   Used, and overused, as a synonym for *speak to, talk with, get in touch with, call upon*.

continue on   The *on* is redundant and should be omitted.

contractions   *Don't, won't, can't, hasn't, wouldn't* and other similar contractions are acceptable for informal use, not for formal (see *don't; its, it's*).

could of   Unacceptable. Understandable because the *of* sound resembles the *'ve* sound of the contracted *could have*.

council, counsel, consul   In nontheological context, council is an advisory or legislative body, as in *a town council*. To counsel is to give advice, and a lawyer who advises is a counsel. A consul is a governmental official representing his country's interests abroad.

> He was elected to the student council. His counsel was sought. He was American consul in Sao Paulo.

couple   A man and wife are a couple. *Couple* is colloquial when used (with *of*) to mean a few (*a couple of singers, a couple of skiers*).

cute   A vague and unadmired way of expressing approval. "She is cute" may imply that she is *alert, intelligent, nice-looking,* even *saucy* or *impertinent.*

Dangling construction   Subordinate constructions not clearly linked to the SVC pattern are said to dangle; see **16e.**

data   Plural of the Latin borrowing *datum. Phenomena, agenda,* and *strata* are similar plurals. The Anglicized plural *datas* is not yet established and is nonstandard.

date   As a noun, meaning an appointment, and as a verb, meaning to make an appointment, *date* is acceptable in informal use especially when dealing with affairs of the young.

deal   Slang for an arrangement or understanding, a *big deal* may mean a remarkable achievement. *A great deal* is not standard in formal English.

definite, definitely   Vague intensifiers, overworked in expressions like *a definitely big deal.*

Dependent clause   See *Subordinate clause.*

Determiner   Articles like *a, an, the* (which see) and other words like numerals (*six* tennis rackets) are called determiners.

different from, different than   *From* is a preposition and requires an object. (He is *different from us.*) *Different than* introduces an SVC. (The arrangement was *different than* we had expected.)

Direct object   The *direct object* is essential to the transitive verb. In *He mounted the stairs, mounted* is the verb, *stairs* the direct object (see Chapter 12).

do   A verb of multiple uses, it is also an intensifier. (*He* does *have a good mind.*) The word is protean in idiomatic uses.

> Anything will *do.* Whistler *did* a portrait. Early settlers had to *make do* without electricity. We can *do* seventy on this road. He could *do* with more money.

For faulty reference with *do,* see **17f.**

don't   Contraction of *do not* but not acceptable as a contraction of *does not,* even in informal writing or conversation.

> He *does not* (or informally *doesn't,* not *don't*) speak correctly.

Double negative   The double negative is generally disapproved in standard Modern English. The mathematician's axiom that "two negatives make a positive" does not fit the thinking of speakers of English.

> We didn't see anything (not *nothing*) of them.

However, various degrees of a positive idea can be suggested with two negatives.

> The tale *was not* too *improbable.*

doubt   If one *doubts that* the tale is true, he disbelieves it. If one *doubts whether* it is true, he is uncertain.

due to   Although frequently used, *due to* is an unsatisfactory replacement for *because of.*

> The bus was delayed *because* of (not *due to*) bad weather.

each and every A legalism unacceptable in most English.

each other, one another These pairs are commonly used interchangeably; precise writers use *each other* to refer to only two and *one another* to refer to more than two persons.

effect See *affect, effect.*

either, neither One of two is *either*; not one of two is *neither*. Not one of more than two is *not any.*

enthuse Colloquial but disapproved by some writers.

equally as Wordy and confused; to be avoided.

etc. Abbreviation for *etcetera* meaning "and others" or "and the like," to be used sparingly, appropriate when statistics or lists justify abbreviation.

everybody, everyone *Body* is firmly established as a synonym for "person" and, although the words are singulars, both are used also with plural force. As antecedents best usage requires a singular pronoun (*Everybody* or *everyone took his choice*). *Every one* is commonly followed by *of* (*Every one of them knows it*).

exactly Because *exactly* means "exactly," it is difficult to use the word in a positive sense. As a loose filler it is best avoided.

except See *accept.*

expect To *expect* is not to "suppose" or to "suspect."

Expletive construction Use of a satisfactorily weightless word to fill the subject slot—like *it* in "it is my duty to tell you." See **14a.**

extra Nonstandard when used to mean "remarkably," and doubly objectionable in the expression "extra special."

fact, the fact that *Fact* connotes tangible certainty; *the fact that* is generally a roundabout way of saying *that.*

> He realized *that* (not *the fact that*) the day would be long.

factor Worn thin by overuse; see *Jargon.*

famed Amateur and untrained journalists use it, meaning "famous."

farther, further Commonly used interchangeably but precise writing demands *farther* in reference to space, *further* when the idea of something in addition does not involve measurement.

feature Used as a verb meaning "emphasize" or as a noun meaning "that which is emphasized," it is accepted but not admired usage.

fellow Colloquial when used as a synonym for *person, friend, man.*

fewer, less The first refers to number, the second to amount.

> The *fewer* the workmen the *less* they will accomplish.

field Worn to shreds, often meaninglessly redundant, when used in reference to studies, scientific disciplines, professions. See *Jargon.*

figure Colloquial and vague when used to mean *think, calculate, anticipate, expect, suppose, conclude*, etc.

fine Not an adverb. "You did fine," is nonstandard.

fix A word of many nonstandard uses generally connoting making ready for use (*fix your hair, fix the car*), but including other unrelated uses. A *fix* may be a predicament; many uses are nonstandard, including those that refer to an illicit arrangement with law enforcers and an injection of heroin.

folks Colloquial for family members, or for people in a small community.

formally, formerly The first means "in a formal manner," the second, "previously."

funny Not a useful synonym for *strange, unusual, erratic*.

Genitive cases See **26g**

Gerund A verb form having at least one unit ending in *ing* and usable as a noun. For pronouns used with gerunds, see *Possessive with gerund*.

get, got When used to mean *must* or *ought* (*He's got to go*) *got* is redundant and colloquial. It is also colloquial in many other expressions: *I get you, The pain gets you in the elbow, Get wise*, "Get going."

good An adjective often confused with the adverb *well*.

good and As an intensifier (*He got good and wet*) it is nonstandard.

gotten Past participle of the verb *get*, it is less used than *got*.

guess Acceptable as a synonym for "think," "believe," "suspect" by most lexicographers, but not by many English professors.

Hackneyed expressions See *Trite expressions*.

had of Wasteful; *had* conveys the meaning obviously intended.

had ought, didn't ought, hadn't ought *Ought* or *should* will do, instead, and should do.

hang The verb is declined *hang, hung, hung*, except when the object is human; then it is *hang, hanged, hanged*.

hardly See *but, hardly, only, scarcely*.

he or she Usage is changing. Perhaps because of the women's liberation movement, this expression is gaining favor as equivalent of *one*; he was formerly the standard inclusive pronoun with antecedents of both sexes.

healthful, healthy *Healthful*, conducive to health; *healthy* possessing health.

heap, heaps It may take a great deal to make a heap, but *heap* or *heaps* are not acceptable synonyms for *a great deal*.

heighth Save a letter! The spelling is *height*.

honorable A title of respect for office holders, it is usually preceded by *the* and calls for use of the full name and, often, the office: *The Honorable John Doe, U.S. Senator from Whatstate*, not *the Hon. Doe*.

however This, and other conjunctive adverbs, tend to modify the entire predication when they introduce it. See **17b**.

human An adjective suited to modify a limited number of nouns: creature, animal, being. *Human* is now becoming a noun in its own right.

idea An abused and overworked word, *idea's* meaning is likely to be better conveyed by a more carefully chosen word.

> My *hope* (not *idea*) is to become wealthy. I was annoyed by his *assumption* (not *idea*) that I would take part in his skulduggery.

Idiom Idioms are expressions developed by use to have meanings not dictated by the literal sense of their individual words; *do away with* and *do in* have meanings reflecting language customs. Unidiomatic writing violates these customs.

if, whether   Both imply uncertainty, but *whether* also implies the existence of an alternative.

> I will go if he does. I will go whether he goes or not.

imply, infer   The writer or speaker *implies,* the reader or hearer *infers.*

> Uncle John *implied* that he really was Santa Claus. The children *inferred* that this Santa Claus was really Uncle John.

in, into   *In* carries the connotation of "within"; *into* suggests movement from without. To say that "the boy wades *in* the brook" is not the same as to say that "the boy wades *into* the brook."

in back of   If it means anything, it means "behind," which is preferred.

in regards to   Nonstandard for "in regard to."

Incomplete sentence   See *Complete sentence.*

Independent clause   See Chapter 12. All SVC's not classified as subordinate clauses are considered independent.

Indirect object   See Chapter 12. It can complete the SVC pattern.

> They wished John (*indirect object*) luck (*direct object*).
> He gave his dog (*indirect object*) a kick (*direct object*).

Indirect question   See **25a.** The direct question demands a question mark; the indirect—often merely a statement that a question was asked—does not. The pitch test aids in identification: if the voice rises at the end, a question mark is called for. If the question is indirect, the voice is not raised.

> DIRECT: The judge asked, "Are you guilty?"
> INDIRECT: The judge asked him if he was guilty.

> For verbs in indirect questions, see *Tense.*

individual   Abused and overused as a synonym for "person," this word can seldom be defended as a noun but is most useful as an adjective and adverb.

> He greeted every *person* (not *individual*) with a handshake.
> He greeted every *person individually* (*adverbial use*) with a hand shake. He greeted each *person* as an *individual* (noun use). Each *individual person* (adjectival use) differs from every other.

infer   See *imply.*

inferior than   *Inferior to* is meant, is standard, and shorter.

ingenious, ingenuous   The *ingenious* person is intellectual, a problem solver; the *ingenuous* person is open and overtrusting.

inside of   The *of* is excess baggage; so is it in *outside of.*

Intensifier   Words that do not much modify the meaning of a head word, but indicate degree or heighten quality, such words as *very, extremely,* and *deeply,* are now called intensifiers.

invite   The verb is *invite,* the noun *invitation.*

irregardless   Since *ir-* is a negative prefix and *-less* a negative suffix, this is a double negative and nonstandard.

it *It* is too often "the lost pronoun" without antecedent and without excuse. "It says in the Bible"—meaning "the Bible says," is a usage common in colloquial speech but is avoided by careful writers.

its, it's The first is the possessive form of *it*, as *his* is of *he*; the second is the contraction of *it is*.

it's me, it is I The standard *it is I* commonly becomes *it's me* in casual speech; it is not acceptable in formal use except in quotations.

Jargon, journalese *Jargon* is vague, wordy, overstated. *Journalese* is an invidious term implying an origin for *jargon*. Such words as *case, condition, circumstances, spectacular, tremendous*, and *great* are favored by writers of jargon.

JARGONIC: The factors in the case were in regard to the university administrator having replied in the negative.

REVISION: The dean said no.

JARGONIC: Priming for the terminal, knockout windup of the hardwood season, State's tournament-bound hoopsters roared through their pennant-planning by giving final checkups to their get-the-points strategies.

REVISION: State's basketball squad used it's last pre-tournament workout running through its basic offensive plays.

kind, sort These words, synonym of *species*, are distinctive, although not unique, in that the singular form is modified by *this* or *that*, the plural by *these* or *those*. In colloquial use, the plural modifier converts the singular form to plural (*these kind*).

kind of, kind of a Colloquial, meaning "somewhat," "rather."

lay Forms may be confused with those of *lie*; see *lie, lay*.

lead, led Present and past forms of the verb *to lead*. To use *lead* as the past form, a common error, is to confuse the metal and the verb.

less For the distinction between *less* and *few*, see *fewer*.

let, leave Where a sense of permission is implicit, *let* is preferred (*Let sleeping dogs lie*); otherwise either may be used: *Leave it* (or *let it*) *alone*.

liable, apt, likely Used interchangeably in speech, these words nonetheless have different meanings. *Liable* carries the sense of liability; *apt* that of aptitude, *likely* that of likelihood.

> She is *liable* to slip. He is *apt* to have the answer right. Rain is *likely* tonight or tomorrow.

lie, lay "*Lay* it down, then let it *lie*" illustrates standard use of these two words. *Lie*, an intransitive verb, has no object. *Lay*, a transitive verb, requires an object. (*I lie down to sleep*, but *I lay me down to sleep*.) The confusion arises in part because *lay* is the infinitive and present form of the transitive verb, but the past of the intransitive verb.

The forms of the transitive verb are *lay, laid, laid*. (*The bricklayer lays bricks; he laid them yesterday*, and *he has* laid *them for years*.) The forms of the transitive verb are *lie, lay, lain*. (*She lies in bed every morning; she lay there yesterday, and she* has lain *there every morning for weeks*.)

like, as Users of standard English insist that *like*, being a preposition, must have an object—*like* English. The same persons insist that *as* is a conjunction leading into an SVC expression—*as* this does. Recently, the use of *like* has increased as a conjunction (*Like* I told you, but is not acceptable in formal English, and is usually not approved at informal levels.

line The flexibility of this word has led speakers to invent and employ a number of nonstandard uses.

> He flattered and deceived her (not *fed her a line*). What do you *do for a living*? (not *What's your line?*) The record was *similar to* a box score (not *along the lines of a box score*).

literally Synonymous with *in reality*, the word is too-often used to mean almost the opposite. The person who says "I'm *literally* dead," probably means that he is rather tired.

loan Until a generation ago, *loan* was a noun and *lend* was its companion verb. Careful users of English still make the distinction.

locate Widely used, but not always accepted in the sense to *take up residence*, as in: *He located in San Francisco.*

lot(s) of Colloquial for *a number of* or *many*.

love Implying deep emotion, *love* is not an acceptable synonym of *like*.

mad In formal usage, not accepted as a synonym of *angry*; common in informal use in this sense, but widely discouraged.

Malapropism A mistake, usually humorous, in the use of a word, from Mrs. Malaprop, a character in Sheridan's play, *The Rivals*, whose "allegory [for *alligator*] on the banks of the Nile" is only one of many blunders.

math Short for mathematics but not common in formal writing.

may A verb having the past or subjunctive form *might*; it implies permission or possibility.

> He *may* go today. (*He might go today* is common but often disapproved.) Mother says I *may* go too. He *might* have gone yesterday. We climbed the hill so he *might* see the river.

might of Use *might have*; for an explanation, see *could of*.

mighty Dialectal as a synonym of *very*. (*That's* very [*not* mighty] *good*.)

Mood English grammarians recognize five moods that can be expressed in the verb; indicative, interrogative, imperative, conditional, and subjunctive. The first states a fact: *Gerry wears a crash helmet.* The second asks a question: *Where is Jane?* The third gives an order: *Sit up straight.* The fourth marks conditions: *If you want to make the squad you must train down.* The fifth, the subjunctive, is disappearing as a distinction in English but survives in some formal use in a few special forms—*be, were*, and the third person singular without the *-s* ending. These forms survive in the following: (1) In an if-clause expressing "a condition contrary to fact," something impossible or highly improbable (*If I* were *you I would shoot myself. Even if he* were *to inherit a million, what good would it do him?*); (2) in that-clauses expressing a wish, a command, or a request (*The regents ordered that the library* be *kept open on weekends*).

moral, morale *Moral* implies righteous behavior, *morale* is a noun referring to attitude, usually an optimistic attitude. *Moral* may be either an adjective or noun, *morale* a noun only.

more than one Although apparently clearly plural, *more than one* is accepted as singular when sense requires it.

> *More than one of* us *is* amused. If there *are more than one* for each player, divide the extras among the substitutes.

most Not standard as a shortening of *almost* (*Almost* [not *most*] *everybody*).

muchly Nonstandard as a substitute for *much*.

must As a noun (*This is a must*), the word is overworked.

myself *Myself* has long been a reflexive pronoun (*I blame myself*) and an intensive pronoun (*I, myself, will see to it*), but it is now widely used in place of *me*. (*They elected Marion and myself.*) Many writers consider the use for *me* an affectation.

nature Often jargonic and redundant. (*Lee's assignment was difficult* [not *of a difficult nature.*)

neither Refers to "not either" of two. See *either*.

neither...nor Like *either...or*, these are correlatives and in standard usage *nor* appears after *neither* as does *or* after *either*.

> He could *either* fish *or* cut bait. She could *neither* fish *nor* cut bait.

nice Colloquial when used as a synonym for *friendly, kindly, generous, affable*, and the like. *Nice* may imply precision.

> Careful writers must make *nice* distinctions between and among words.

nice and As an intensifier, this is nonstandard.

> The breeze was *pleasantly* (not *nice and*) cool.

Nominative case See *Subjective case*.

none As a number, *none* is fewer than one, but in writing it takes a singular or plural verb according to the sense.

> None of his generation is now alive. None of us are (or is) going.

not as, not so Interchangeable. *Not so* is preferred by some.

Noun The conventional definition that "a noun is the name of a person, place, or thing" will not stand examination. *Green* is the name of a color, but it often functions as a modifier; many verbs can be names of actions. But if nouns are hard to define, they are easy to recognize. They are the kinds of words that can serve as subjects, and all native speakers know what parts of sentences are the subjects.

nowheres *Nowhere* is the word.

Objective case, object case Case form for objects can now be observed only in some pronouns (see *Pronoun*). Theoretically, the following are in the objective case: the head word in a prepositional phrase (*among them*); all complements not felt to be subjective (*I detest him, I gave her the memo*); and most subjects and objects of verbals.

of   A splendid word in its place but its place is not where *have* is meant. See *could of, might of.*

off of, off from   *Off* is what is meant. Omit the *of* or *from*, but a traveler may be *off to* his destination.

on   May be redundant in a date.

> The meeting will be on Friday. I may see you (not *on*) Friday.

one   The formal third-person pronoun. To avoid stiffness some writers substitute *he* or *his* after the first use of *one* or *one's.*

out of   Like *off*, *out* usually needs no support from *of*, although *of* occurs in some senses. (*We are out of butter. They are out of my jurisdiction.*)

outside of   *Outside* is better off alone except when *outside of* is used colloquially to mean except.

outstanding   Overworked and common in jargonic writing (see *Jargon*).

over with   Colloquial in the sense of *ended, finished.*

overall   Often jargonic when used to mean "in general" (see *Jargon*).

party   Not, except in legal documents, a synonym for **person** (*an elderly person*, not *an old party*). In the jargon of telephone operators it seems essential.

past, passed   Past means that which has gone before or refers to it; *passed* is a form of the verb *to pass.*

> The *past* is known, the future unknown. He used the *past* tense. The police car *passed* once. We were *passed* by the police.

people, persons   Persons are individual entities, who in a group are people; persons are generally countable. A group of persons or people may be people or a people. The Chinese are a people, and the Chinese and Japanese are Asian peoples.

per-, pre-, pro-   The first prefix, *per-*, usually means "through" or "by" (*per annum, perceive*). *Pre-* means "before" (*preliminary*, and *prelude*). *Pro-* signifies "for" in the sense of "favorably disposed toward" (*pro-reform* as against *anti-reform, proceed*).

> The pin *perforated* the diaphragm. The *preface* may *precede* the foreword. Life is *procreant* and man is a *procreator.*

phase   A useful word when precisely used, especially in the physical sciences, it is too often used vaguely. See *Jargon.*

phenomena   The plural of phenomenon; see *data.*

phone   Shortened form of *telephone*, which is used in formal writing; common in informal use. *Phone up* is nonstandard for *call up* or *ring up.*

picture   An overused word. (*You get the picture? Can you picture that? This is the picture.*) Compare: *Do you understand? Can you imagine* (or *visualize*, or *conceive* of) *that? This is the way matters stand.*

piece   Nonstandard use as a synonym for "short distance."

plenty   Nonstandard as an intensifier (*superb*, or *excellent*, not *plenty cool* or *plenty sharp*).

point   Worn thin by overuse; prefer a more exact word (see *Jargon*).

poorly Dialectal for "in poor health." Prefer a more exact term.

pore, pour Spelling, not meaning, seems to be a growing problem with these two words. The student *pores* [not *pours*] over his textbook while the waitress *pours* his coffee.

Possessive case. See **26g**.

Preposition. See **17d**.

prejudice A noun. With *d* added, the word becomes a modifier. *Prejudiced people have prejudices.*

presence A noun. The corresponding verb is *present*.

> Your *presence* is required. Will you please *be present*?

principal, principle As an adjective, *principal* refers to that which is first, primary, of greatest importance (*the principal person, the principal reason, the principal sum* on which interest is paid). Meanings of the nouns are related (*the high school principal, the lawyer's principal, the principal of the loan,* on which interest must be paid). *Principle,* referring to a law or belief, is always a noun. (*A rascal has no principles.*)

Principal parts Most verb forms can be derived from their principal parts or basic forms, listed in dictionaries: for example, *play, played; begin, began, begun.* Variations like *drug* for *dragged* or *blowed* for *blown* are nonstandard.

prof. Depreciative as a common noun, *professor* is the formal word. The abbreviation may be used only with the full name in standard English (*Prof. John J. Jones*), and is written out in formal English, even in a title.

Pronoun, types and forms Where repetition of the same noun would be wearisome or objectionable, pronouns—words serving for the nouns—are used to serve the functions of nouns. Pronouns must agree in sex, number, and case with the antecedent noun that, for the reader's guidance, must be clearly identified with the chosen pronoun. First-person pronouns, *I, me, my* or *mine* are matched by the second-person forms, *you, you, your,* or *yours,* and those of the third person, *he* or *she* or *it, him* or *her* or *it,* and *his, her, hers,* or *its.* The first-person plurals are *we, us, our* or *ours.* The second-person plurals are identical with the singular forms, and the third-person plurals are *they, them, their,* or *theirs.*

Some personal pronouns preserve a distinction that has been lost in the noun, that between the subject or nominative case, forms that can be used for the subject (*I, he, she, we,* or *they see*) as against the object or accusative case, which can be used for objects: The spy saw *me, him, her, us,* or *them.* For the possessive case, see **26g**.

The relative pronouns *who* and *whom* are readily confused. A guiding rule is that *who* will be the subject in any SVCS in which it occurs, *whom* will be the object of the verb, or of a preposition. *About whom, from whom, with whom, of whom, to whom* are all standard constructions. But when the preposition and the pronoun are separated, the writer may miss their connection. "*Who* are you going to talk with about this?" may not be recognized as equivalent of "With *whom* are you going to talk about this?" And since *who,* the subject form, appears in the subject position, it is growing in acceptance. *Whose* is the genitive form of *who* (*The girl* whose *books I had uninten-*

tionally picked up was waiting at the door), but since English has no possessive form for *which, whose* is used for animals in all but formal writing (*The whippet* whose *foot was injured in the starting gate started to lose ground*). For relative or subordinating pronouns and relative conjunctions, see **17e**.

Indefinite pronouns—like *anyone, everyone, everybody, everything, each, any, all*—and demonstrative pronouns—*this, that, such, these, those*—do not change form. For agreement with indefinite pronouns, see **17g**; for distinctions between *anyone* and *any one, everybody* and *every body*, see *anyone, any one; everybody, every body*; for reference of demonstrative pronouns, see **17e**. Reflexive pronouns (*I blame myself*) and intensive pronouns (*He did it himself*) appear in identical forms. For the use of *myself* instead of *me*, see *myself*.

proved, proven *Proved* has better standing than *proven*, but the two are interchangeable.

providing, provided Historically, *provided* and *providing* had separate uses; compare:

> According to the story, Raleigh threw his cloak into a mud puddle, thus *providing* dry passage. I will buy it, *provided* the price is right.

The use of *providing* is growing, except at formal levels, for both uses.

put across A stretchable, flexible, slippery expression. See *Jargon*.

quite Almost an intensifier, *quite* connotes "*really and truly*" or "*entirely*." A problem may be "*quite* elementary," or a robbed till "*quite* empty." Colloquially it is used to mean "somewhat" or "rather," as in "*quite hot*."

raise May be confused with *rise* (which see). Growers *raise* cattle, oranges, wheat and, of recent decades, parents *raise* children, although purists still use *rear*. Monuments are *raised*, but new buildings *rise*. Old buildings are *razed*.

rate Slang in uses like *That chick doesn't rate with me*.

re Standard in legal and acceptable in business writing to mean "about."

real Colloquial as an intensifier. "A *real* close basketball game" might be better described as one in which the score spread was never more than four points, or simply as a close game.

really A meaningful word, relating to reality or essential truth, it is often used jargonically.

VAGUE: She was really something.	REVISED: She charmed all the men because she was pretty and had an answer for everything.
WEAK: It was really cold.	REVISED: It was well below zero, with a stiff wind blowing.

reason is because See *because* and **13c**.

reason why Redundant because the *why* is implicit in *reason*.

reckon Acceptable in the sense of *accounting*, unacceptable except colloquially in the sense of *guessing, supposing*. It is dialectal in the sense of *agreeing*, "*I reckon so*."

regard, regards In formal and standard usage, *regard* is a useful word. *Regards* is unacceptable in *in regards to*.

Repetition Careless repetition makes writing sound wordy and amateurish. The second *that* in the following represents a common lapse of attention: "The teacher announced *that* if anyone wanted extra help *that* he should see him after class."

respectful, respective Confusion of these words suggests unfamiliarity with the meanings of the suffixes—*ful* and *-ive*. The first conveys the meaning *full of*; the second *relating to* or *of the nature of*. *Respectively* has an idiomatic use indicating order. (*He subpoenaed the father, the mother, and the various children, respectively*.)

reverend Often, like *honorable* (which see), misused in both unabbreviated and abbreviated form. The abbreviation, *Rev.*, is found in standard English only preceding the full name of the divine: *The Rev.* John Doe, but The *Reverend* Mr. Doe (not *Reverend* Doe).

right Acceptable in informal writing as an intensifier—*right now, right away*—but less acceptable as a synonym for *very* as in *a right good meal*.

right on A recent development, rapidly gaining acceptance, but at this writing, still slang or colloquial in various uses.

rise, raise *Rise* means that the subject moves. (The sun *rises*. The people *rise* in rebellion.) *Arise* may replace *rise* but not *raise* (See *raise*).

said Past of *say* or *says*. Not acceptable as a modifier except in legal writing, as in: *It was this* (not *the said*) *John Jones*.

same A modifier meaning *this* or *not another* or *identical, same* is standard. As a pronoun, especially as the object of the preposition *in*, it is awkward with a quasilegal sound.

scarcely A negative. See *Double negative*.

seem A word overworked in wordy writing. "If this *seems* to imply...." can be said as well in three words: "if this implies...." *Seem* carries the connotation of *pretence* or *falseness*, which its synonym, *appear*, does not.

seldom ever Unacceptable for *almost never* or *seldom*.

set For confusion with *sit*, see *sit*.

set up Slang for a certain, future, victory or an easy one in the past. Jargonic for an arrangement or organization. Acceptable in technical usages.

shall, will The schoolbook rule calls for *shall* with *I* and *we* to indicate future action, *will* to signify determination, with the roles reversed for the second and third persons.

> I (we) *shall* try to speak correctly; in fact, we *will* speak correctly. You and he *will* try to speak correctly and, if I have my way, you and he *shall* speak correctly.

Although this supposed rule has no historical standing and has never been generally followed, it is insisted upon in some formal writing. *Shall* has some special legal and governmental uses. (*He shall be* hanged until dead.) In general, *should* and *would* follow, in future use, the same pairing practices as *shall* and *will*. However, *should* implies duty and *would* willingness and these are overriding influences.

shape   Colloquial in the sense of athletic training. The training regime had brought him into good *condition* (not *shape*).

should   See *shall, will*.

should of   Nonstandard for *should have* (See *could of*).

show   Technical term in horse racing, colloquial term in "show business," slang term meaning "chance" or "opportunity."

show up   Colloquial in two senses, "to arrive" and "to be exposed." (*Henry didn't* show up *at the meeting. Beulah's story* showed him up *as a fraud.*)

sic.   See abbreviations in Chapter 24.

sign up, sign up for, sign up with   Colloquial in sports and business; not acceptable in formal or most informal English.

Signal words   See Chapter 17.

sit, set   A man *sits*, a court *sits*, but the sun *sets*, and a man *sets* goals. Generally, despite the sun, and broody hens, which also *set, set* is a verb that requires an object. *Sit* does not. We *set* a dish on the table, the law *sets* a speed limit, we *set* ourselves to meet adversity. But we *sit* and talk. Sit has two forms, *sat* sufficing for all the past. *Set* has but the one form, *set*. I *sit* here. I *sat* here yesterday. I *have sat* here for a year. I *set* the plan here and now. I *set* the plan yesterday. I *have set* the plan again and again.

situated   Redundant in *situated in*.

situation   Often redundant, as in *The party was in a losing situation*.

size   Acceptable as an adjective modifier (*This is a size twelve*) but not acceptable as a noun modifier (*She wants it in a size twelve*). It is, however, acceptable as a noun. (*The dress can be had in all sizes from eight to eighteen.*)

so   Overused and carelessly used to join independent clauses; see **16a**.

so as   To be distinguished from so that. See **17c**.

so long as   See *as long as*.

some   Not standard to express approval (a *delicious* [not *some*] dinner!)

somebody's else   See **26g**. The possessive sign goes with the last word, and it is *somebody else's*, maybe your *mother-in-law's*.

sometime, some time   A time other than this is *sometime*; a time of definite but unspecified length is *some time*.

somewhat of   Nonstandard, not even widely used as an idiom.

somewheres   The final *s* is superfluous; nonstandard.

sort   See *kind*.

sort of, sort of a   Colloquial modifiers meaning "similar *to*" or "of a kind or sort," they are too nonspecific to serve a writer well.

speak, speech   Readily confused in spelling.

state   To use *state* as a casual synonym for *say*, or *remark*, or *observe* is to deny the formal quality of the word. To *state* means to make a formal *statement*.

The mayor stated that he would revoke the ordinance.

stationary, stationery   The first is an adjective, the second a quite unrelated noun. A *stationary* engine does not move about. Letter paper used for correspondence is *stationery*. The *e's* in *letter* may serve as a clue to the spelling.

stress   Fear and pain are psychological and physiological forms of *stress;* so are the emphases used in speech. Both kinds have many gradations.

such   Useful as an indefinite pronoun (*as such*); see *Pronoun.* As a vague intensifier it is much overused.

Subjective case   Nouns and pronouns used as subjects or as complements equivalent to the subject (*It is I*) are conceived to be in the subjective or nominative case. The case form is now apparent only in certain pronouns (I, we, he, she, they, who). See *Pronouns* and Chapter 12.

Subordinate clause   A subordinate or relative clause contains a subject and predicate but is not a complete sentence (see Chapter 12). It is introduced by a relative pronoun or conjunction (see *Pronoun*). For punctuation of subordinate clauses, see **25e**.

suspicion   A noun, not a verb; the verb is *suspect.*

sure   Colloquial or dialectal as an intensifier:

> You are *quite,* or *certainly,* or even *surely* (but not *sure*) right.

take and   Generally nonstandard.

take sick   Dialectal.

Tense   Tense, or evidence of time in verbs, is shown partly by phrasal combinations (*am going, will shoot*) and partly by form. The present tense appears without ending in the first person singular (*love, ride*), and the past tense most commonly appears with *-t, -d,* or *-ed* as an ending (*loved, slept*). Dictionaries record irregular forms. The sequence of tense can give trouble; following are sentences that illustrate some of the ways in which tense forms show relationships.

> When the boss *had finished* (past perfect), I *received* (past) my pay. When the boss *has finished* (present perfect), I *receive* (present) my pay.

terrible, terribly   Overused and misused as blanket terms. Carefully used, these words connote terror. Common in several loose uses (*She was terribly funny. I had the flu and felt terrible*). See *Jargon.*

terrific   So extensively used to mean having a superlative quality—in size, in performance, in excellence—the word is likely to be misunderstood in its standard sense: "causing terror."

that   the commonest relative conjunction (*This is the house* that *Jack built*), is often best omitted. (*I said I would go,* rather than, *I said that I would go.*) *That* may be necessary to avoid misreading, as in the following:

> John knew *that* all men, black and white, were considered equal (not *knew all men, black and white . . .*). See **17e**.

that there   Not standard when used as a unit. The *there* is superfluous.

that, which   Relative pronouns with similar uses. However, *that* can be used instead of *who* when the reference is to a person; *which* cannot. See *Pronoun.* Some writers prefer *that* for restrictive clauses, *which* for nonrestrictive; see **25e**.

the   The definite article, *the*, often refers to something distinctive and widely known—*the sea, the sky, the Great White Whale*. When New Yorkers speak of *the* city, they mean New York. New Englanders may mean Boston.

The may identify an object among others of its class. Compare:

> He works in *a* mine. He works in *the* mine I spoke of.

The can refer to something previously mentioned. See above.
The can replace a personal pronoun in referring to part of the body.

> Pat the top of your head with *your* (or *the*) left hand, and rub your stomach with *your* (or *the*) right.

Since *the* often refers to something previously mentioned, it should not be used to introduce a noun new to the context.

> Walking slowly up the road to the cemetery came *a* (not *the*) man with a lunch box.

The would suggest that the man had been previously introduced. Some special uses such as "*the* average man" and generalized ones such as "*the* time of day" call for the definite article.

their, there, they're   The pronunciations are as alike as the spellings are unlike, and the similarity leads to confusion in spelling. *Their* is a pronoun, the possessive form of *they*. (*It is theirs.*) *There* is a place other than *here*. They're is a contraction of *they are*.

these   See *this*.

these kind, these sort   See *kind*.

they   See *Pronoun* and **17e**.

this   When used as a determiner, *this*—like *the*—signifies that the antecedent to which it refers has been identified previously. See **17e** and **16a**.

> As she drove along the road, *a* (not *this*) policeman drew abreast. She knew she was speeding and thought *this* was the reason.

this here   As in *that there*, the second word is worse than useless.

tho   Short for *though*. It is rational but not formally used.

those   As an intensive with no reference, as in "*those* trout we caught!" *those* is colloquial.

thusly   Nonstandard for *thus*.

to, too, two   To is called a "function word." It serves as a preposition (*the train to the city*) and as part of a verb (*to sing, to sweat*). *Too* implies something in addition (*too weak to walk*). *Two* is the number.

toward, towards   Interchangeable and equally acceptable.

trait   Redundant when used with *character*; use either alone.

Trite expressions   The person who first called his wife his "better half" may have seemed clever, but contrived expressions usually cannot stand frequent repetition. Phrases like "this great land of ours" or "beautiful but dumb" or "by leaps and bounds" usually seem hackneyed, trite, and worn-out by overuse.

try and   *Try to* is standard.

type   As a noun, *type* is a synonym of *kind*. Most uses as a modifier are nonstandard (*this type of knife*, not *this type knife*).

unique   See 16c.

used to could   Nonstandard for "used to be able."

Verb   A verb is the middle word or phrase in the SVC pattern. In *Avery hates potato chips* the verb is *hates*. See Chapter 12.

Verb set   In Modern English a verb may combine with a particle to make what are called *verb sets* or *merged verbs*. In *As for smoking, he decided to give it up*, the particle *up* is better thought of as part of the verb set *give up* than as "a preposition at the end of a sentence."

very   Because it is so useful, *very* is overused. Good writers use it with caution, partly because apt modifiers may be stronger without the supposed intensive. *It was hot* sounds hotter than *It was very hot*. An almost archaic rule proscribed its use before a past participle without an intervening *much*— *very much honored* [not *very honored*].

Voice   Voice is a characteristic of many verbs in English. If the verb is in the active voice the subject occupies the subject position. (*A dog bit him.*) If the verb is in the passive voice, the object appears in the subject position. (*He was bitten by a dog.*)

wait on   Nonstandard in the sense of "*wait for*." *Wait on* is standard in the sense of *serve*.

ways   Whether referring to a *long way* or a *short way*, the *s* is excess.

we   The plural of *I*, *we* may refer to as few as two persons and as many as the writer wishes to include: (*We, the people of America* . . . or *we, the peoples of the world*). In journalistic writing, the antecedent of the so-called *editorial we*, are anonymous editors or publishing executives or the anonymous nonperson whom its readers refer to as "the paper." An author may use *we* to include the writer and the reader. (*Next, we shall consider the chemistry of the question.*) Or he may refer to a body of persons of whom he is one. (*We now know that viruses cause some colds.*)

weather   Not to be confused with *whether*.

well   An adverb, not to be confused with *good*, usually an adjective, which is similarly compared: (*well, better, best; good, better, best*).

what   Usually not standard as a relative pronoun.

> We liked *what* he said, but we didn't like the restaurants *that* (not *what*) he recommended.

what all   The *all* is usually redundant.

when   *When*-clauses are usually to be avoided in definitions; see 13c.

where   Sometimes ineptly used for *that:*

> I saw on the bulletin board *that* [not *where*] classes have been canceled.

where at   The *at* is usually superfluous.

whether   See *if*.

which   For most uses; see *Pronouns*; for *which* after *and*, see *and which*; for distinction from *that*, see *that, which*.

while   In most precise usage, *while* refers to time (a *long while ago, only a little while, while in college, wait while I dress*). It is less precisely used as a synonym for *although* and for *and*.

Although [not *while*] the instructor did not approve, he let the misused word stand. While one of them watched for the owner, the other would pour sugar in the gas tank.

who, whom   See *Pronoun*. When the pronoun appears at the beginning of an SVC, few have difficulty in deciding on *who*, even when *whom* would be standard. *Who are you?* fits the rule. *Who do you think you're talking to?* does not; the purist would insist on *Whom do you think you are talking to?* because the pronoun is the object of the preposition *to*. That is, historically, *who*, the subject form, is required if the word is serving as subject; *whom*, the object form, is required if the word is serving as an object, whether the object of a verb or the object of a preposition. Since the first word in the SVC pattern is usually the subject, however, *who* is now generally accepted if it is in the subject position, whether or not it is serving as the subject of a verb.

who's   The contraction, not the possessive. *Who is (who's) going?*

whose   The possessive, not the contraction. *Whose car is that?*

will   A future form of the verb *to be*. See *shall, will*.

wire   In the sense of message sending, *wire* is informally used as both noun and verb. (*Send me a wire. Wire me.*)

wise   Acceptable in words like *otherwise* and *sidewise* but nonstandard in recent coinages. (*The omelette tasted all right*, not *It was okay tastewise.*)

without   Not synonymous with *unless*.

> John wouldn't go *without* Jane. John wouldn't go *unless* (not *without*) Jane went along.

wood, woods   Interchangeable, meaning forest.

worst kind, worst way   Not acceptable as substitutes for *greatly, very much, exceedingly, excessively.*

worthwhile   A blanket word worn thin by overuse; see *Jargon*.

would of   See *could of*.

you   To be used only with caution as an impersonal pronoun; see **17g**.

you-all   A logical form but dialectal, and hence likely to be frowned on even in informal writing.

27A   The word *shimmy* is in common use as a name for "a marked shaking, vibration, or wobble, as in automobile wheels." It is recognized by standard dictionaries as the name of a dance popular in the 1920's, but most college students have never seen it, and probably would not use the word in this sense. Very few college students would now know that *shimmy* was once common college slang for women's underwear. In the following blanks try to list slang words current on your campus, which you cannot find used in this sense in your dictionary. Try to define the words accurately.

	Word	*Definition*
1	_____	_____
2	_____	_____
3	_____	_____
4	_____	_____
5	_____	_____
6	_____	_____
7	_____	_____
8	_____	_____
9	_____	_____
10	_____	_____
11	_____	_____
12	_____	_____
13	_____	_____
14	_____	_____
15	_____	_____

27B The following essay contains slang, colloquialisms, and unidiomatic expressions. Some of the numbered and italicized expressions are acceptable in college composition; for them write *A* in the corresponding numbered blank at the right. Others are unacceptable because they are not standard English; for them write *F* in the corresponding numbered blank. If in doubt, consult a good dictionary.

Not all thieves are interested in the big (1) bread; some are notably (2) camp. A professor at St. Norbert College reported that 350 trained cockroaches which he was using in an experiment had been (3) *swiped* from his car, and a home in Wolcott, N. Y., was twice (4) *burgled* of goldfish. Piety must (5) *rate* with some people because 720 (6) *typed* sermons were stolen from a Mississippi minister and in Long Beach, somebody got so (7) *enthused* by the names and telephone numbers of a hundred unmarried women that he broke into the Friendship Center and (8) *snitched* them. (9) *Irregardless* of the watchman, six men stole 700 teddybears from a British toy factory, and some (10) *newfangled* (11) *rustlers* stole the wooden horses off a (12) *merry-go-round* in New Jersey. What the (13) *deal* is in Vienna, West Virginia, the (14) fuzz (15) *don't know*, but some thief steals chocolate milk off doorsteps but never touches the homogenized milk. Some thieves apparently (16) *go* in for weighty objects: a 1600-pound bell vanished from the Comanche, Texas, church; ten (17) *cannon balls* rolled away from Warsaw, N. Y. Somebody in St. Paul (18) *up* and (19) copped a plea with nearly two tons of paving blocks pried out of the (20) *approach* to the state capitol. One cannot help (21) *speculating* why a New York thief stole two hundred phonograph records, all of hog calls, why an Indianapolis thief stole a fingerprinting kit from a (22) *hobbyhound* (leaving the (23) *dopester* no fingerprints to work on), why a Chicagoan stole 637 safety stickers, and why some (24) *phonies* in Ohio (25) *glommed onto* six thousand (26) *yo-yos*. There was (27) *poetic justice*, however, in the case of the Indiana (28) *gippos* who stole eighteen dollars' worth of boys' shirts labeled, "I'm a Little (29) *Stinker*." Under the general heading of (30) *homey* housebreaking, there are plentiful entries. A Des Moines housewife (31) *phoned* police that the (32) *grub* for dinner had been stolen out of her oven, and a (33) *dope* in Dallas, Tex., reported that he awoke to observe the blanket (34) flaking off toward an open window. The (35) *deal* was this: somebody had thrust a wire through the screen, (36) *hooked* it into the blankets, and was pulling the bed clothes toward the open (37) *casement*. Nor is petty (38) *larceny* solely an occupation of (39) *teenagers*, if the inference from Willoughby, Ohio is valid. The aged must be busy with it too, for some (40) *crutch* broke into a crutch and cane factory there and stole thirteen pairs of crutches.

1 _____
2 _____
3 _____
4 _____
5 _____
6 _____
7 _____
8 _____
9 _____
10 _____
11 _____
12 _____
13 _____
14 _____
15 _____
16 _____
17 _____
18 _____
19 _____
20 _____
21 _____
22 _____
23 _____
24 _____
25 _____
26 _____
27 _____
28 _____
29 _____
30 _____
31 _____
32 _____
33 _____
34 _____
35 _____
36 _____
37 _____
38 _____
39 _____
40 _____

27C Many of the sentences following contain jargon, journalese, and re-
dundancies. If the sentence seems clear and precise to you as it stands, write
C in the space provided; if not, rewrite the sentence. In rewriting you may
need to add concrete material since jargon and journalese characteristically
obscure meaning.

EXAMPLE: When he started to give his angle the Russian ambassador
literally exploded.

Answer: When he started to state his views, the Russian ambassador exploded, shouting vituperation.

1 After investigating the university budget, the committee reported that
unfortunately a complete breakdown of the university seems impossible at
this time.

2 The way the play was presented made it seem to make me feel that it
could really have actually happened to me.

3 He went to the meeting without knowing the deal but knowing that any
angle he put across would be diametrically opposite on the other side
from me.

4 I am definitely going to be in attendance at the track meet because
I am interested in that phase of athletics.

5 *The Faerie Queene* can be called a serious poem due to the fact of
the underlying factors of the story which depict the seriousness of the times
of that day.

6 The journalist who wrote that only a few enlistments were required
"to top the year's bullseye" was forgetting that bullseyes, like golf balls, are
better hit in the middle than topped.

7 The propositions which came as a response to this questionnaire show deviations of approach to the problem which introduce factors which relate to the differing recommendations of the report instigated by the committee, and to include some modifications of the initial objectives, which the committee previously instituted at an earlier date.

8 *The New Yorker* presented unfavorable comments on the play to the highest degree, which I think is to the extreme in this respect.

9 In any particular municipal government setup, which is almost always somewhat unique, some co-operative working together is definitely, more or less, imperative, in a deal like this.

10 The decision which was the result of the conference by three leading physicians was that his eyes were on their last legs.

11 To all intents and purposes, the bankruptcy of the company was due to the fact of the inability of any member of the board of directors to see the light of dawn in any respect of the market situation.

12 As the student progresses a slight increase in religion should also progress with him, thus giving an emphasis to his overall characteristic traits.

27D In the following essay, words and phrases are numbered and italicized. For those that seem to you clear and expressive, write *C* in the corresponding blank at the right. For those that are faulty because they are jargonic, redundant, or pompous, write *F.*

(1) *Climatology* has become an entrancing subject, partly because weather affects all of us, and thus we are interested (2) *in this respect,* but also because each year (3) *definitely* brings an (4) *actual* contribution to our understanding of why we freeze and why we (5) *swelter.* Scientists, have long known about pressure areas, but some years ago climatological thinking was revolutionized by the theory of air masses and other (6) *facets of the air situation.* Then the jet stream was thought to be a (7) *factor in the circumstances*, but just what the (8) *deal* was concerning the jet stream was a puzzler, (9) *more or less.* Then came the (10) *anticyclones.* They are weather disturbances (11) *which upset the weather by disturbing it.* There are two of them, and since they travel clockwise, one travels clockwise in the Atlantic and one travels (12) *clockwise* in the Pacific. Both the anticyclones promote (13) *conditions* which (14) *trend toward* changes which have an effect upon various parts of the country (15) *respectively.* Resulting from this (16) *as a consequence* are increased tornadoes along the eastern (17) *coastal* seaboard and cooler weather being in store for the western counterpart. These changed (18) *factors* in weather (19) *background* may influence world conditions detrimentally (20) *for the worse.*

1 _____
2 _____
3 _____
4 _____
5 _____
6 _____
7 _____
8 _____
9 _____
10 _____
11 _____
12 _____
13 _____
14 _____
15 _____
16 _____
17 _____
18 _____
19 _____
20 _____

Obviously this essay does not say much because it is weak and lacks facts. On separate paper, rewrite the essay as clearly and tellingly as you can. You will doubtless need more facts. Here are some notes that may be useful:

jet stream, not really a stream, seldom moves at speed of 300 miles per hour once attributed to it, and probably influences weather but little; Atlantic and Pacific anticyclones seem to be altering weather markedly; called anticyclones because they move clockwise and cyclones move counterclockwise; great sweeps of air, one in each ocean; Atlantic anticyclone moving clockwise brings tropic air to eastern U. S.; also brings tornadoes; this accounts for recent increase in tornadoes; in United States during years 1916–1920 tornadoes averaged about one hundred a year; during 1956–1960 the average was nearly six hundred, which was about three times the average for the previous half century; anticyclones moved north and caused difference; in west, anticyclone, likewise clockwise, brings cold air to Washington, Oregon, California, and mountain states; net result is warmer weather, however; slight change may be cataclysmic; temperature dropping average of fourteen degrees would return North America to ice age; rising temperature may melt polar ice cap and flood great ports like New York, London, and much of states like Louisiana and Mississippi, along with vast stretches of Siberia.

27E   In the blanks to the right, insert the proper first-person singular form and be prepared to explain why you preferred this form to another.

1   He had to (lie, lay) down and crawl across the field before he dared (rise, raise) and advance erect.   _____

2   The railroad (lie, lay) in that direction.   _____

3   The plan was to (rise, raise) up an army of zealots to (lie, lay) the tyrants low.   _____

4   He has (lie, lay) down a rule to govern us all.   _____

5   The picnickers were told to (sit, set) on benches with the line of lunch boxes (sit, set) before them.   _____

6   When you get upstairs (sit, set) the tray on the bedside table and (sit, set) down in the rocking chair.   _____

7   The rescue squad let him (lie, lay) where he was (lie, lay) until his leg was splinted.   _____

8   (Lie, lay) the pine boughs in the snow and let them (lie, lay) there until spring.   _____

9   After she had (lie, lay) down for an hour, she (rise, raise) to help him (lie, lay) the carpet.   _____

10   The authority to (lie, lay) down the law has never (lie, lay) with his office.   _____

27F   Insert the appropriate verb form in the blanks below, and be prepared to explain why you preferred it.

1   If Jane _____ (be) here she would help.

2   If a truck _____ (be) past, there would _____ (be) visible tire tracks as recently as yesterday.

3   Suppose it turns out that nobody could _____ (be) there?

4   If anyone _____ (see) the wreck, it would _____ (be) the crossing guard.

5   If that _____ (be) not a *non sequitur*, I am quite mistaken.

6   John often wished Jane _____ (be) prettier than she _____ (be).

7   Jane often wished John _____ (be) appreciate her as she was.

8   They _____ (can) stop quibbling if they _____ (wish).

9   Neither _____ (be) break the pattern if the other _____ (persist) in continuing it.

10   When my turn comes, you may be sure I _____ (be) ready.